CW00747249

LONDON'S LAST TRAMS

by Hugh Taylor

Published by Adam Gordon

FRONT COVER

Working on route 46, E3 1940 is seen at New Cross on the last day that trams operated in London. 1940 picked up a plough at Lee change pit and is working on the conduit system; following is a car on the 38. The colour of the wording on the Last Tram Week posters matched the livery of the fleet. (Peter Mitchell)

TITLE PAGE

E3 1925 crosses Westminster Bridge during the last week that trams ran in London. During that time they were probably a bigger tourist attraction than Big Ben and the Houses of Parliament, seen in the background. In most parts of London, trams ran in the centre of the road. On Westminster Bridge this was not so and trams heading away from town hugged the nearside kerb; those going the other way ran against the traffic flow. No doubt many unwary motorists got caught out by this phenomenon. The LAST TRAM WEEK posters were iconic. (London Transport Museum U53504)

It was balmy weather on Last Tram Day and people came out in their thousands to say farewell to London's trams. Moving from Westminster Bridge onto the Embankment and passing a large queue for a southbound car, this unidentified tram on route 72 passes onlookers on both pavements. No side route boards are carried, for by this time attention to detail was unimportant. Young ladies are out in their summer dresses; men are more formally attired in sports jackets. (Jack Wyse)

ISBN 978-1-874422-94-5
Publication no. 98
Published in 2013. Reprinted with minor alterations in 2015
by Adam Gordon, Kintradwell Farm, Brora, Sutherland KW9 6LU
Tel: 01408 622660 E-mail: adam@ahg-books.com

Design & production: Trevor Preece – trevor@trpub.net

Printed by: Henry Ling Ltd, The Dorset Press, Dorchester DT1 1HD

CONTENTS

Typifying Saturday 5th July 1952, a queue of people wait at a tram stop on the Victoria Embankment; they are about to board E3 1932 on route 36. The 'ON JULY 5 1952 WE SAY GOODBYE TO LONDON' poster is starting to peel away from the side of the car. (London Transport Museum U22790)

Because it was a priority to replace many ailing and ageing motorbuses in the immediate post-war period, the overhauling of trams continued as they would need to run for a few more years. Trolley-less HR2 114 is seen outside Westminster Station on the Victoria Embankment on route 35; its destination blind appears to be brand new. With gleaming paintwork 114 has recently been out-shopped from Charlton Works. The white painted line between the tracks indicates where the driver has to stop. (Fred Ivey)

AUTHOR'S NOTE

The opening words of Ken Blacker's book 'Trams of Bygone London' are: 'It was well towards midnight* on Saturday 5th July 1952, when tramcar No. 187, filled to overflowing with boisterous passengers, left Beresford Square, Woolwich, on its last journey of the day. After cruising slowly along Westhorne Avenue and through Lee and Lewisham she finally groaned to a halt outside New Cross depot. And thus was history made. For No. 187, looking much the worst for wear, and robbed of light bulbs, mirrors, seat springs and sundry other internal fittings by acquintry travellers, was the last London tram of all.' This account is confirmed by a number of enthusiasts who were at New Cross in the early hours of Sunday 6th July. Ken's statement held true for about three decades but about twenty-five years ago, former Charlton Works employee Ken Thorpe told me that after 187 had arrived at New Cross, there was still another tram running on the London metals. This book tells the enchanting story, courtesy of a dedicated tram crew and a man on a bicycle.

So........

It was about 2am on Sunday 6th July 1952 when tramcar No. 87, with a fair number of passengers on board, left New Cross on its last journey of the day. After travelling quickly through Lewisham and Lee she finally groaned to a halt at Woolwich Free Ferry. And thus history was made. For number 87, looking much the worse for wear and robbed of light bulbs, destination blinds and sundry other internal fittings by acquisitive travellers was the last London tram of all.

I only travelled on a London tram once – when teachers at Edgware infant's school, who were aware that it was Last Tram Week, took my class for a ride on one along the Victoria Embankment. I recall climbing the narrow stairs to the top deck. Much has been written about the tram to bus conversion in the early 1950s; I have therefore sought to use as much new material and unpublished photographs as possible and to prioritise on the last day of each conversion. Those who have written personal chapters were last day participants and the opportunity is taken to relate some of their earlier tram experiences.

*was actually just after midnight.

There is only one man that this book can be dedicated to and that is of course Peter Davis who not only saved tram 1858 from being scrapped, but ensured that it would operate again. I would like to thank those who have assisted one way or another: George Cook, Peter Davis, Fred Ivey, Martin Jenkins of Online Archive, Dave Jones of the London County Council Tramways Trust and Ken Thorpe. I also acknowledge the assistance given by Felicity Premru and Simon Murphy of the London Transport Museum. I was aware that Ken Blacker had travelled on tram 187 on what, for many years, had been thought to be the last tram in service, so I asked him to write the chapter titled '187's Last Journey' especially for this book. I appreciate his contribution. I was very pleased to re-establish contact with a former bus driving colleague Vic Peters who was willing, in his retirement, to relate his tram days. Vic worked with conductor Ernie Mole at Edgware Garage, and I with Fred Collins (a tram driver at Hampstead depot and then a trolleybus driver at Colindale depot). Now and again Vic and I were paired together and it was on one of these occasions that he told me that he was moving trams until 2am on 6th July 1952. He was obviously the man I needed to locate as a contributor to this book. A search of the London Transport archives has produced much hitherto unpublished material. Last, but not least, my devoted wife Catherine who typed the manuscript and spent many hours on the last hurdle of bringing the book to completion.

Hugh Taylor, Edgware, Middlesex

Seen on the Victoria Embankment at Savoy Street on 28th June 1952, E3 1911 has already had LAST TRAM WEEK posters fitted. With so many cars to deal with, a start was made before the first day of the cars' last week which was 29th June. (John Gillham)

INTRODUCTION

As part of its 1935-1940 New Works programme, the London Passenger Transport Board had replaced more than half of the tramway system it had inherited in 1933; in the main, trolleybuses were operating in their place. Heavier passenger loadings than expected saw frequencies improved on a number of routes and at Bexleyheath the demand was so great that spare and brand new higher capacity vehicles were drafted in to meet the demand. Revenue was up and costs were down and the LPTB were very satisfied with the conversion. However, as early as 1937, concerns were being voiced as to whether those trams remaining after the final tram to trolleybus changeover in June 1940 were to be superseded in this manner. A decision had to be made and in November 1946 it was stated that when the time came the trams still running would be substituted by buses and not trolleybuses - there was the more pressing need to replace time-expired motorbuses. This meant that trams would continue to run for a number of years to come. It was not an option to patch up the buses and get rid of the trams first, as buses were being condemned by the day; in fact vehicles were being borrowed the length and breadth of the country to make up the shortfall. Despite this, London Transport (as it was otherwise known) put a tramway replacement scheme together and on 23rd December 1948, the British Transport Commission gave approval in principle to the conversion of the remaining London trams to oil bus operation; they required that all matters connected to it should be submitted for approval.

It was announced on 5th July 1950 that the start of the tram scrapping programme would commence on 1st October that year; it was ironic that this statement was made two years to the day when trams would last run in the capital. At the time of the July 1950 announcement all but three routes in North London had gone; those that remained traversed the Kingsway subway. In South London only a few services had succumbed to the trolleybus; in fact, many areas of this part of London were solely or predominantly served by trams.

London Transport staff prepare the Penhall Road site. These top two photographs show "Men at Work". (Phil Tatt)

The lower pair of photos show wooden sleepers, with tram track and span wires attached to the traction standards – running wire will be strung later on. The work was carried out to London Transport's usual high standard. (Phil Tatt)

PREPARING PENHALL

A site was required for the disposal of the trams. The only suitable one along the routes that were to be abandoned at the last stage of the replacement scheme was on land adjacent to Penhall Road, Charlton, which was a thoroughfare off Woolwich Road. The site was, usefully, only about a mile away from Central Repair Depot (CRD) - more commonly known as Charlton Works. To the public, the first tangible sign that the 'South London trams' were to be scrapped occurred in October 1949 when London Transport moved on to this land. Opinion was sought by the legal adviser as to whether there was any statutory obligation to submit details of the track or overhead equipment at 'Penhall depot' to the Ministry of Transport. He stated that there did not appear to be any but there would be little doubt that the 'depot' would be regarded as a factory and come under the auspices of the Factory Act. Hence, it would be necessary to conform to the requirements of the Act particularly regarding the generation, transmission, distribution and use of electricity; it was further agreed that the site should be under the control of the Works Engineer, Charlton. At one time it was anticipated that access would be restricted to daylight hours; this was entirely unfeasible as movements at each conversion were myriad. It was found necessary for entry to be available at any time during the day or night - access at night though (possibly until 3am) was by arrangement. The work was considered to be new construction and termed Penhall Road Disposal Site Approach. Mileage was 0.01 miles of single track - this equates to eighteen yards and was the distance between the highway and the scrapyard entrance. With 34 tracks in the yard, it was estimated that there was about a mile of track on the site. Traction standards were planted and overhead wiring erected outside the yard, on Woolwich Road, for access to the yard - presumably an arrangement was made with the local authority to allow this.

In August 1949 the Chief Engineer, the Chief Mechanical Engineer and the Operating Manager submitted costs for the preparation of the Penhall Road site. It was approved under 'Special Expenditure'.

Permanent Way Engineer (Trams)	
Levelling site, laying tram tracks, constructing traverser pit, concreting surface, laying ashes, etc.	£15,000
Distribution Engineer (Trams & Trolleybuses)	
Overhead equipment, cables, conductor rails and insulators, brackets and insulators for lighting, etc.	£1,000
Works Engineer, Charlton	
Provision of traverser, adaption of old trams as offices, cloakrooms etc. (for site staff), sundries and fire appliances	£2,000
Signal Engineer (Trams and Trolleybuses)	
Provision of lighting and heating	£325
Architect	
Fencing site and provision of lavatories, etc. including fees	£2,200
	£20,525

The foregoing estimate was based upon the use of second-hand permanent way materials laid by direct labour and the work proposed and costs involved were formulated with 'full regard to every aspect of economy'. No figure, however, had been included to cover administration expenses or the cost of clearing the site upon completion of the tramway conversion. The extent of tram movement to and from the site for storage and scrapping was far more extensive than was originally assumed, and it would be necessary to augment the current supply arrangements by providing a pair of second-hand DC cables from Charlton sub-station. The additional cost was estimated at £2200 although the cables would have a recoverable scrap value of £1000 after the yard was vacated. The original £20,525 cost had risen to £21,000 by May 1950; this meant that the full amount for equipping the site was £23,200. The fencing and lavatory block was provided by J. Whymann & Son of Hackney at a cost of £1865. 9s. 7d - seems a lot for a few toilets and some fencework! Their contract ran to 54 pages such were the intricacies of the plumbing and fencing.

A two-part lease was obtained from Walmont Properties Ltd. The part of the land furthest away from Woolwich Road

This spring-back point sent the majority of the trams withdrawn between 1950 and 1952 to their fate. Especially constructed on the eastbound track in Woolwich Road, Charlton, it was set westbound – for trams going into Penhall Road scrapyard.

The trolley-less HR2s could not move under their own power in the scrapyard because the site was fitted with overhead wires. There were only two places where ploughs could be removed from these cars; inside CRD and the entrance to Penhall Road yard. This scenario is happening at Penhall Road to 144 which is about to be given a helping hand by one of the on-site London Transport tractors on 6th October 1951; the driver will bring the tram to a standstill in the yard by using the handbrake. (Clarence Carter)

consisted of 0.9 acres and cost £175 per annum; the lease was for four years renewable thereafter annually – it started on 30th September 1949 and finished on 29th September 1953. None of these tracks were wired and trams were shunted on and off this part of the yard. The land nearest Woolwich Road was 1.9 acres with the lease being for fourteen years subject to a break after three, four or ten years; the lease started on 26th March 1949 and concluded on 25th March 1963 at a cost of £850 per annum. This part of the premises was wired and fed with electricity. By the spring of 1950 all was ready for the reception of trams and well in advance of the start of the conversion scheme – by having the site ready in good time a clean start could be made when the first stage occurred. 150 trams could be accommodated; more could be squeezed in if necessary and 158 service cars and eleven miscellaneous specimens were there on 6th July 1952 – even then a few more could have been shoe-horned in. It was estimated that George Cohen and Sons who had scrapped London trams in the 1935-1940 era, and who were awarded this scrapping contract, could deal with ten a week, or 32 a month. It was anticipated that the maximum number to be withdrawn at any stage was 130; it turned out that the greatest number to be taken out of service at any one time would be 117 – at stage six. 'Penhall' was a name that made any tram passing its gates nervous!

Access to 'Penhall' was via a single line off Woolwich Road. The spring-back point was in favour of those going in; cars worked 'wrong road' for a few yards before entering. Just inside, a plough change-pit was installed; principally for

5th April 1952 and E3 202 has carried its last passengers; this is confirmed by the word 'SCRAP' chalked on its dash. Illumination above the highway is provided by lights strung between lamp standards; when erecting overhead here, London Transport staff had to ensure that they did not foul the local council's overhead lighting arrangements. When trams were arriving en masse at Penhall Road yard, slick movement was needed as many tram services still passed along Woolwich Road. (Clarence Carter)

E1 1793 is being moved onto road 21 by the traverser; the London Transport staff member on the platform is smartly turned out. For after dark operations, of which there were many, the traverser is fitted with a headlight. (Don Thompson)

'Marshalling condemned trams at Penhall Road' is the caption to this view taken on 30th September 1950. Two E1s, one rehabilitated and one not are being manoeuvred by an LT tractor. One car has its blinds removed; the other shows BORO & LONDON BGE. (London Transport Museum U50143)

1231 was used as an office at 'Penhall Depot'. The only part of the top deck to remain was the roof which was placed on the top of the lower deck; it still has its trolley retaining hook in place. All trams arriving at the yard were recorded by a London Transport employee inside this half-car. (Fred Ivey)

arrivals, it could also be used by those returning to service, Felthams going back to CRD, etc. When trolley-less cars entered, they coasted downhill once they had 'shot the plough.' They were then marshalled into position by one of the on-site LT tractors; when they left they were pushed up the slope to the change-pit with the assistance of another tram. On conversion days, when large numbers of cars were expected to arrive in a short space of time, either an LT breakdown truck or one of the aforementioned tractors would be on hand in the Woolwich Road to push into the yard any trams reluctant to enter a place from which they would most definitely never return.

Upon arrival, cars were parked on the 'south and east' sides of the property; the positioning of the condemned trams depended on the number withdrawn at each stage. The unwired tracks were used first; when they were full the wired tracks were utilised (at times Felthams, spare cars and service trams were parked thereon). Trams were usually sold in batches but it was London Transport staff who oversaw the movement of each car to Cohen's – these men had been tram

A close-up of a plough being taken out of its carrier; this view was taken at the entrance to Penhall Road yard on 6th October 1951; E1 1802 is the unlucky car. Bearing in mind that this area is not part of the public highway, was it really necessary for a man with a red flag to be in attendance? (Clarence Carter)

101 is pushed across the traverser and on to a siding for use as a 'spark shield'; it is the last of four trolley-less HR2s to make this short trip. The traverser had a tower placed on top of it to which a trolley base with a trolley wheel was fitted – this had a wide conducting roller for sideways movement. It was no wonder that Beatalls Furniture factory (seen in the background) had concerns about the scrapping of trams so near to their premises. Cohen's employees work in well-ordered fashion. (Don Thompson)

1727 acted as the canteen at Penhall Road for two years; the fact that it has come straight out of service is shown by its farechart still in position. Batteries power the trams' light bulbs for use in winter months. A frying pan is hooked to its holder – presumably there is a cooker in 1727 for workers to make a hot meal. Some lower deck seats have been removed and conditions are rudimentary. The 'white collar' man is not one of the scrapmen; maybe he is a London Transport employee on administrative work. (John Wills)

drivers and would either drive one on to the traverser and pull the trolley arm down, after which an LT tractor would push the doomed tram on to the burning area, or organise a tractor to push one on to the traverser which ran on wheels in a specially constructed pit. In the dismantling area, trams were set upon with voracious speed; the more they broke, the more money Cohen's men made as they were on 'piecework.'

Charlton Works adapted four trams for general purpose use at 'Penhall.' 1231 was to be the office and sent to CRD on 6th July 1950 where its top deck was removed. The roof only, which retained its trolley hooks, was lined with canvas in order to make it waterproof; it was then fitted to the top of the lower deck to give more strength to it – the remains of the top deck were scrapped. The work is recorded as finishing on 21st August after which it was towed to Penhall Road; it retained its trucks. 1231 had interior lighting though it is not known how it was 'juiced up.' 1727 was converted into a canteen (in 28th September/out 31st October – involving little more than the removal of seats and installation of tables). 1730 and 1768 became cloakrooms (1730 in 29th September/out 24th October: 1768 in 2nd October/out 30th October). The scrapping staff must have had makeshift arrangements while the three cars were being prepared. London Transport is renowned for recorded and actual date of transfers being at variance with each other; to illustrate this, 1727 went to CRD on 29th September and 1730 was in service on 30th September and noted going to CRD at 2pm that day. 1768 was also in service on 30th September.

Works car 02 and passenger car 1322 went to Penhall Road in advance of the hundreds that would follow; this allowed tests and trials to take place. 1322 was stripped by LT staff and burned on 26th July 1950; a few others 'met their maker' before mass scrapping began. A problem foreseen at Penhall was that the burning of cars would cause ash to fall on to neighbouring premises. The owners of Beatall's furniture factory, which was very close to the burning area, were understandably alarmed and made immediate representations to London Transport about the danger; they were so concerned that they proposed to the LTE solicitors that the Executive should accept full responsibility for any conflagration. The London Fire Brigade spent some time at Penhall and despite a number of residential and business properties situated nearby, gave their approval. The LFB stated that a 'firewall' should be provided and Beatall's fears were to be addressed by placing four metal-bodied trams between the burning area and the factory. With no metal-bodied trams due for immediate scrapping, E1s 1743, 1763, 1764 and 1771 were initially provided (if there had been a fire, not only would the wooden-bodied cars have fanned the flames, but difficult questions would have been asked of the LT hierarchy). These four E1s were scrapped by the end of 1950; they were followed by various other cars and by the summer of 1952, the firewall was metal-bodied HR2s 101-104. However, their trucks were required for sale to Alexandria in Egypt so E3s 175, 183, 185 and 186 replaced them as the 'spark shields'; this was for a just few weeks towards the end of 1952. The LFB told Cohen's that they could only burn if there was a favourable wind; this meant that there were days when no cars were dealt with. London Transport referred to the disposal of trams as 'burning,' not 'scrapping.'

The stacking of trams at Penhall Road was a highly sophisticated operation. The scrapping of London Transport's motorbuses, trolleybuses, and its trams prior to 1940 was not in this vein; vehicles were brought to a site and broken up virtually where they stood. At each stage of this conversion, trams were parked on specific 'roads'; this had been planned in advance so as soon as a car arrived at Penhall, a number was chalked on its dash – it was then positioned on the relevant road. This enabled LT staff to know which line each car was on; its location could be readily identified but with all of them going to be broken up anyway there seemed little point to it all. However, London Transport is known for its efficiency and there was a method in it all. Spare parts were needed to keep the remaining trams serviceable and rather than manufacture new items, major units after removal were returned to CRD for further use. CRD knew which cars they wanted parts from; when 'given the nod,' these trams were cannibalised. Even at stage eight, many were marked up as to which road they were on.

Although macabre, the work carried

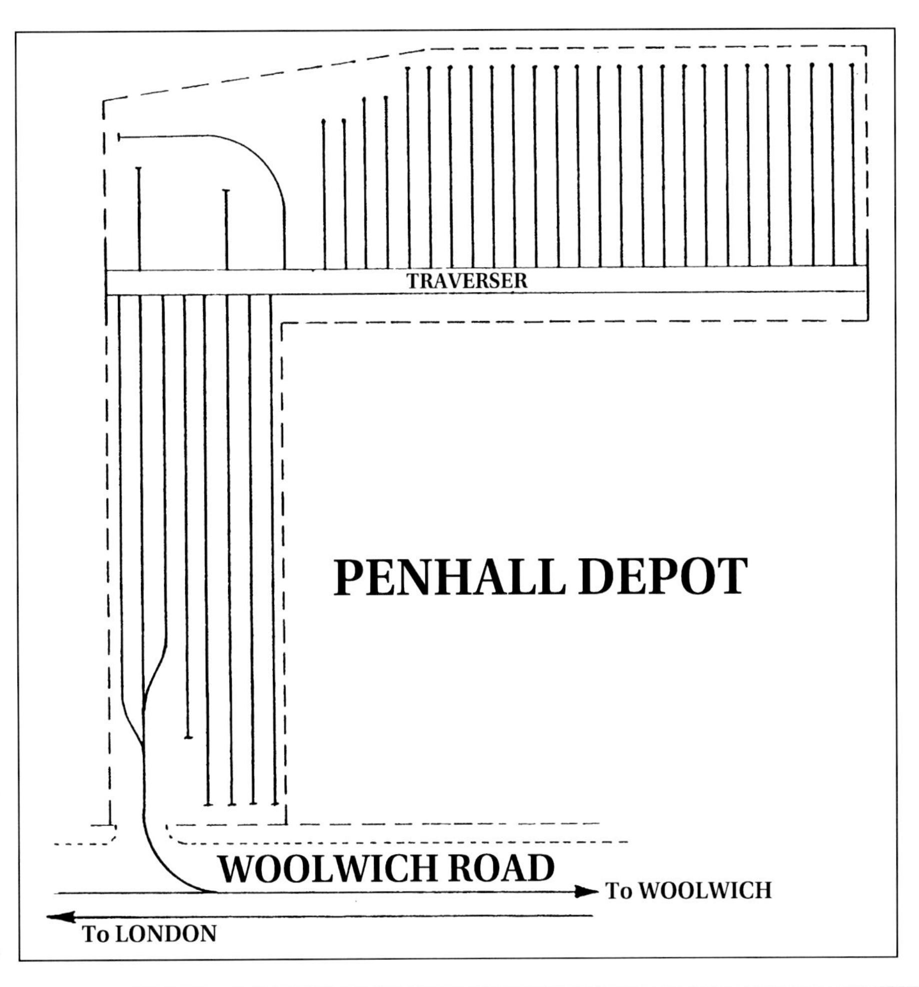

A number of cars were used as 'spark shields' during the scrapping period; temporarily assigned this task were two former West Ham Corporation trams. One is 327 which is amongst the remains of a number of cars that have already been broken up; the other West Ham car can also be seen. Some E1s have been parked in the same position for some considerable time; weatherworn, their adverts are peeling off. The practice of numbering traction standards on the public highway has been perpetuated in the scrapyard by London Transport construction staff. (Don Thompson)

George Cohen and Son secured the contract for breaking up London's trams in the 1950-1953 period. They were known as the 600 group, this number being their 'public face'. When car 600 was ready for scrapping in the summer of 1951, they sent a photographer to the scene. The first view shows the oxyacetylene burner cutting into 600; the second shot sees a hawser attached to the car to pull it on its side. The third view shows a Gaumont British News film unit on site that day. (Ronald Harrington)

out at Penhall Road was paramount to the scrapping of the trams; the close proximity of Charlton Works to the yard was very convenient. Large numbers of trams would appear at each stage of the conversion programme and their arrival and subsequent demise was a well co-ordinated programme, efficiently seen through by London Transport and Cohen's. Because this was profusely photographed, the opportunity is taken to illustrate the situation from their arrival at the yard until they were turned over and burned.

The *'Kentish Independent'* described in great detail the destruction of Metropolitan Stage Carriage No. 4347 – this was tram 162 which was one of the cars sent for scrap in the days leading up to 5th July. The reporter describes how he was 'in at the death' at the London Transport Crematorium, and monochrome images record the murder of a tram. When the workmen have carried out part of their day's work, all that remains is a smouldering wreck which only a little while before was clanking, lurching, groaning and banging along the Woolwich Road. The *KI* representative took a ghoulish delight at being in at the death of one of the last of the old brigade. With glee he laughed maliciously as a husky workman darted forward to tear off the licence number plate as tram 162 entered the yard. It had carried this plate for many a year but the reporter whooped with joy as 162 groaned its way along the 60 yards of track leading to the place of sacrifice. Intently he took note of the men as they tore out the seats, the electrical equipment, the glass, etc, and there was a little holiday in his heart. A spidery little crane approached the almost helpless monster, and our man leaned forward with the air of a Roman patrician waiting for the gates of the lion's cage to open. And then it happened! In the most business-like manner possible, the crane's jaws gripped the top of the tram's shell, shook it like a terrier shaking a bone and pushed. Three seconds, that was all the time it took that tall shell to fall. But in that brief space of time a hundred, nay a thousand memories flitted through the reporter's mind. He remembered the days when clutching his mother's hand he had tried to pull her up those steep stairs so that he could sit looking down from his exalted position at the parallel lines along which the car was running. He remembered the fascination of sitting close to the driver's cabin and watching the seemingly motiveless spinning of what he now realises was a brake. He remembered the fun of arriving at the terminus and being allowed to help with the small miracle of changing the direction of the seats by giving the backs a strenuous shove. He remembered too, the swaying, jerking and general uncomfortableness of these mighty beasts, the waiting in a queue, followed by the sight of as many as ten trams apparently stuck together, and the noise as the trams 'yam-yam-yammed' down the hills sounding for all the world as though their wheels were square. But in those three seconds laughter died. Then the burning started. Black smoke billowed, giving way to sheets of bright flame. Within ten minutes the whole interior was ablaze. An hour later brought the realisation that even with so much fire about this was no holocaust. True, the complete shell had disappeared, but no. 4347 contained a great deal of non-ferrous metal. Valuable stuff this and not to be despised. After the cooling down the workmen came forward again bringing with them their acquisitive little crane to collect the tons and tons of scrap that once formed the backbone of London Transport tramcar 162. Outside the gates to the crematorium, new shining buses rushed triumphantly past. They are the victors and we must now travel in them. But we who lived with trams will never forget them; although we hated them at the time, we knew even then that they did have a personality of their own. MSC licence plate 4347 somehow survived and is in the Acton depot of the London Transport Museum.

STAGES ONE TO SIX

A strange feature to arise just before the conversion started was the renaming of a tram depot. On July 12th 1950, Central Buses, and Trams and Trolleybuses came under the same operating umbrella: Central Road Services. A number of bus garages and trolleybus depots had the same place name. One was Holloway; to avoid confusion the bus garage kept its name but the tram and trolleybus depot became Highgate depot. For many, the old name persisted, but on some internal documents, London Transport's northern tram depot was known as Highgate. There was also a Norwood tram depot and a Norwood bus garage; with the former only having a limited lifespan, neither location altered its name.

Local newspapers gave details of the thirty-seven daytime and six night tram routes that were to be replaced by buses. The impending changes were advertised in the trams themselves and in timetable panels of bus and tram stops. 'Buses for Trams' leaflets have only been seen for stages six, seven and eight. The Press comprehensively covered each stage of the conversion.

In 1950, there were many elderly tramway staff; some had been in service since horse tram days. It was estimated that there would be a 5% failure rate of men not reaching the required standard to make the grade of bus driver. In fact it increased to 8.5% at depots that featured in the later stages of the conversion due to their more advanced age; this was because they had transferred from their 'home' depot to places such as New Cross and Norwood. Out of 2069 men put through the bus driving course, 1904 passed; the 7.97% failure rate was considerably higher than anticipated. A numerical coincidence saw 1904 tram crews replaced by 2212 bus crews – an increase of 308, a large reduction from what was thought to be at one time, 580. New men were taken on to drive trams (albeit for a short time) while established tram drivers went through their bus driving course; this was a well thought out policy as the new recruits would then go on to drive buses.

On 1st July 1950 tram track mileage was 102. Cars were housed at ten depots: Wandsworth, Clapham, Purley, Streatham (Telford Avenue), Camberwell, Norwood, Holloway, Brixton Hill, Abbey Wood and New Cross; Brixton Hill was an annexe to Streatham. There were 833 passenger cars and 25 works cars. With replacement buses on order, tenders were sought for the conversion of tram depots into bus garages – there would also be a number of brand new garages in South London.

Tram staff had to work in appalling conditions while depots were being converted into bus garages. In the run-up to the final chapter of the London tram, repair and maintenance facilities were primitive at many depots. Whereas trams had previously been under cover, some were now out in the open; this view at New Cross shows the degradation of it all. All these trams have both trolley poles at the same end – this enables cars to be tightly packed within the remains of the building.

The state of affairs at Abbey Wood was never as bad as that at New Cross. The roof of the depot is being replaced and girders of what will become Abbey Wood bus garage are in place. In later years, there was a preponderance of former East Ham and West Ham cars working at Abbey Wood; illustrating the West Ham contingent are 338, 297, 337 and 342. E1 1177 represents the former LCC fleet. (Peter Mitchell)

Route 34 operated between Blackfriars and King's Road Chelsea. Owing to a ship colliding with Battersea Bridge on 23rd March 1950, the route was cut back to the south side of the structure where a crossover was fortuitously sited. At the revised terminus, 1933 awaits departure for Camberwell Green. (Fred Ivey)

During the reconstruction of the tram depots, it was necessary to retain their inspection pits until conversion day. An ever dwindling pit accommodation caused much shunting of trams from filled-in pit areas in order to bring them over pits still remaining open. A lot of the servicing had to be done in the open and during wet and cold weather, conditions were severe. The engineering staff had to carry on with sections of roof missing, walls removed, steelwork being removed or installed around them with builders' plant and materials absorbing useful space. Despite all these difficulties the trams went out in a safe and clean

After the Battersea Bridge incident, route 34 trams initially showed LATCHMERE (a nearby hostelry). Such was the efficiency of London Transport that even though the route would be withdrawn in six months time, a BATTERSEA BRIDGE display was provided; the words just fit in the width of the blind – normally BRIDGE was abbreviated as BGE. It looks as if 189 has a new blind but it is not known if all Camberwell's cars were thus provided or whether some had an insert panel; it is assumed that this was the last new display on London tram destination blinds. 189 passes 'The Astoria' in Brixton Road. (Fred Ivey)

Going at stage one was route 34. Seen at Gresham Road change pit in Brixton, 1381 is about to swallow up a large number of passengers who are waiting at a 'dolly' tram stop. 1381 has just picked up a plough; the driver comes to have a word with his conductor who is removing the trolley arm from the overhead. Note the plough fork in the right foreground. (Fred Ivey)

A casualty of stage one was trolleybus route 612 on which D3 511 is seen in Tooting. Operated by Wandsworth depot there were no plans for motorbuses and trolleybuses to work from the same building – therefore the 612 had to go. The route is in its last phase of life and 511 will transfer to Walthamstow shortly; later it will go to Hammersmith depot where it will return to this area and work on route 630 on a regular basis until April 1959. (Fred Ivey)

condition and on time. The management appreciated this, along with all the efforts and enthusiasm made by all grades of tram staff in their new jobs. Tram drivers and engineers had undergone training courses on buses with displaced permanent way staff being accommodated one way or another. Even a continuous day and night canteen service for each depot was maintained throughout the conversion period; a staff benefit saw new canteens and recreation rooms being provided at six locations. Placed on record was the spirit of co-operation displayed by staff; this was particularly so during the course of rebuilding as there were many occasions when recreation and club rooms had to be closed.

As soon as the Saturday midday peak hour of 30th September 1950 was over, trams started to arrive at Penhall Road; 1355 from New Cross depot was one of the first. Instructor Stan Collins oversaw some of the operations that day and is on the platform. A number of onlookers can be seen; two doff their hats at the condemned car. The man in civvies is Richard Elliott, a senior employee at Charlton Works. The bespectacled man on the right is Mr Gratton, the senior London Transport official at the yard; LT employees received a warm welcome from him and were given free access here whenever they wanted it. An X on the fender indicates that 1355 is for scrap. The plough shift at the entrance to the yard can be seen; to avoid mishaps, ploughs were drawn out manually. (London Transport Museum U50138)

The last 26 from Borough was Clapham's 1777 which, despite exterior bracing, is in pristine condition; it had received a 'partial' overhaul in August 1950. It was involved in a three-car shunt in December 1950; despite its recent overhaul, it was not deemed worthy of repair and Cohen's relieved London Transport of it on 28th of that month. Each conversion attracted mourners and historians; although the number at Borough is small, they increased as the programme progressed. (London Transport Museum U1754)

The 12.23am departure from the Bloomsbury crossover on route 31 on Sunday 1st October 1950 was by E3 195; it will soon dive down into the Kingsway Subway and head for Wandsworth depot where it was due at 1.02am. The wet evening does not deter driver Henry Lancaster from posing in front of 195; maybe the London Transport photographer asked him to do this. (London Transport Museum U50144)

On a different vein, London Transport expressed concerns about the lack of progress at Clapham and Wandsworth depots which were being transformed into bus garages. Continued pressure had to be made on the contractors whose response was that there was a 'lack of spirit in the labour employed' rather than any weakness in supervision Change pits and overhead wiring had to be installed at some depots as it was necessary to dispense with conduit operation while construction work was taking place.

Tramway conversion committee meetings regularly took place at 55 Broadway; such was their frequency that the one on 13th March 1952 was number 57. These were presided over by Mr J.B. Burnell (Operating Manager, Central Road Services) with much of the business centring on progress reports on all aspects of the changeover; another man to the fore in the conversion was A.A. Durrant (Chief Mechanical Engineer, Central Road Services). There were problems from time to time. One was the great difficulty experienced in purchasing 37 Clapham Park Road and it was proposed in 1950 to include this property in the next Parliamentary Bill – an early example of 'Big Brother' state and compulsory purchase; it was required in relation to the building of the new bus garage there. With it being anticipated that facilities at Clapham would not be ready in 1951 for motorbus operation, an adjoining vacant site was required for temporary

SATURDAY ROUTE 31 CREW SCHEDULE FOR HOLLOWAY DEPOT DATED 10TH NOVEMBER 1948 AND IN FORCE UNTIL 30TH SEPTEMBER 1950

LONDON PASSENGER TRANSPORT BOARD
(TRAMS AND TROLLEYBUSES)

DUTY SCHEDULE

REGISTER NUMBER 923L

DAY OF OPERATION Mon-Fri. COMMENCING ~~20 OCT 1948~~ 10 NOV 1948 Holloway DEPOT

Route number	Time schedule number	Relief point	Travelling time allowance
31	CNON	Islington Grn	18"

"D" Indicates reliefs on down track

DUTY NUMBER	Commencing time including all allowances	Route number	Running number	From Time	From Place	To Time	To Place	Finishing time including all allowances	1st & 2nd spells H. M.	Total time H. M.	Relief H. M.	Spreadover H. M.	Spreadover allowance H. M.	Overtime including enhanced rate Mins.	Cash allowance s. d.
1	4 52		1	5 2	Dr	8 41			3 49						
			7	9 21		11 8		11 36	2 15	6 4	40	6 44		x	1 —
2	5 10		4	5 20	Dr	8 59			3 49						
			11	9 41		11 32		12 0	2 19	6 8	42	6 50		x	6
3	5 28		7	5 38	Dr	9 21			3 53						
			7	11 8		1 0		1 28	2 20	6 13	1 47	8 0		x	6
4	5 51		11	6 1	Dr	9 41			3 50						
			11	11 32		1 24		1 52	2 20	6 10	1 51	8 1	1	x	6
5	5 57		12	6 7	Dr	8 4			2 7						
			4	8 59		12 36		1 4	4 5	6 12	55	7 7		x	6
6	7 36		12	8 4		11 40			4 4						
			7	1 0		2 52		3 20	2 20	6 24	1 20	7 44		x	x
7	8 13		1	8 41		12 20			4 7						
			11	3 16		5 4		5 32	2 16	6 23	2 56	9 19	1 19	x	x
8	11 12		12	11 40		1 32			2 20						
			4	2 28		6 25	Dr	6 35	4 7	6 27	56	7 23		x	x
9	11 52		1	12 20		2 12			2 20						
			7	2 52		6 35		7 3	4 11	6 31	40	7 11		x	x
10	12 8		4	12 36		2 28		2 46	2 38						
	3 27		18	3 32	Dr	7 42	Dr	7 52	4 25	7 3	41	7 44		x	x
11	12 56		11	1 24		3 16			2 20						
			1	4 4		8 4	Dr	8 14	4 10	6 30	48	7 18		x	x
12	1 4		12	1 32		5 16			4 12						
			7	6 35		8 25		8 53	2 18	6 30	1 19	7 49		x	x
13	1 44		1	2 12		4 4			2 20						
			12	5 16		8 55		9 23	4 7	6 27	1 12	7 39		x	x
14	4 36		11	5 4		7 9	Dr	7 14	2 38						
	8 7		7	8 25		12 31	Dr	12 41	4 34	7 12	53	8 5	5	x	x
15	8 27		12	8 55		1 2	Dr	1 12		4 45	—	4 45		x	1 —
									Total	94 59	16 40	111 39	1 25		4 —
									Average	6 20	1 7	7 27			

22
18
36
[illegible]

CH. 83 13
RI 6 0
P 10
TT 6 36
SU –

94.59

195 was the last tram of stage one; it is at the junction of Jews Row and York Road, Wandsworth. Whether it went into the depot or was left in York Road and went straight off to Streatham depot is not known. 195 spent time at Streatham, Norwood and New Cross depots before meeting a fiery end at Penhall Road scrapyard. A 'NOT FOR BURNING' inscription has been chalked on 195's front dash. A trolleybus trailing frog is seen in the top left-hand corner; with route 612 being withdrawn at the same time, it will be removed for use elsewhere on the network. (London Transport Museum U50145)

This photograph encapsulates stage one. Brand new RTLs, all meticulously blinded for route 45 and showing 'CLAPHAM LT GARAGE' are perfectly aligned and ready for work on Sunday 1st October 1950. The canteen is open all night to provide sustenance for those on duty; maybe the canteen lady has come out to see if anyone wants a cup of her best Griffin tea (London Transport's own brand). (London Transport Museum U24574)

The first bus on tram replacement route 44 was RT 3272 which leaves Wandsworth garage at just before 4.30am on Sunday 1st October 1950. A number of staff observe the first stage of the tram to bus conversion take place. (London Transport Museum U24559)

open air parking nearby. The owners of two properties refused offers made by the LTE, and a senior member of staff went to see them personally; presumably they co-operated but on their terms. At Stockwell, the building of the new bus garage saw nineteen houses pulled down with new flats provided for the fifty families rendered homeless; though they commanded rents of £3 10s per week on the open market, they were let to the dispossessed families at the rents they were previously paying – some at less than £1 a week.

There were to be nine stages which would take place on the first weekend of nominated months: October, January, April and July. The first conversion would take place on Saturday 30th September: 'Last Tram Day' would be Saturday 4th October 1952. The changeover would take place in a west to east configuration, allowing access to CRD until the end. The £9 million tram scrapping scheme was officially titled 'Operation Tramaway'.

A bittersweet effect of the conversion was that some staff had no alternative but to move from a tram depot where they had spent a long time at to a bus garage which was some considerable distance away. Norwood crews had to go to Brixton, Camberwell, Rye Lane and Stockwell while New Cross staff were sent to Peckham and Rye Lane garages. This inconvenience was met by paying a generous one-off disturbance allowance. The upside of this was that for some staff their new base was nearer to their homes. Staff temporarily displaced were paid 'travelling time' between their home depot and the temporary base; e.g. New Cross crews going to Peckham, Camberwell and Rye Lane. Thornton Heath staff moved to a re-opened Purley depot on 1st January 1950; this was due to Thornton Heath depot being demolished before work could start on a new bus garage. Thornton Heath staff did not return until 8th April 1951 – presumably a double financial arrangement was made in this case. As London Transport was not going to mix motorbus and trolleybus operation at Highgate depot, the tram crews and buses were operated from nearby Holloway bus garage.

Stage one took place overnight Saturday 30th September/Sunday 1st October 1950. Wandsworth depot was converted to bus operation in one go; part of Camberwell's and Clapham's allocation went too. That night, some depots 'jumped the gun' and observed in Penhall Road on Friday 29th September were 1145, 1219, 1654, 1656, 1744, 1762, 1770 and 1773, along with works cars 05 and 034. Noted at 1am in Wandsworth depot on 30th September was 1766 which was waiting to be taken to Penhall – alongside was 1958 which would accompany it but would bring 1766's crew back. Wandsworth were short of cars on their last day – it would be a trait of the programme and it did not matter that getting cars away early meant that a full service could not be provided on 'last days'. Despite the imminent implementation of stage one, CRD was working at full pelt; on 29th September there was a wide variety of cars receiving attention one way or another – a total of twenty-one in fact (86, 155, 186, 187, 193, 326, 333, 391, 590, 599, 994, 1212, 1547, 1727, 1782, 1793, 1796, 1837, 1968, 1980 and 1986). At all stages, as soon as the Saturday midday peak was over, trams due for scrapping started to move to Penhall. Volunteer crews, on overtime, were obtained for these movements; with New Cross cars going for scrap at each stage – their staff made good money. Also going at this time was trolleybus route 612 which was operated by Wandsworth depot; there had been joint tram and trolleybus operation here since 1937 and the changeover enabled a Tooting to City service to be re-established.

Cohen's were "open for business" on Monday 2nd

Scrapping at Penhall Road started on the morning of Monday 2nd October 1950. The Press were invited to the first conflagration which saw 1656 dismantled and burnt the same day – it had been in service the previous Saturday. London Transport aptly captioned this photograph 'Dismantling old trams before burning'. No mercy was shown by Cohen's staff; the windows have been broken and the dash cut away to allow a good draught for the car to burn. The controller has been removed and may well find its way back to Charlton Works for re-use. (London Transport Museum U50165/U50168)

October and made an immediate start on scrapping; first to go that day was 1656 (intriguingly London Transport did not formally sell this car until 3rd October). The Press were invited to witness its destruction and by the end of the day a conflagration engulfed its remains; 1647 went on 3rd October with 1170 due to be burnt the following day. Trams that had been working for their living one Saturday had been stripped of all valuable spares and their remains burned within the week. Cohen's had to ensure that no backlog occurred and this was closely monitored by London Transport. It was noted in October 1951 that there were 82 trams on site; two bodies a day were required to be dealt with if a backlog was to be avoided. London Transport was its own worst enemy at this time for the previous month it was noted that 43 motorbuses were awaiting scrapping; this was far more than was anticipated but Cohen's got the blame for the bottleneck of body-burning. Concerns were raised that the scrapping was not being done as quickly as hoped and that an alternative site at Erith was being examined. If such an option had been taken up, trams would have had to be taken on a low-loader from Abbey Wood depot.

The carnage was relentless and the funeral pyre and smoke was to be a familiar sight in the area for more than two years. On average, Cohen's would scrap about seven or eight cars a week, though there were times when double figures were reached. There were weeks when none were scrapped and for much of summer 1951 not one tram was burnt; Cohen's were concentrating on scrapping motorbuses. When there was an influx of trams (at a conversion) the number scrapped per week rose and in the six weeks following stage six, 75 were dealt with. The highest number scrapped in any one week occurred during the week commencing 20th January 1952 when fifteen E1s were broken up. The highs and lows of scrapping also depended upon which way the wind was blowing! Cohen's scrapped 741 passenger cars and 24 works cars; Leeds City Transport bought 90 UCC Felthams and the prototype LCC car number 1. It is thought that 1231 was taken away for further use by Cohen's and not scrapped at Penhall Road.

Stage two occurred on 6th/7th January 1951 when the rest of Clapham's trams were withdrawn, along with many from Streatham and some from Norwood. It was policy for newer trams to replace older ones and at each stage there were many inter-depot transfers with New Cross participating every time; not a single car working at New Cross depot on 5th July 1952 had been there on 30th September 1950.

Four depots were involved at this stage: Brixton Hill, Clapham, Norwood and Streatham; at the next conversion Brixton Hill, Norwood, Purley and Streatham were affected.

Stage three took place on 7th/8th April 1951 and saw the end of trams at Streatham and Purley depots. Although stage one drew little local interest, droves of people turned out to see the last trams pass through their boroughs at stages two and three. The Infantile Paralysis Fellowship Association used these occasions as a means of raising funds, and hired trams on a number of 'last nights' (participants paid a fare with the profits passing to the needy). At this stage, the remainder of the Felthams were taken out of service (bought for £500 each by Leeds with £40 loading costs); they were stored at Penhall Depot pending removal to Charlton Works and ultimate transfer to Leeds. Although there had not been any tram vandalism at stages one and two, London

London Transport title this as 'Burning of old trams as seen from the upper deck of one waiting its turn' on 2nd October 1950, the first day of scrapping. The photographer has composed the view very well; the silhouette shows the traverser trolley arm, and a burning tram. (London Transport Museum U50166)

Stage two not only embraced Clapham and Streatham depots but also impinged on Norwood who operated route 10. E1 560 has been unusually loaned from New Cross to Norwood to cover for a shortage of cars; it is seen in Streatham High Road on its way to CITY & SOUTHWARK. (Fred Ivey)

Two of the three last cars on route 1 stand outside Streatham depot on the night of 5th/6th January 1951. When 2107 returns in a few hours time, it is likely that it will go out on daytime work later. The next night the crews will be taking out a motorbus on route 287. (Alan Cross)

This view at Wimbledon sees trams 1810 and 1812 waiting for departure time one wet evening. Oakey advertised prolifically on London's trams. In the background is a Q1 trolleybus.

Conversion stage two: 1812, the last 24 is at Westminster tram shelter; the crew wave. Going the other way is 1576 on route 38; both were scrapped early in the conversion programme. (Both photos by Don Thompson)

A moment in time: New Cross, 3.30pm Saturday 6th January 1951. Passing through is Feltham 2098 which was decommissioned at Streatham depot a short while ago. 802, the lowest numbered E1 in service at the time, has been working on route 52 and rather than go through to Grove Park has been curtailed at Catford – the conductor has failed to change the blind to NEW CROSS GATE. 802 has come to a halt outside New Cross depot; once the crew have left the car inside, it will be decommissioned and sent to Penhall Road. In view are six other cars carrying out their normal duties. (Fred Ivey)

Londoners had great affection for their trams and the last to run through many boroughs was met by large throngs of people who came to bid farewell; the size of the crowd in Balham and Tooting on the night of 6th/7th January 1951 was enormous. London Transport allowed organisations to use trams after the last service car had passed through. 1829 was hired by the Infantile Paralysis Fellowship for a journey from Balham Hill to Tooting Broadway and back; it was a total sell-out. Among the crowd were Don and Elsie Lewis who had come to say goodbye to an old friend; Don has provided many of the photos and the majority of the press cuttings for this book. (London Transport Museum U50750)

The last route 10 was E1 996; there was a shortage of route blinds for rehabilitated cars at Norwood depot at the time. A metal route plate used on the sides of trams has been sourced and will suffice until 'close of play'. It is 10.44pm on 6th January 1951. When it reaches St Georges Church, 996 will return to Tooting and then proceed to Norwood depot. (London Transport Museum U50734)

Last car from Wimbledon was 1847 on the night of 6th/7th January 1951– the Mayor of Wimbledon has left his comfy armchair and warm front room to shake hands with its crew. (London Transport Museum U50739)

LONDON TRANSPORT

SOUTH LONDON CONVERSION
STAGE II

MOVEMENT OF TRAMCARS PRIOR TO JANUARY 7TH, 1951

At the completion of Stage II of the South London Conversion scheduled for January 7th, 1951, the undermentioned tramcars will be transferred between the depots indicated on Saturday, 6th January, 1951, in readiness for the revised services commencing on January 7th.

The transfer arrangement as hitherto will be in the hands of the Operating Department, who will move the cars either by diversion immediately on completion of service or from the home depot later, dependant on local conditions, but to ensure a satisfactory movement, the usual full co-operation will be necessary between the Rolling Stock and Operating Staffs.

NEW CROSS:

Eighty cars to be moved for scrapping to ....PENHALL ROAD SITE

802; 836; 940; 948; 960; 978; 981; 984;
993; 1005; 1007; 1030; 1032; 1088; 1090;
1092; 1094; 1163; 1171; 1175; 1182; 1195;
1211; 1215; 1216; 1218; 1223; 1233; 1244;
1246; 1247; 1251; 1267; 1273; 1291; 1350;
1362; 1363; 1375; 1381; 1415; 1486; 1488;
1489; 1491; 1496; 1501; 1503; 1504; 1520;
1530; 1533; 1563; 1570; 1577; 1587; 1588;
1589; 1592; 1595; 1597; 1601; 1606; 1608;
1621; 1624; 1626; 1629; 1636; 1640; 1642;
1643; 1644; 1646; 1657; 1659; 1662; 1667;
1671; 1674.

NORWOOD:

Nine cars to be moved for scrapping to ....PENHALL ROAD SITE

1357; 1359; 1365; 1388; 1393; 1399; 1401;
1500; 1506.

ABBEY WOOD:

Three cars to be moved for scrapping to ....PENHALL ROAD SITE

1137; 1225; 1398.

BRIXTON:

Twenty-one U.C.C. type cars to be moved (for sale) to....PENHALL ROAD SITE

2068; 2079; 2089; 2090; 2092; 2094; 2095;
2098; 2101; 2102; 2103; 2104; 2106; 2107;
2110; 2111; 2112; 2114; 2117; 2119; 2123.

BRIXTON:

Twenty-three Class E3 cars with 116 AY motors and 013 Controllers to be transferred to .... NORWOOD

161; 163; 164; 167; 170; 171; 172; 174; 177;
181; 188; 189; 190; 191; 192; 193; 194; 195;
196; 197; 198; 199; 200.

NORWOOD:

Fourteen Class E1 cars (Rehabs) with 121/124 type motors and 07 controllers to be transferred to ....NEW CROSS

1353; 1366; 1368; 1369; 1386; 1387; 1391; 1392;
1398; 1402; 1492; 1502; 1507; 1514.

-2-

CLAPHAM:

Sixty-three class E1 cars with 31C type motors and 09 controllers to be transferred to ....NEW CROSS

1312; 1777; 1778; 1779; 1781; 1782; 1783; 1784; 1785;
1786; 1787; 1790; 1791; 1793; 1794; 1795; 1796; 1797;
1798; 1799; 1801; 1802; 1803; 1804; 1805; 1806; 1809;
1810; 1811; 1812; 1813; 1814; 1815; 1817; 1818; 1819;
1820; 1822; 1823; 1824; 1826; 1827; 1828; 1829; 1830;
1832; 1833; 1834; ~~1835~~; 1836; 1837; 1838; 1839; 1840;
1841; 1843; 1844; 1845; 1846; 1847; 1848; 1849; 1850;
1851;

NEW CROSS:

Three E1 class cars with 121/124 type motors and 07 controllers to be transferred to ....ABBEY WOOD

1042; 1144; 1177.

NOTES:

(1) Where service requirements permit, shunts may be carried out on Friday, 5th January, but it is essential that all movements are completed by Saturday, 6th January.

(2) Any removable equipment which can be conveniently removed, such as boards, blinds and stencils on cars being moved to Penhall Road site, which may be required at the depot, may be removed, but in any case, the Works Engineer will later remove any equipment which he desires for Works use and other equipment on request by depots to a limited amount.

Tool boxes and as many lamps as possible should be removed, (except on U.C.C. cars).
On cars being transferred to other depots, blinds, boards and stencils may be removed if desired for further use after agreement with the receiving depot, but on no account may blind gear or any other equipment be removed which will prevent the car entering immediate service at the new depots.

(3) Ploughs on cars entering Penhall Road site will be stacked for collection by the Works Engineer and redistribution to the depots, - spare ploughs can be removed at the depot before transfer to Penhall Road site.

(4) In view of the unavoidable period between the preparation of this list and the car movements, it is probable that some adjustment will be necessary on car numbers, due to accidents, repairs and similar contingencies, and it will be necessary for District Engineers or their deputies to advise Mr. Deacon at this office of such changes without delay.

DIVISIONAL ENGINEER

C.21/VLD.
22nd November, 1950.

An agreement between London Transport and Leeds Corporation saw the BTH equipped Felthams despatched first; they were ex Metropolitan Electric Tramways with the 'GEC' cars being ex London United Tramways. All 'BTH' cars had been withdrawn by stage two (though 2079 was reinstated). 'BTH' 2104 is having a plough inserted into its carrier at the exit of Penhall yard on 18th January 1951 – it is about to go to CRD for preparation for service in Leeds. Stage two withdrawals, an E1 and a Feltham are on stabling tracks; flames will consume the E1. The Feltham will be more fortunate and soon will be seen at exotic places such as Harehills, Hunslet and Temple Newsam! (Fred Ivey)

RTL 1135 is working on route 168 to Putney Heath and straddles the tram tracks on the Embankment on 2nd February 1951. It is adjacent to rehabilitated HR2 1890 which has just terminated at Savoy Street. The tram stop here is only for cars on routes 33 and 35 which have just come out of the Kingsway subway; the next stop westbound will be for all tram services. (Clarence Carter)

London Transport title the picture below, taken on 27th January 1950, as 'Streatham Tram Depot before conversion to Bus Garage'. At the time, Streatham's allocation was predominantly Felthams and a number are in view; a few ex Walthamstow cars are also seen and it would appear that the two types are segregated. On the left, a large number of ploughs are ready for use. In the centre is the traverser that moves cars across the width of the depot. As it approaches the traverser pit, the conduit slot slews towards the running rails – this was to accommodate the mechanics of the traverser. Traversermen had to be inch-perfect when lining up trams to running rails. (London Transport Museum U15794)

Transport was mindful of what had happened at some of the pre-war last tram nights, and at this stage and this stage only, put out some old E1s to be the last into Purley (839) and Streatham depots (947). They needn't have worried as the crowds, though boisterous, did not attempt to strip them. Three depots simultaneously closed to trams that night – Brixton Hill, Streatham and Purley. Streatham depot was renamed Brixton garage to avoid confusion with Streatham bus garage. Route 42 was withdrawn at this stage; along with route 44 which survived until Last Tram Day, they were the only two post-war tram routes that operated solely on overhead wires – all other routes in this era were conduit equipped either fully or partially.

Stage four occurred on Wednesday 11th July 1951 involving routes 68 and 70 – these were known as the 'slow routes' on account that lower horse-power motored cars were used. Route 72 was withdrawn from its Hop Exchange terminus

No.1 was used spasmodically in south London; this was due to the small number of men qualified to drive it. It was often used as an EXTRA and, working in this capacity to Streatham Library, is seen above in Brixton. Behind are two motorbuses – an STL on the 59A and an RT on route 95. (Fred Ivey)

Feltham 2145 basks in the sunshine at the Purley terminus of route 16 on 24th March 1951; another Feltham is behind. Crews take their stand time here; 2145 will soon pull forward, one pole will be raised and the other lowered and it will move over the crossover to pick up passengers. Routes 16 and 18 were busy services and many passengers will board and alight on the trip to Embankment; with no stand there, this tram will not return to Purley for another two and a half hours. Purley had always been the southernmost terminus of the London tramway system. 2145 was one of seven Felthams that did not enter service in Leeds and which were burnt, still in their London Transport livery.

Now it's too quiet

AS I told you last week, the staff and patients at Croydon General Hospital were glad to see the back of the noisy old tramcars and so were the staffs of most of the offices in Croydon High-street, who for years have been unable to open their windows, even on the hottest summer days, because the clanging and grinding of the trams made it almost impossible to hold a conversation on the telephone.

But in contrast to this, I hear that quite a few people have missed the tramcars greatly since Saturday night, so much so that they have been unable to sleep. A colleague who lives in London-road near Thornton Heath Pond tells me, "It's so darned quiet at nights now that I can't get off to sleep. After being used to the clatter of the trams for so long, the new silence is most disturbing."

Noises in the night

I suggested that until he gets himself "acclimatised" to the new conditions, my colleague ought to employ a couple of small boys to kick a pile of old tin cans and buckets around in his front garden at intervals throughout the night. (His reply is unprintable).

One of the older Croydon residents who lives in George-street told me this week, "I know how the people who live on the main road are feeling. After the trams were scrapped on the George-street-Addiscombe route, I slept badly for several nights. I had to get used to the strange silence."

The conversion of trams to trolleybuses saw temporary or permanent overhead wiring arrangements made at a number of locations where these vehicles crossed paths. After June 1940 there were only four: 1) junction of Knee Hill and Abbey Wood Road for access to Abbey Wood depot: 2) Wimbledon Town Hall; 3) Beresford Square, Woolwich; 4) London Road, Croydon at its junction with Tamworth Road and Station Road. 2133 followed by a tram on route 16, passes through the Croydon crossover which was used by trolleybuses on routes 630 and 654. (David Watson)

Four ex-Croydon trams were rehabilitated in the mid 1930s; one was 380 seen on route 42 which ran between Croydon and Thornton Heath Pond. 380 is about to pass under a section feeder in Croydon. (Fred Ivey)

All tram depots south of the River Thames converted to bus garages changed out of all recognition both internally and externally. 2133 leaves Streatham depot to take up service on route 20. Owing to the extensive work being carried out, some of Streatham's allocation on routes 16 and 18 had been transferred to Norwood depot at stage two. (Fred Ivey)

Information about the tram to bus changeover was given in various ways. Bus stop information panels, such as this one at The Oval, were ideal; the one illustrated here is for stage three. Details are given of tram routes 16, 18 and 42 being replaced by motorbuses on Sunday 8th April 1951. (Fred Ivey)

Allocated to New Cross depot, 839 and 947 were to be discarded at stage three. It was thought that revellers might strip the two hired trams so they were sent especially to Purley and Streatham depots for the day. The cars survived remarkably intact. They were the two lowest numbered cars at New Cross, maybe the reason for their selection.

A trio of pictures illustrate 947 being hidden away in Brixton Hill depot at 1pm on 7th April 1951; prior to this the Streatham Ratepayers Association had placed their banners on it in Streatham depot. In the top photo, 947 turns off conduit track on to one of the two single lines of approach to the depot. In the middle view, the trolley has been raised but unusually is at the driving end. In the lower photograph, 947 disappears into the depot to await its crowning glory later on. A unique arrangement applied here; on the depot forecourt are two plough-shifts – one for cars arriving/departing south, the other for those arriving/departing north. Trolleybus-style hangers are used here. (Peter Mitchell)

The Infantile Paralysis Fellowship in conjunction with the Croydon and Purley Chamber of Commerce hired E1 839 for a sum of £4 for a trip from Purley to Thornton Heath on the night of 7th April 1951. In daylight at Purley depot 839 is prepared for its time in the limelight; the night shot shows it prior to departure. (*Croydon Times*)

Thornton Heath depot could not be adapted for motorbuses; it had to be demolished and a new bus garage built on the same site. Therefore from 1st January 1950, all its trams and staff were transferred to Purley depot which was re-opened – staff returned to Thornton Heath on 8th April 1951. An unusual visitor to Purley depot on 7th April 1951 was Feltham 2155; it has probably been curtailed short of its destination. (Alan Cross)

and now terminated at Savoy Street on the Embankment. It was anticipated that this stage would embrace routes 33 and 35 (the remaining subway routes) as well as 48 and 78; various factors dictated against this and all were converted later on. There was some reluctance to do this as fourteen miles of single tramway track would have to be retained in excess of that which would otherwise have been made redundant for a period of nine months. It also meant the continuance of the current supply for this period and the retention of 46 trams over what had been anticipated at this stage; there would also be the utilisation of 64 buses less than the number which would have been brought into service. The payroll week for staff finished and started on a Tuesday/Wednesday; conversion stages were planned to take place on a Saturday night/Sunday morning when matters were quieter. This changeover took place midweek owing to its complexities.

A boy scout with a bugle played the 'Last Post' for the last

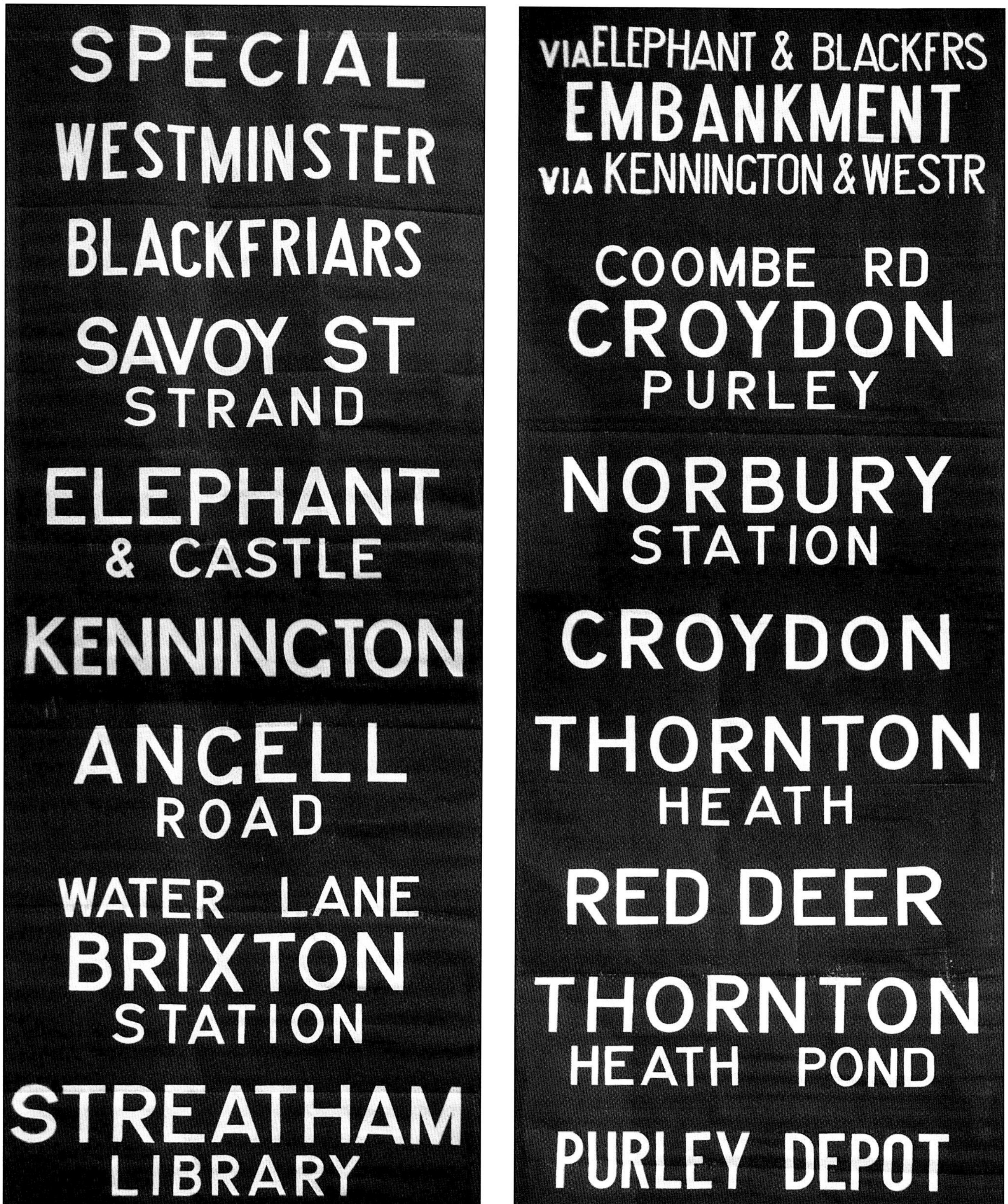

SPECIAL
WESTMINSTER
BLACKFRIARS
SAVOY ST
STRAND
ELEPHANT
& CASTLE
KENNINGTON
ANGELL
ROAD
WATER LANE
BRIXTON
STATION
STREATHAM
LIBRARY

VIA ELEPHANT & BLACKFRS
EMBANKMENT
VIA KENNINGTON & WESTR
COOMBE RD
CROYDON
PURLEY
NORBURY
STATION
CROYDON
THORNTON
HEATH
RED DEER
THORNTON
HEATH POND
PURLEY DEPOT

When Thornton Heath depot closed, lock, stock and barrel moved to Purley depot. 'Stock' included the trams and everything about them and they went with their blinds which could continue in use. Wear and tear, old age and leaky blind boxes saw new destination blinds supplied to Purley depot just seven weeks before tramcar operation ceased there. This blind is dated 15 FEB 1951, and is unused.

After 15th October 1938 there was only one area on the London Transport network where trams rubbed shoulders with country area buses; this was between Croydon and Purley. Taken at 2.33pm on the wet afternoon of 7th April, RT 3146 is a few minutes into its journey on route 409 to Caterham Station and is passing E3 1911 at 'The Greyhound' terminus of route 42 in Croydon. The destination blind is one supplied for rehabilitated cars but which has found its way into 1911. Purley depot predominately used ex-Croydon cars but a few E3s were also allocated. (Peter Mitchell)

Top. The last Felthams came out of service on 7th April 1951. Approaching Camberwell Green at 3pm is 2132 – three standard cars are in the background.

Right. 2141 and another are seen at New Cross Gate at 3.30pm. Both head for Penhall Road where they will be temporarily stored; all have their destination blinds turned to blank. The Felthams are strangers in this area. (Clarence Carter)

Left. 2155 has reached the entrance to Penhall Road on 7th April 1951. One of the trolley arms has been hoisted on to the overhead and, in contrast to most other trams entering this foreboding place, 2155 will re-emerge in due course. 2155's destination and route blinds have been turned to the blank parts of the blinds. This car was one of seven Felthams not to enter service in Leeds. (Fred Ivey)

The last 16 from Blackfriars was 384; the light against the offside of the car is a street light and not part of 384's external lighting. A number of 'hairies' (Don Jones is one of them) are on the top deck ready for the run to Purley depot on the night of 7th April 1951. The moustachioed driver, with heavy leather gloves and scarf, looks the part. (London Transport Museum U51185)

56 Thornton Heath Garage

A new Garage on the site of the old tram depot in London Road, Thornton Heath will be brought into operation on Sunday, 8th April, 1951 in connection with Stage 3 of the Tramway Conversion Scheme.

This garage is in District 22, the District Supt. is Mr. A. Watson and the Chief Depot Inspector is Mr. S. H. C. Weatherhead. The running letters are T.H. Telephone Number— THOrnton Heath 3835 (2 lines).

PURLEY DEPOT
This depot will be closed after 7th April, 1951, when tram operations cease at Stage 3 of the Tramway Conversion Scheme.

The Streatham Ratepayers Association hired E1 947 for a late night run on 7th April 1951 and was given free rein to decorate it in whatever manner they wanted. A number of inscriptions were emblazoned while 947 stood in Streatham depot in the morning; the messages differed on each side of the car. At the controls is driver Stan Collins; conductor is Bert Edwards. Standing on the platform is the deputy mayor of Wandsworth (Alderman A.E. Carr) who had earlier driven the gaily decorated 947. A banner states that this is the last tram to and from the Astoria; someone needs to go back to school and see how 'faithful' should be spelled. (Wykeham Studios)

SOUTH LONDON CONVERSION - STAGE 3

Instructions for inter-Depot transfer of tramcars and the transfer of tramcars to Penhall Road, Charlton site

1919

1. On Saturday, 7th April, 1951, inter Depot transfer of tramcars and the transfer of tramcars to the Penhall Road, Charlton, site will be made consequent upon the introduction of Stage 3 of the South London Conversion Scheme as follows:-

SUMMARIZED MOVEMENT OF TRAMCARS

Purley	Depot to	New Cross Depot	32 cars	
Abbey Wood	"	" Penhall Road Site	3 "	
Brixton	"	" Penhall Road Site	40 "	U.C.C.
"	"	" New Cross	10 "	
New Cross	"	" Penhall Road Site	58 "	
" "	"	" Abbey Wood Depot	3 "	
Norwood	"	" Penhall Road Site	3 "	
"	"	" New Cross	19 "	
		TOTAL	168 cars	

2. The cars affected in this movement are shown in detail on the attached Summary of the Divisional Rolling Stock Engineer. The Superintendent of each district concerned will detail a Road Inspector and the Instructor outlined in para. 12 to be present at each Depot concerned to supervise the despatch and reception of tramcars as indicated in the Summary, and they will maintain a close liaison with the Depot Engineer for that purpose.

3. Volunteer crews will be obtained by the District Superintendent in co-operation with the Depot Committee, and the Instructor will be responsible for the briefing thereof and full instructions to each Driver as to the route to be traversed, as set out in Appendix 'A'.

Arrangements will be made for the reception of cars into Penhall Road Site from 2.0 p.m. on Saturday, 7th April, 1951. Superintendents concerned should, therefore, arrange in conjunction with the Depot Engineer for tramcars listed by the Divisional Engineer for transfer, to be allocated as far as possible to running numbers scheduled to run into depot after mid-day peak.

It is important that the allocation of such cars should not be varied by "change overs" by Control Point Officials and a list of cars involved in the movement should therefore be supplied to them with instructions to this effect.

The details of proposed departure timings for movement of tramcars from each depot, to be supplied to the Divisional Superintendent, for collating, and if necessary modification, to ensure an even flow of tramcars into Penhall Road site and receiving depots.

District Superintendent to advise Divisional Office by 9.0 a.m. on Thursday, 5th April, 1951, that the necessary crews have been obtained.

4. District Superintendent Sharp, New Cross Depot, will, in conjunction with the Chargehand of Bowles Road Breakdown Gang, obtain a volunteer Gang for duty at Penhall Road site from 2 p.m. Saturday, April 7th, to cover the period of reception of cars at Penhall Road. They will be stationed there with the tender and will be responsible for the marshalling of cars from the carriageway to the site.

In this connection the following must be observed:-

(a) When cars are proceeding from down track onto the site, a red lamp warning must be given to oncoming traffic.

p.t.o.

(b) The ploughs shed from oncoming vehicles must be stacked for subsequent removal.

(c) Drivers to be warned to proceed "Dead Slow" over sleeper tracks on site, and when assembled into position, handbrakes to be set under retaining hook and controller key and trolley booms removed.

(d) Every care must be taken to reduce noise to a minimum at the site entrance, so as to avoid annoyance to residents in the vicinity.

District Superintendent Dunn and selected Instructors will be in charge at this point and the Works Engineer, Charlton, will be responsible for marshalling cars on site.

5. It is important the U.C.C. (Feltham) cars do not pass cars travelling in opposite direction on Greenwich Church Curve and Canal Head, Peckham. Drivers concerned to be instructed accordingly. Instructor Bain will be responsible for observance of this condition at these points.

6. Staff Buses will be operated to enable staff engaged in shunting to return to their home depots, and timings will be supplied in due course.

7. Arrangements are being made with the Welfare Officer for the provision of Canteen facilities at Penhall Road and Depots concerned in the transfer and the volunteer crews engaged, will be provided with a note as per attached, signed by the Road Inspector at the despatching depot, authorising the free provision of refreshments at the receiving depots and site.

8. The Divisional Superintendent and Divisional Rolling Stock Engineer will be on duty during the period of transfer at the Divisional Rolling Stock Engineer's Office, and Mechanical Inspector Rutland will be responsible for liaison between Traffic and Engineering Officials during the transfer, and will be available at Divisional Rolling Stock Engineer's Office during the period of transfer.

9. The completion of each phase of the transfer is to be reported to Mechanical Inspector Rutland as soon as each movement is completed.

The Road Inspector at each depot will record the name of each crew, the number of the car for which they are responsible, the time engaged and the booking for work performed.

10. Should any problem or difficulty arise prior to or during the transfer, contact should immediately be made with the Divisional Rolling Stock Engineer's Office.

11. The Permanent Way and Electrical Distribution Divisional Engineers have been requested to defer track operations to avoid single line working during this movement.

12. Mechanical Inspector Rutland will arrange with Superintendents for Instructors to be on duty at the undermentioned Depots and points:-

5th [illegible]il, 1[illegible]51,

Brixton
Purley
New Cross
Penhall Road
Greenwich Church
Canal Head

DIVISIONAL SUPERINTENDENT (S.E.)

22nd February, 1951.
D25/

SOUTH LONDON CONVERSION - STAGE 3

APPENDIX 'A'

1. PURLEY DEPOT

To New Cross Depot: As tram routes 16, 18, via Croydon, Streatham, Brixton Rd. to Magee Street, Kennington and Turn, thence as Route 40, via Camberwell New Road, Peckham High Street.

2. ABBEY WOOD DEPOT

To Penhall Road Site: As tram route 36 via McLeod Road, Plumstead High Street, Beresford Square, Beresford Street, Woolwich Road.

3. BRIXTON DEPOT

To Penhall Road Site: As route 16, 18 via Brixton Hill, Brixton Road to Magee Street, Kennington and turn, thence as route 40, see No. 1.

To New Cross: As in No. 1

To Norwood Depot: As route 16, 18 to Brixton Station, turn and as for routes 78, 33.

4. NEW CROSS DEPOT

To Penhall Road Site: As route 40, see No. 1.

To Abbey Wood Depot: As tram route 40, via New Cross Road, Deptford, Greenwich Church, Woolwich Road, change over Free Ferry, Beresford Street, Plumstead High Street, McLeod Road, to depot.

5. NORWOOD DEPOT

To New Cross Depot or Penhall Road: As tram route 48 via Herne Hill, Milkwood Road, Coldharbour Lane, Camberwell Green and turn, thence as tram route 40, see No. 1.

District Superintendents will arrange for the posting of an Official at crossovers on routes where shunting is taking place, as follows:

Magee Street — Kennington Park Road
Camberwell Road — Camberwell Green
Church Lane — Charlton
Brixton Station

These Officials must be provided with red hurricane lamps, and continue supervision of cars turning until completion of movement.

J. R. Garratt.
DIVISIONAL SUPERINTENDENT, S.E.

Distribution:
J. B. Burnell, Esq. (2)
P. G. Gibbins, Esq. (2)
A. E. Butler, Esq. (12)
J. H. Giffin, Esq. (6)
District Superintendents (3)
J. Schofield, Esq.
H. L. Buckman, Esq. (3)
H. A. Wickham, Esq.
E. C. Gezzele, Esq.
Mr. M. I. Rutland
Mr. G. Long

22nd February, 1951.
D25/

The first bus to leave Brixton Garage on the morning of 8th April 1951 was RT3278 on route 109. The garage staff have positioned the blinds perfectly; the qualifying display of EMBANKMENT split on two lines is unusual; this feature did not last long. (London Transport Museum U51195)

Left: Ninety Felthams were sold to Leeds Corporation in 1950/1951 with modifications being undertaken at CRD; they were stripped of trolley booms and bases, retaining hooks, plough carriers and lifeguards. Many then went to 'Penhall Store' and back to CRD for despatch to Yorkshire. 2141 left CRD for Penhall on 1st June and has been pushed up 'Penhall slope' by 2129 on 4th July – an LT tractor pulls it onto Woolwich Road. 2141 will be towed to CRD by 2129 seen at the yard entrance; the tractor will follow them to the entrance of the works. Movements took place under heavy supervision as tram services still operate along Woolwich road. *Bottom Left:* 2129 has pulled 2141 from Penhall Road to the outskirts of CRD; shunting at a nearby crossover, the tractor will finish the job by pushing 2141 inside. Both cars still have their number blinds in. *Bottom Right:* Having been freed of its companion (seen in the far distance under tow), 2129 is just outside CRD and in Fairthorn Villas. Soon it will be prepared for shipment to Leeds Corporation who fitted the Felthams with bow collectors. STL349 is on learner duties – maybe for works employees who will be driving staff buses before long. (Fred Ivey)

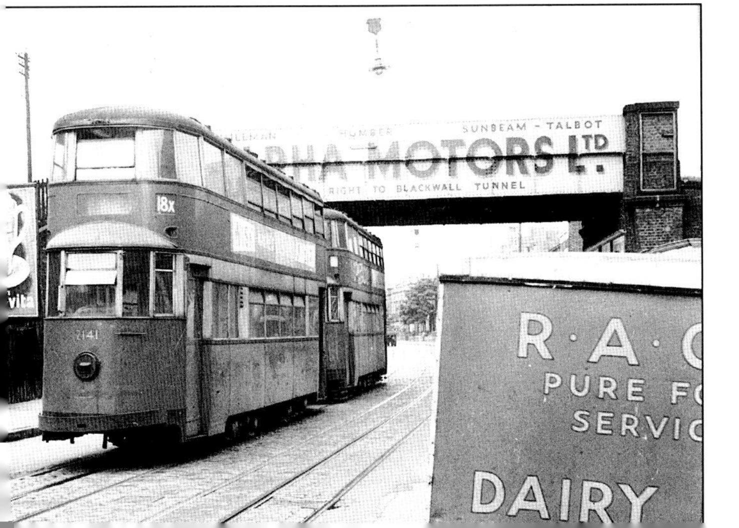

The delay to Cohen's scrapping trams in 1951 was through no fault of their own, but by London Transport sending many motorbuses to be broken up at the Penhall Road site. There is not much left of G127. Feltham 2124 and some sister cars will soon be in Leeds. (Fred Ivey)

The permanent way needed to be maintained in good condition until the end; there is more than a year to go though, when 304 was photographed on Shooters Hill on 21st April 1951. The track maintenance staff needed power to operate their equipment; they obtained this by hooking a device onto the running wire as seen here. A 'TRACK UP' sign was used when maintenance work was being carried out. Note the customary tar boiler in the foreground. (Clarence Carter)

160 was originally an HR2 car. After its EMB trucks were positioned under LCC Number 1, a pair of maximum traction trucks were fitted to 160 leading to its reclassification as an E3 (the only member of this class not to be fitted with trolley gear). Allocated to New Cross depot, 160 turns from Tower Bridge Road into Tooley Street; it is working on route 68 from Waterloo to Greenwich. Also in view is RT 1212 on route 78 to Dulwich Library; in the background is Tower Bridge. (Peter Mitchell)

2048 is at a deserted Borough terminus during the time that route 72 operated to this point. An informative destination display of LEE & BERESFORD SQ tells passengers that the 72 travels to Woolwich via Lee and not Greenwich. (Peter Mitchell)

Between stages one and four of the conversion, route 72 worked to London Bridge; no display was provided so the conductor has used the LONDON BGE route 70 panel and 'wound it down a bit'; 1844 passes over Blackfriars Bridge on 7th July 1951. It had been a Clapham depot car for many years and was one example of E1s moving in and out of New Cross depot between 1950 and 1952. E1 1844 is fitted with external bracing for body strengthening. (Peter Mitchell)

The 552-601 batch of cars led interesting and varied lives; many saw service in North London in their early years. Some were fitted with low horse-power motors; others had a high horse-power rating. The low-motored cars were assigned to the 'slow routes' – the 68 and 70. Trams and buses on route 68 could be seen alongside each other at Waterloo; E1 561 and RTL 1186 illustrate this on 7th July 1951. (Peter Mitchell)

As stated in the caption to the photograph on the previous page, the 552-601 class of car led varied lives. One of the most useful connections made in the change from trams to trolleybuses was in North London. Until October 1936, route 23 had turned at the 'Ferry Boat Inn' on Ferry Lane with people wanting to travel west having to walk to Tottenham; with the introduction of route 623 the gap was bridged. Seen at the Ferryboat Inn, in about 1935, E1 586 has just arrived from the east. (Hugh Nicol)

70 from Tooley Street on the Tuesday night; it was almost midnight when it left and people in Bermondsey and Greenwich turned out in their hundreds to say goodbye and farewell to a sight and sound which had been part of their lives for nearly fifty years. Football rattles and whistles were added to the shouting. People hung out of their windows of houses and flats, waved union jacks, towels and pillowcases and cheered; some brought children in pyjamas out into the streets. Said an old "customer" of the tramcars, "I am sorry they're gone; we got used to the noise. It was like an alarm clock; you learned to pick out the individual noise that would tell you the time without having to lift your head from the pillow". There was an escort of motorcyclists and at the junction of Rotherhithe Tunnel and Jamaica Road the crowd was so dense that police had to force a way to let the tram through. London Transport allowed a private tram to run after the last service car; this was E1 587 with appropriate signage on the advertisement panels.

The fifth stage took place on 6th/7th October 1951 and in one stroke, Camberwell's cars succumbed to the motorbus.

1648 is an inappropriate tram for routes 68 and 70 as they were normally the preserve of slower cars. Dockers are boarding at Surrey Docks; despite showing WATERLOO STN, the car is heading for Greenwich. (Fred Ivey)

Stage four saw the end of trams at Waterloo and London Bridge; the last 70 from London Bridge was crewed by driver Jimmy Jameson and conductress Nora Dooley. Driver Jameson waves to the crowd as 580 leaves Tooley Street. Once 580 had departed, Nora punches tickets from her short rack. (London Transport Museum U51859/U51858)

Far more people wanted to ride on 'Last Waterloo' than on 'Last London Bridge'; this may have been because it would be the last service car through Deptford. 936 is at Waterloo; close inspection of the 68 route stencil indicates that it is an 89 plate that survived the war.
(London Transport Museum U51868)

London Transport allowed a special to run after the last service car from London Bridge. Banners were positioned on both sides of 587 stating that it is the last tram through Bermondsey.
(London Transport Museum U51861)

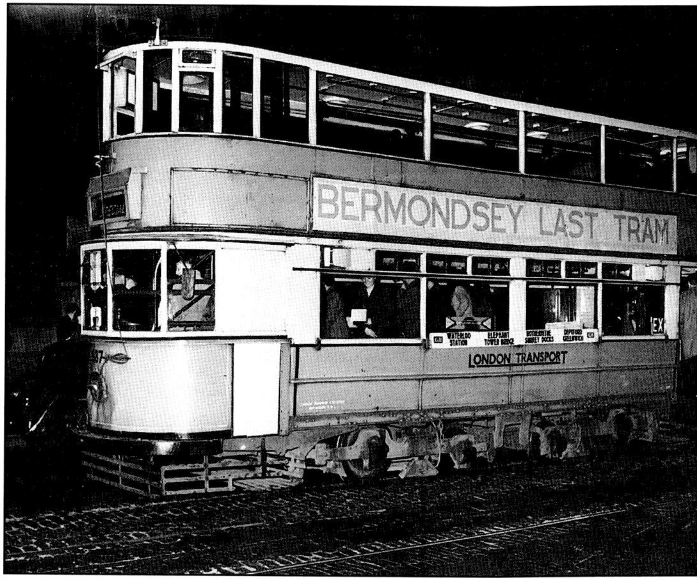

The special is seen between London Bridge and Greenwich; crowds mob the tram which is full up. Eventually the well-wishers will move aside and allow 587 a path to proceed to Greenwich and then on to New Cross depot. (London Transport Museum U51863)

This stage saw the end of trams on Dog Kennel Hill and heavy inroads made into the HR2s; however, many of these powerful cars, along with their share of route 35, were transferred to New Cross at this time. The conversions at stages four and five only embraced conduit track. Camberwell tram depot was named Walworth bus garage at this time; this avoided confusion with Camberwell bus garage which was almost opposite it in Camberwell New Road.

Stage six occurred on 5th/6th January 1952 with New Cross now losing large numbers of routes and trams. It was at this conversion that chalked inscriptions started to appear on cars; not by well-wishers or those mourning their passing, but by crews. Not only were the last Croydon and Walthamstow cars taken out of commission, the last pedigree E1s went too. The important inner London tram terminus of Victoria was now lost – the last car was despatched by cheering and singing crowds. Until the fifth stage there were enough trams to cover for the maintenance and overhaul of the remaining fleet. However, at stage six the number required for service reduced dramatically with London Transport being aware that if there was a sudden increase in failures

HUNDREDS SAY GOODBYE TO LAST TRAMCAR

THE people of Bermondsey and Greenwich turned out in hundreds early this morning to bid farewell to a sight and a sound which have been part of their lives for nearly 50 years.

The last tramcar was going home from Tooley-street, near London Bridge, to Greenwich.

The last tram was a special hired by The Electric Traction Group—enthusiasts in all forms of trams, trolleybuses, railways.

All along the route, at cross-roads and side turnings, were crowds who had stayed up especially to say goodbye.

There was an escort of motor-cyclists, and at the junction of the Rotherhithe Tunnel and Jamaica-road the crowd was so dense that police had to force a way to let the tram through.

LAST TRIP

★ As a Boy Scout with a bugle played the Last Post, the last tramcar on the No. 70 route left Tooley Street, Bermondsey, for Greenwich depot—and the scrap heap.

It was almost midnight, but people were out in hundreds to say good-bye. Football rattles and whistles were added to the shouting.

People hung out of the windows of houses and flats, waved Union Jacks, towels and pillow-cases and cheered. Some brought children, in pyjamas, out into the streets.

Said an old "customer" of the tramcars: "I am sorry they're gone. We got used to the noise. It was like an alarm clock—you learned to pick out the individual noise that would tell you the time without having to lift your head from the pillow."

The rear of Camberwell tram depot on 6th October 1951. A number of new RTLs have been brought to the premises and are ready for the next day's service; RT 43 is also in evidence – it has probably been used to train tram drivers. The next day, this place will be known as Walworth bus garage; much work still needs to be done and was a feature at many garages during the changeover. (Clarence Carter)

OCTOBER 6, 1951

MORE TRAMS OFF

London Transport will take the trams off 56 more miles of routes from the Embankment to Camberwell, Catford, Peckham, Forest Hill, Dulwich, and Greenwich, all S.E., at midnight tonight.

they could find themselves short. Therefore, fifteen HR2 trolley-less cars were classified as 'emergency spares' and parked at 'Penhall' in that capacity. This was odd as they could work on a conduit-only route – the 35 from New Cross depot. 118, 121, 122 and 132 were reinstated at New Cross and operated on the 35. They were withdrawn at stage seven when twenty E class cars became the emergency spares. Of these, only 192 was reinstated – the other nineteen had gone by the end of June. At this stage, northbound cars on route 35 were diverted at the Elephant and Castle to run via London Road and Westminster Bridge Road (the same as the southbound routeing). This enabled the tracks in St George's Road, which had only been used by the 35 since stage five, to be taken out of use.

Not scrapped immediately was trolley-less HR2 138 which had one last unexpected task before it went to meet its maker. Sent for use in the trimming shop at CRD on 1st February 1952, some wooden decking was assembled on the roof – no more than a frame to prevent staff falling to the ground. Some heavy lifting gear located in the ceiling of the works had to be dismantled once museum cars 290 and 1025 had been overhauled. As tower wagons were not tall enough, a tram without a trolley was needed – hence 138 was commandeered from Penhall. The work done, the framework was removed and 138 was driven back to Penhall on 14th May. This was her second visit – there was to be no reprieve this time; she outlasted all other trolley-less cars and was not scrapped until the week of 25th May 1952.

Hampstead depot closed to trams on 10th July 1938; the two and a half mile track connecting it to the rest of the system at Holloway depot was retained in reasonable condition as access would continue to be required. Its main function was for the scrapping of trams – this continued until early 1940. Later it was used to store and in some cases upgrade cars for a return to service during the war; scrapping recommenced in 1945, but following a fire on 1st October 1946 when five cars were destroyed, the fire authorities put a block on any further scrapping there. Some of the Hampstead cars were towed to Brixton Hill for dismantling; Purley depot took on this task in the late 1940s. On 14th December 1950, it was stated that consideration was being given to restoring the tracks between Holloway and Hampstead depots to a suitable condition as it

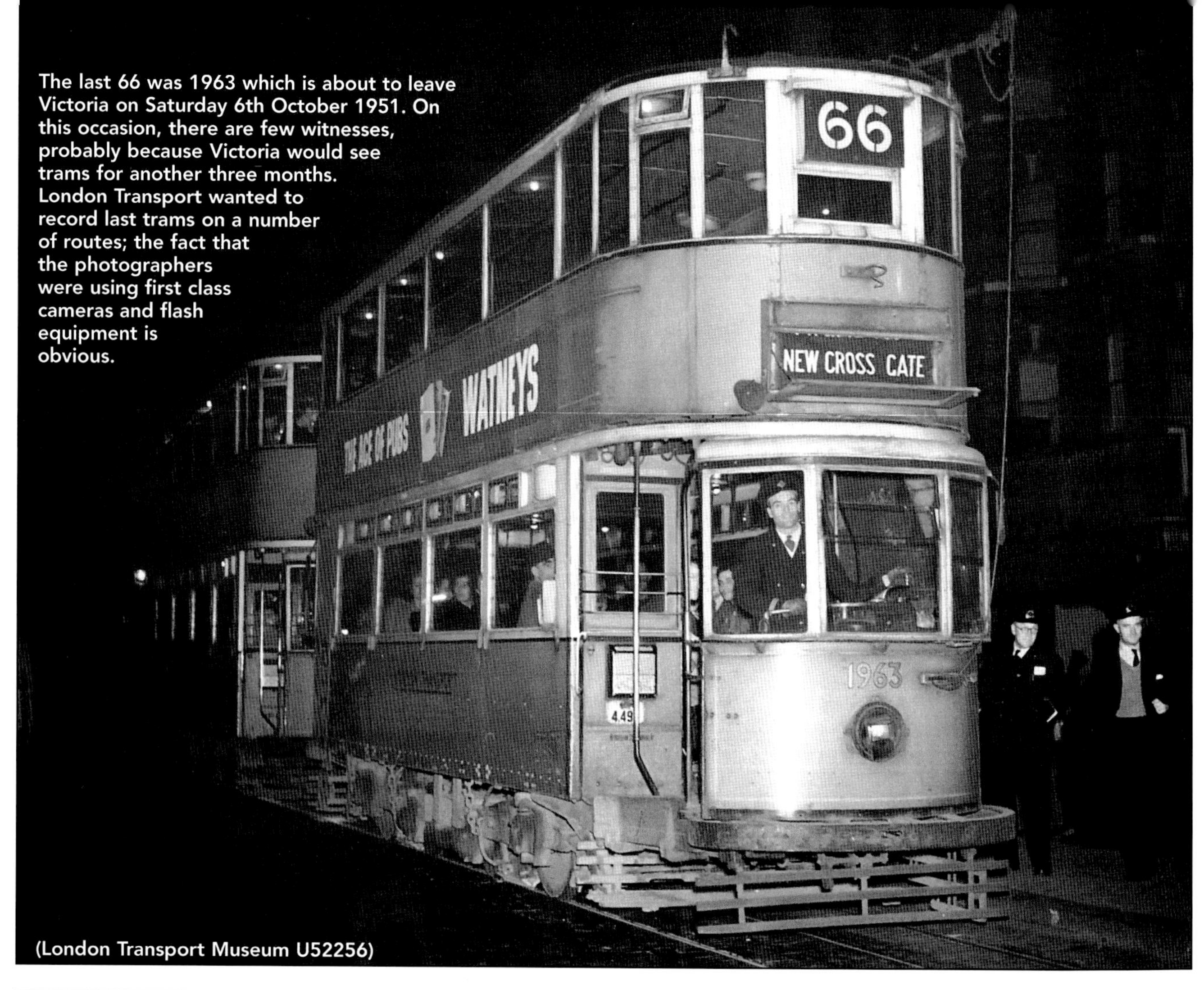

The last 66 was 1963 which is about to leave Victoria on Saturday 6th October 1951. On this occasion, there are few witnesses, probably because Victoria would see trams for another three months. London Transport wanted to record last trams on a number of routes; the fact that the photographers were using first class cameras and flash equipment is obvious.

(London Transport Museum U52256)

Final 62 was HR2 134. The conductor is ready to leap off at Camberwell, shortly before it enters the depot as stage five comes to its conclusion. In a couple of minute's time, the driver's working life on a tram will be over. (London Transport Museum U52250)

London Transport captions this view as '5th stage tram conversion. Last service 58 tram at Camberwell Green'. This is incorrect as 1855 is followed by a rehabilitated HR2 going to Vauxhall on route 58. The number of people to see the last cars into Camberwell depot is not large; this may have been because trams would be running through Camberwell until July 1952. (London Transport Museum U52249)

QUESTION **Has anybody been caught speeding while driving a bus?**

FURTHER to earlier answers, in the Forties my father was caught speeding while driving a London tram. He could scarcely believe he was doing more than 40mph.

Back at New Cross tram depot, he learnt that he had been driving a tram borrowed from the No 58 route that had more powerful motors fitted to enable it to negotiate the steep Denmark Hill in South-East London.

My father was fined the equivalent of 38p. I believe his trade union assisted with paying the fine.

D.A. LUNAN, Lytham St Annes, Lancs.

A question asked in recent times in the *Daily Mail* showed a pitfall for New Cross drivers who were unaccustomed to HR2 cars. These powerful cars had formerly been at Camberwell depot working on Dog Kennel Hill routes.

was thought that Hampstead could be used as an annexe to Penhall Road for scrapping (access from south London would be at night via the Kingsway subway). It was stated that A) defective trams could be towed there by lorry (as would trolley-less cars): B) trams with ploughs could get there under their own power. In the case of 'A', it would not be difficult to restore the continuity of the rails and carry out ancillary works to render the track suitable for towing purposes; the estimated cost would be in the order of £3,000 and would take eight weeks to complete. With regard to 'B', it was impossible to give an approximate estimate as the condition of the sub-surface could not be ascertained without opening the road. It might cost as much as £13,000 and take three months to complete providing the materials were readily available ('B' entailed re-vamping conduit track). Neither option was taken up. An oddity that now appeared was that the track between the two depots was embraced in the South London scheme.

An Abandonment Notice was served on 11th April 1951 with maintenance liability ceasing on 12th July 1951, more than thirteen years after trams had regularly used it. It could only be accessed by travelling 'wrong road' at a number of locations – these were the tracks that were in the best condition and able to be kept in operational order; whether maintenance was retained to the end is doubtful as the track was in parlous condition in post-war years. Driver Skinner took the periodic statutory car from Holloway to Hampstead and back until July 1951, enabling London Transport's legal obligations to be maintained. It is thought that otherwise these tracks were last used in 1947.

2105 is in Fairthorn Villas on its way 'up north' on 9th October 1950. The body is on the low-loader and the trucks on the towing wagon. London Transport placed metal sheeting around front windows of cars going to Leeds to protect them from getting broken by trees. This meant that if a Feltham went into the works 'A' end first, metal sheeting was fitted at 'B' end. Fairthorn Villas (the road leading to Charlton Works) was later named Felltram Way in honour of a former LCC tramways manager.

At the end of the Saturday mid-day peak hour on 5th January 1952, the last 52 is 'chalked up' by 2043's conductor at Southwark; maybe a few more fares were taken because of this. Trams used to go about a hundred yards further north until the terminus was cut back owing to bomb damage. (Geoffrey Ashwell)

This view exhorts passengers to hurry up if they do not want to miss the last 52. This last-minute passenger heeds the slogans' advice in Great Dover Street at 2.09pm. 2043 did not reach New Cross depot until 3.30pm. (Peter Mitchell)

Top. Unusually, two consecutively numbered trams have arrived at the scrapyard together; this has happened at 3.30pm on Saturday 5th January 1952. Both are former Walthamstow cars that have come out of service following the midday peak hour surge. 2046 still has its 54 route plate on as it moves off the highway for the last time; 2047 will follow it in. The sequence of arrival of these four cars outside Penhall Road is 2046, an E3, 2047 and a West Ham car.

Centre. A man with a red flag holds back a former West Ham car and any other road traffic that may attempt to come up on the nearside. A large crowd watch trams go to their place of execution. A BEWARE CARS CROSSING sign is installed here. 2047 enters. (both Clarence Carter)

Below: Last tram of all from Victoria was 1998, a 78 to West Norwood on the night of 5th/6th January 1952. The car is packed; those at the stop have either been unable to board or have come to say goodbye. London Transport was keen to name those who staffed their last trams; crewing 1998 is driver Douglas Coleman, with his brother Pat as the conductor. Note that the car is showing VIA KINGSWAY SUBWAY – a metal plate that could have covered this panel has not been used. (London Transport Museum U52701)

138 was used to remove some redundant items from the roof inside Charlton Works. Some primitive decking was fitted to the top deck – this can be seen in this view. (Ken Thorpe)

This view in Hampstead depot in 1946 shows some trams that had spent much of the war here. Most of these trams operated from Poplar depot until June 1940; this explains the white paint on their fenders. They have been mothballed in case they were needed during the rest of the conflict. Nearest the camera is 1754 which still has a route 36 plate in position. Also identifiable are 1304 and 1774; further along is one with a windscreen. The car at the end is scorched, having been involved in the 1946 fire here. All these cars were broken up without being used again.

The closed Hampstead depot was a place where even London Transport employees, wishing to have a look round, could not get in. Somehow this has been achieved; maybe the watchman was warming himself somewhere on the premises. This is the forlorn snow swept scene on 29th March 1952; at this time, Hampstead depot is still considered to be part of the tramway system. (John Gillham)

ANYBODY WANT A TUNNEL?

Stage seven took place on 5th/6th April 1952; this embraced routes 33 and 35. Route 35 was the last all-conduit route and the last to have an all-night service. The closure of the Kingsway subway occurred now along with the last routes in north London; apart from the 31, which had been withdrawn in October 1950, the previous conversion in this part of the capital had been in December 1939. For all that time, Holloway depot had operated trams and trolleybuses, this being the longest period of joint operation by any depot. A continuing problem though, had been the manning-up of trams there as drivers had to have six months service before they could drive in the subway. To meet the ruling, they had to complete this period by driving in South London (remunerative, as they were paid travelling time to and from Holloway). Even that did not completely solve the problem and therefore to provide a full service

London Transport officials would normally co-operate with those who wished to photograph buses, trams and trolleybuses on the Executive's premises. The unknown photographer would have asked the official standing alongside 1912 if it would be alright to stand behind the tram and take this view. 1912 heads south for Forest Hill; another car waits at the Holborn northbound platform.

Photographers had to be patient to get trams passing each other at either end of the Kingsway subway; this has been achieved at the northern end with E3s 1944 and 1942. The former car retains its corner advertising frames; 1942's have been removed. 1942 has received a wooden windscreen while 1944 retains its original metal one. (Fred Ivey)

Towards the end of March 1952, just a week before trams last ran in North London, a heavy snowfall swept across the capital. Approaching Highgate depot, E3 169 is seen in Pemberton Gardens. Tram crews had to be hardy to work in this sort of weather; there will be a short respite from the cold though, when 169 is in the warmth of the Kingsway subway. (Peter Mitchell)

The weather has played havoc with Norwood's 1940. With snow still falling heavily, smoke billows out of one side of the tram at Manor House. The problem could not have been too great as 1940 was repaired and worked on the subway services on 5th April 1952; with its transfer to New Cross depot, it also operated on 'Last Tram Day'. (Peter Mitchell)

ANYBODY WANT A TUNNEL?

Aldwych tram station, looking north on 30th March 1952. The 'THIS SIDE FOR TRAMS' sign informs passengers which tram they should board for various destinations. The exit stairs in the middle of the picture lead into Kingsway; in the far background, a northbound tram is at Holborn Station. In this part of the subway trams ran in a single tunnel; this section is well lit. (Alan Cross)

A top deck view from a tram heading out of the Kingsway subway on 5th April 1952; the car is travelling northbound. Those travelling through the subway were used to its hollow sound. (Clarence Carter)

This is a view that passengers waiting for a tram at Holborn Station would see; daylight falsely indicates that there is not a great distance between the station and the exit of the tunnel. A NO ENTRY sign warns passengers not to walk along the tramlines; stairs leading to Kingsway are on the left. (Alan Cross)

Seen in Rosebery Avenue on route 35, HR2 127 has the appearance of a rehabilitated car. Severely damaged during the war, only the lower deck survived; the top deck was replaced with an E1 type top deck. 127 is running late and has been curtailed at Nags Head which was famously known as a major junction on the trolleybus system. (Fred Ivey)

On the evening of 3rd April 1952, the two last snowbrooms in North London left Highgate depot. 037 will be followed by 035; they will travel through the Kingsway Subway and on to Penhall Road scrapyard. (D.W.K. Jones)

Seen at West Norwood, 186 has a blank destination blind on 5th April 1952. Note the 'dolly' tram stop and the bus stop with the flag covered. When 186 moves forward, its trolley wheel will touch the skate in the overhead; this will change the traffic lights to green, giving it priority over other traffic.

Three trolley-less cars were running on 5th April 1952 – HR2s 118, 121 and 132. Seen at Highgate on route 35 that day is the highest numbered of the trio – 132. There were no conduit-only tracks left after this so Cohen's will take 132 off London Transport's hands in a few days time. (Clarence Carter)

Rail grinder 02 is seen in Penhall Road yard on 5th April 1952; Cohen's made short work of miscellaneous cars and would have dismantled 02's wooden body in minutes rather than hours (the tank contained water which was sprayed on tracks). 1A on the front dash indicates that it was parked on this road on arrival at Penhall Road (a magnifying glass shows that G Cohen has been scrawled above 1A). Also just in view is 122 which is next for the chop; it was not due for withdrawal until 5th April – for some reason it has been disposed of prematurely. Both trams are not on tracks. (Peter Mitchell)

The LRTL hired two cars on 5th April 1952. One was 199 which is seen south of Aldwych station and in the part of the subway where the northbound and southbound tracks ran in separate tunnels. This could only have been a short stop as service cars still pass through; not only are a number of adults on board but the tour also attracted some youngsters. The tunnel was generally a dry area, but damp marks on the rails imply water seepage. Is there a bus enthusiast on board as 199 shows 36 VICTORIA? – the 36 tram did not go there but the 36 bus did. (Alan Cross)

210 has been lavishly adorned with flags, bunting and flowers; this was carried out by the West Norwood Chamber of Commerce in Norwood depot on Saturday 5th April 1952. Step-ladders have been used to put a well thought out decoration plan into practice. 210 was the highest numbered car of a batch of fifty that was originally owned by Leyton Corporation.

Norwood depot was going out in style and there were three 'last trams' for its closure. 197 was hired by the Lambeth Borough Council and is seen at the borough boundary at Addington Street. (London Transport Museum U53095)

The last service tram (1994) for West Norwood on route 33 passes a special (210) at Effra Road at 11.50pm on Saturday 5th April 1952. The two trams have stopped in a position that allows people, on the top deck, to shake hands. 210 will reverse and follow 1994 back. No photographs have materialised of the last 33 at Manor House. (London Transport Museum U53089)

Virtually unnoticed because of the publicity given to the Kingsway Subway aspect of route 35, the last car from Forest Hill was 1936 which had plenty of room for one and all. She waits for departure time of 11.40pm on 5th April 1952. The stained glass KINGSWAY SUBWAY sign was illuminated at night. Route 35 was the last tram route to serve Forest Hill. (London Transport Museum U53101)

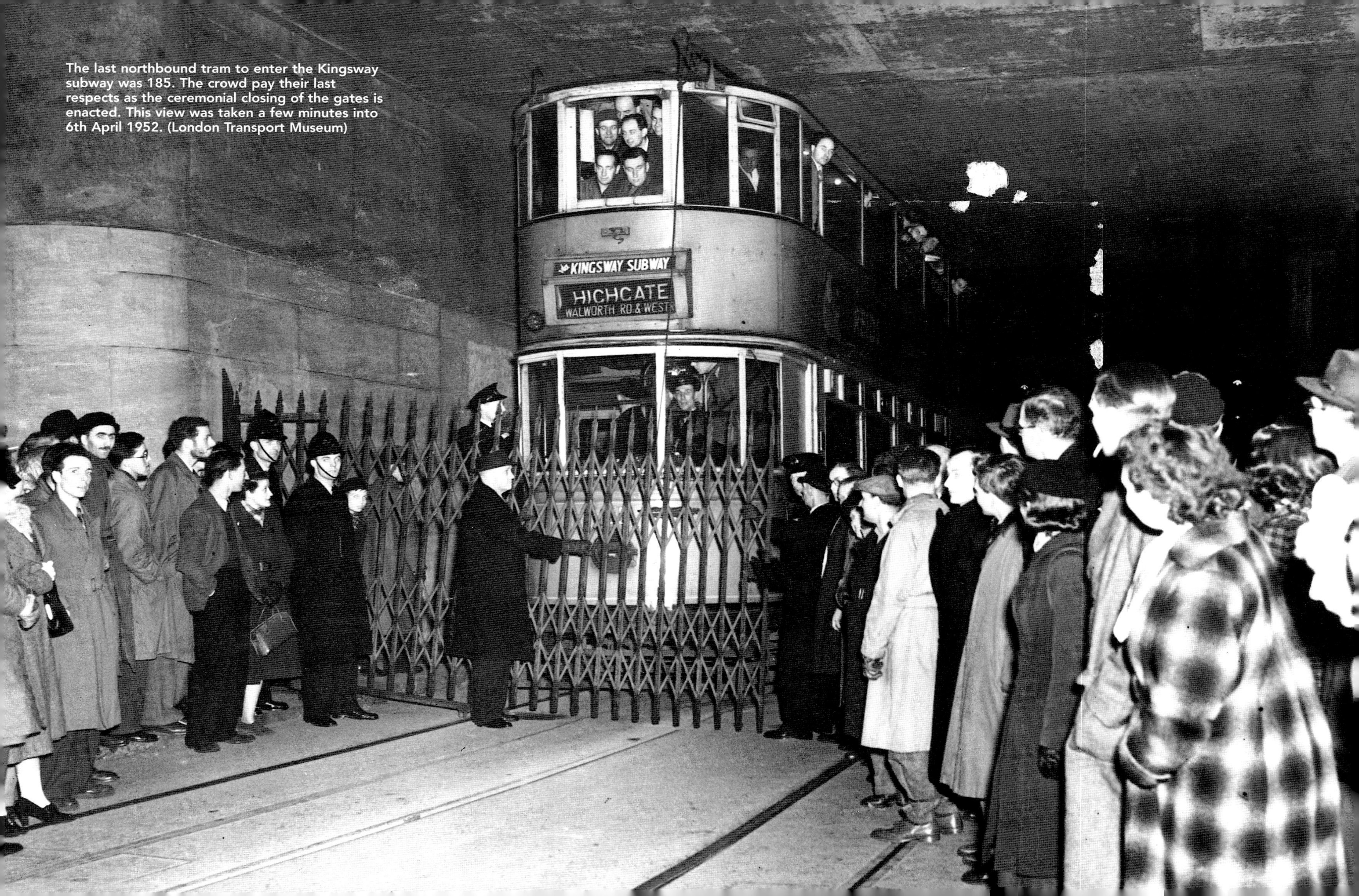

The last northbound tram to enter the Kingsway subway was 185. The crowd pay their last respects as the ceremonial closing of the gates is enacted. This view was taken a few minutes into 6th April 1952. (London Transport Museum)

MONDAY, APRIL 7, 1952

Last tram puts them in a hole

LONDON Transport is in a hole over a hole.

The Kingsway - Embankment tram tunnel shut down early yesterday morning.

Both ends are closed with steel gates, and intermediate entrances are also gated, with notices: "*Tram services will cease to operate. . . .*

Scrawled by a tram - lover under the Holborn notice is a plaintive: "Wot! No trams?"

TOO NARROW

Now—what's to do with the hole? (Cost, *since* it was dug in 1906, £500,000.)

A Ministry of Transport committee has been to Paris to see how they use tunnels for traffic over there. But Kingsway Tunnel is *too narrow for two-way traffic.*

Bus route? Car park? *Too expensive to convert.*

Meanwhile the lights are on, and a man patrols it day and night, to guard against flooding.

The last tram, a No. 35, was sent off to Highgate by Mr. Paddy Walker, 65-year-old subway inspector for 24 years, who came out of retirement to see it home. It left behind The Hole Nobody Wants.

THE OBSERVER, SUNDAY, APRIL 6, 1952

Sentimental Journey Under Kingsway

By Paul Jennings

THE last tram has trundled through the Kingsway Tunnel: new bus routes—30 miles of them —are now in use, and the old dim way underground is closed.

Yesterday a sad, cold air blew through the subterranean tram stations of Holborn and Aldwych. Both had the stripped air of a house that is to be sold. All the advertisements had been pulled off; the only printed words were a notice beginning: "Tram services will cease to operate"—and underneath was chalked "Why?"

When he was working on the subway services, driver Alf Keir probably never thought he would meet any London Transport 'top brass'. When he brought 185 into Aldwych Station, the chief operating manager, Mr J.B. Burnell, shook hands with him. Keir displays his tram driver's MSC badge on his left lapel; on the right lapel, his PSV badge is turned the wrong way round. His next turn of duty will be as a bus driver – he will need to reverse the badges. (London Transport Museum U53071)

With the formalities over, 185 will proceed to Holborn tram station, up the northern ramp, through Bloomsbury and on to Highgate depot. 185 is packed to the gunwales; a bouquet has been placed on the dash cleat – it is 12.19am on Sunday 6th April 1952. (Alan Cross)

As soon as the last service car had passed Holborn Tramway Station, workers take down the signboard outside; this was top-class efficiency by London Transport. The gates to the station are being closed to passengers for the last time. (London Transport Museum U53070)

some trolleybus drivers were asked to return to tram driving for a while, which they did. London Transport referred to the closure of the subway as 'The Kingsway affair'.

The last day of operation through the subway aroused great interest and as the day wore on the number of people travelling through it increased. Last passenger car through the subway was 185 whose journey started at Westminster; on entering the southern entrance there was a ceremonial 'closing of the gates'. The Mayor of Holborn and the London Transport Chief Operating manager were at Aldwych station to shake hands with driver Alf Keir - not to be forgotten was conductor John Hawes. Behind all the frivolity, a lament was made by a piper at Holborn Station. Then, 'Paddy' Walker who had retired just three weeks previously, and who had been invited back, called out "Take her away". There were so many people on board 185 that when it climbed the slope at Bloomsbury, the circuit breaker blew; a quick thinking passenger knocked it back in, thus preventing 185 returning to Holborn Station! 185 was not the last to arrive at Highgate depot as 184, working short from Bloomsbury, followed 185 into the depot. In the early hours of Sunday 6th April, Highgate TGWU representative, Tom Fitzpatrick, drove the last out-of-service car through the subway, handing 184 over to a New Cross crew at Westminster. Even at this stage, inter-depot transfers took place. The Highgate and Norwood cars were considered to be in excellent condition and apart from 182 at Highgate and 1997 at Norwood, lived to fight another day (in fact many more days) at New Cross. The Highgate and Norwood cars used the subway day in and day out and only the best would do for those traversing the centre of the capital. Also at an end now was the racing of trams and trolleybuses over their common sections north of the Kingsway subway.

The closure of the subway was high profile and was

Last tram to run in North London was E3 184 which ran empty from Highgate to New Cross depot in the early hours of 6th April; 184 heads down the slope of the subway and into the tunnel. It is followed by a London Transport private car; KLB was a registration usually associated with buses. (Alan Cross)

mentioned in the House of Lords and House of Commons. The latter institution is not known for its humour, but in a reply to Mr Lennox-Boyd in December 1954, Lieutenant-Colonel Lipton asked the right honourable gentlemen if he wanted to sell it to road hauliers or keep it as a hide-out for himself. The LT Chairman (none other than Lord Latham himself) wished to walk through the subway in order to familiarise himself with its characteristics in connection with its future use. It was not possible during traffic hours, and as the last northbound tram entered the tunnel at 11.45pm and the southbound one at 12.03am, it was decided to make the visit starting at the Embankment end at 11.45 pm on Monday 5th March 1951. Mr A.B.B. Valentine and Mr P. Groom-Johnson (chief engineer), and presumably some others, accompanied him and arrangements were made to keep the lighting on during the visit.

With the conversion of the tramways to oil bus operation, the Kingsway subway featured high on LTE's agenda; at peak times, 30 cars an hour used it each way carrying approximately 15,000 passengers a day. There were two stations within the 1100-yard long tunnel; these were located with island platforms at Aldwych and Holborn. A ramp carried the subway to the surface at the northern end in Southampton Row; at the southern end, the tracks led directly on to those used by the Embankment services. In its present physical form the subway was not suitable for the passage of buses and many alterations would have to be made to adapt it for their use. Tram tracks would have to be removed, the width of the subway increased, and a ventilation system would have to be installed to deal with exhaust fumes. A major problem would have been the alteration of the northern ramp from a 1 in 10 gradient to 1 in 15 or 1 in 20 which was considered the maximum gradient practical for bus operation – an alternative was for the ramp to be extended. The

After the last service trams had passed through the Kingsway subway there were still a number in Highgate depot that needed to use the tunnel – running empty, they were destined for New Cross depot or Penhall Road yard. One by one they came through with the last being 184 which was driven by depot TGWU representative Tom Fitzpatrick. Most of the well-wishers who had earlier been at the southern end of the subway have left; just a few diehard enthusiasts, a policeman and inspectors remain to see 184 arrive. Its destination box window has dropped down – whoever removed the blind did not lock the box up afterwards. Fitzpatrick will take 184 to Westminster where another ferry crew will take it to New Cross depot. The Highgate men will be taken home on a staff bus. (London Transport Museum U53081)

capital cost of altering just the subway would have been one and a quarter million pounds, with £114,000 for other expenses. An option of using the subway from the Stoll Opera House to the Embankment for southbound buses, and to operate northbound buses on the surface at a cost of about £325,000 was also considered. Abandoning the subway came to less than £150,000. From both a financial and practical view the subway was to be abandoned as a means of transport in the capital. London Transport considered the effect on traffic receipts on abandoning the subway, and stated that a surface route would always be more popular than a subway route because it attracts more people and there are more stops, particularly in this instance at Temple Station and The Strand areas. It was estimated that alterations to the tunnel for bus operation would take about two years. There were those who supported the retention of the subway, bearing in mind that additional buses were to be used in lieu of the trams.

As with all subterranean tunnels, the Kingsway subway accumulated dust and detritus. The stations within the subway were kept tidy by on-duty personnel, and cleaning of the tunnel had been carried out for some years but had stopped in 1939. The sweeping and cleaning of the track and floor was carried out by tram staff who usually devoted their Easter holidays to this task! However it was not popular for, after working a night in the Subway, the men's faces were black and their clothes thick with dust. In June 1947, representations were made by the TGWU regarding the dirt that had accumulated on the tracks and which had never been swept up. The complaint was followed up by the Divisional Superintendant, Trams and Trolleybuses at Manor House offices, who got in touch with the Permanent Way Engineer, Trams, asking for the track to be cleaned one night; a driver and tram fitted with a rotary broom could be provided. The Permanent Way Engineer was not interested! A suggestion was made that an additional two-pence an hour be paid to Permanent Way men when carrying out this work in the Subway, owing to the dirty and dusty conditions. However, there was no authority to pay 'dirty money' on Permanent Way operations. Correspondence went back and forth between various departments and eventually an agreement was made which is shown below. The subway now got a yearly 'deep clean'. Staff had to provide their own clothing (probably old uniforms), with London Transport providing the cleaning materials. Bearing in mind that there would be a full night's pay at Sunday rate, this was 'a nice little earner' and there was never a shortage of volunteers. Bearing in mind that the cleaning generally took place at about Easter time, it has to be assumed that the deep clean of 1951 was thc last occasion on which it occurred.

Upon closure, lighting in the subway was maintained, telephone facilities retained and precautions taken against trespassers. The LTE were free to let the subway – it was under the control of their Estate Agent and Rating Surveyor. They stated that it was subject to occasional flooding by the River Thames (though there are no reports of this), and that there was water seepage from unknown sources. The ventilation system would need to be inspected and effective sanitary and drainage systems installed. The LTE stated that it was improbable that the subway could be used for commercial purposes without the construction of additional entrances and exits; artificial lights and a much improved lighting system would also be required, as would consent under the provisions of the Town and Country Planning Act.

Much correspondence took place about what use the subway would be put to after its closure; various organisations approached London Transport who suggested that it could be used as a through road for motor coaches, a motor coach station or a parking place for coaches. Another proposal came from a group of theatre companies in central London whose patrons were having difficulties parking; another wanted to store theatrical props and there was an approach to use it as a television studio. Mr Kenneth Mason of St Pauls Cray in Kent wanted to use it as a 'kind of Caledonian market'; he also had ideas of adapting part of it as a beer cellar or an underground café. This was eventually achieved for in the 21st century a wine bar opened at the southern entrance to the subway underneath Waterloo Bridge. It was thought that a building licence would need to be obtained for some of the proposals, and considered improbable that local authorities would sanction additional openings in Kingsway owing to traffic congestion. Consideration was also given to the possibility of constructing transverse subways to link the main subway with adjoining buildings and so provide additional entrances, on the assumption that the occupiers of one or other of the important buildings would be interested in leasing the subway for storage purposes - this was deemed impractical because of the presence of sewers and water mains.

Other applicants were: photographic chemists; store for plywood importers; demonstration of the Kearney high speed railway (monorail); the training of naval personnel by the Admiralty Surveyor, and a Health Week Exhibition in March 1953, with the applicant being the Medical Officer of Health for Holborn Borough Council. All told, there were fifteen applicants; another was the Ford Motor Company at Dagenham who wanted to store motorcars there - their main purpose was for the storage of vehicles prior to delivery to export customers from their Regent Street offices; 450 cars a month passed through this office and adequate storage space, enough for about 300 cars, was impossible to obtain in the West End. The LTE thought that, on a short term, this was an ideal solution and that the subway would be useful and remunerative. Fords offered the most meritorious consideration as they had a two year lease in mind at a cost of £4000-£5000 per annum. Although there would be an expenditure of £175,000 in adapting the subway to accommodate 95 motorcars, it was thought that little alteration would need to be made - safeguarding the cars against theft by the fitting of doors was thought to be the only requirement. London Transport concluded that the most likely use to be made of the subway was for storage purposes, a wine cellar or a safe depository. On 12th May 1953, the Home Office wished to earmark the Kingsway Tunnel for shelter purposes, but on 12th August 1955 the BTC approved the leasing of the subway to the Royal Opera House, Covent Garden for the storage of scenery for a term of five years at a rental of £2,000 per annum. The lessees were to pay rates and carry out internal repairs; however, this did not occur and in 1956 Henleys Limited wanted to store motor cars there at a weekly rental of £60. All of these ideas were rejected.

S.G. Young wanted to use the subway for the storage of machinery and machine tools for a sum of £1,000-1,300 per annum; they had wanted a lease for twenty-one years but the reaction of the Home Office and Ministry of Transport had to be sought as they were interested in its future and may not have been particularly inclined to part with possession for that period of time. Eventually the subway was let to S.G. Young in 1957; planning consent was obtained on a temporary basis (until 1st August 1962). A tour of the subway was made by the Tramway Museum Society in 1958; they found that the internal London Transport telephone was still live and were sorely tempted to make a call to the switchboard girls about a tram that was ensconced there! In 1962 Young's vacated the subway.

The subway could catch out the unwary and a visiting motorist to London might see a gap in the traffic at Southampton Row, whizz through it, only to find himself going down a steep incline with a tram accelerating past him on the other track. Usually the motorist was able to reverse back but for those who kept going they could find themselves tailgated all the way to the Embankment by an angry tram driver in hot pursuit. There are those who have driven a motorcar through for a bet, and on the last night a military looking gentleman implored the Sergeant in charge of a sizeable squad of police, "Be a sport, old boy, let me through". He did and a 1904 Oldsmobile car, belching smoke preceded 173, the mayor of Holborn's special tram. Asked rhetorically in an Islington local paper what the significance of the closure of the subway was, the question was answered thus: to the young, the last of the outmoded rattling monsters and another example of internal combustion engine superiority: to the middle-aged, another link broken with their youth: to the older, a sad farewell to those nostalgic creatures of a faded era: to London Transport - stage seven of the tram replacement scheme.

This notice was posted at the Embankment end of the Kingsway Subway before stage seven of the tram to bus conversion programme. Trams last ran through the tunnel on the night of 5th/6th April 1952 – this photo was taken on 22nd June 1952, there being little deterioration to the poster. (John Gillham)

It is 5pm on Sunday 6th April 1952. The last tram to use the Kingsway subway has passed through.With the tram traffic lights being illuminated, it is reasonable to assume that power is still available in the conduit. (Clarence Carter)

RTL 1262 is at the former West Norwood tram terminus of route 33; it will shortly reach the Thurlow Arms on 12th April 1952, the first Saturday of route 171. Tram tracks and overhead are still in position; before long they will be removed. (Clarence Carter)

5th April 1953, exactly a year to the day since trams last ran on route 33. The tram lines and conduit channel are exposed, and are in the process of removal. This view was taken in Rosebery Avenue where electric road transport still operates – trolleybuses on route 581. (Clarence Carter)

A CHANGE OF PLAN

Sunday 29th June 1952 was the first day of Last Tram Week; that morning 165 moves from Knee Hill into Abbey Wood Road. Presumably it is going to park on the stub track. The first and last days of Last Tram Week were blessed with good weather. (Phil Tatt/Online Transport Archive)

In early 1952 the London Transport Executive stated that it was very pleased with the results of the tram conversion; such were the financial savings that on 31st January the LTE stated that it wanted stages eight and nine to occur simultaneously. Investigations took place with two sticking points being identified. One centred on the delivery of new RT/RTL type buses; it should be borne in mind that the Government still had a restriction in place on the supply of new vehicles in the UK. Second, there would not be enough room to hold 200 trams, including works cars, in Penhall Road in one go. Three options to deal with this were nominated: 1) trams over and above those that could get into the scrapyard be temporarily accommodated at Charlton Works. 2) retain some temporarily at Abbey Wood depot – motor-buses could be parked in 'Saunders Yard', an off-site facility. 3) advance stage nine only to 20th July as this would lessen the difficulty of disposing of such a large number of cars in one go. The Rolling Stock Engineer was of the opinion that the task of transferring some 360 vehicles (buses and trams) on 5th/6th July was excessive bearing in mind that some of the STL buses needed were stored at such distant places as the Argent Street garage at Grays, and in aircraft hangers at Stansted, and favoured 20th July. Notwithstanding the conceived problems, a decision was made that the trams would run for the last time on Saturday 5th July 1952. Although there were murmurings within the London Transport hierarchy that this could not be achieved, it was. Not only was the LTE pleased with its statement, but it received an appreciation from the British Transport Commission on 15th May that completion would occur in advance of the planned timetable. A contingency plan allowed twenty cars to be stored at Abbey Wood depot after stage eight if required; this would require the tracks between Abbey Wood and Anchor & Hope Lane, Charlton being maintained. The concept of ridding London of its trams was so high profile that even the Chairman wanted to know whether the tracks would be required after the night of 5th/6th July 1952. A plan was devised and revealed in a document issued on 22nd May, in which the numbers of the 183 trams 'on the books' were quoted: 127 at New Cross and 56 at Abbey Wood (there was an error as car 192 was replaced by 183 at stage seven). A number of trams would be withdrawn before 5th July so that the momentum of the burning programme could be kept up (not so as Cohen's were up to speed; LT was on a mission and that was to rid London of its trams by 'close of play' on 5th July). It was stated that a full peak hour service of trams would not be able to be provided in the days leading up to 5th July, but this policy would ensure that all would be in Penhall Road that night. By 4th July, twenty-five* had gone there under this edict; some were scrapped virtually on arrival.

A formal closing ceremony was a 'must' but on looking at the schedules it was found that the last tram of the night was

*93, 98, 162, 166, 188, 300, 338, 557, 601, 1860, 1866, 1868, 1870, 1874, 1876, 1919, 1944, 1949, 1958, 1960, 1963, 1968, 1986, 1990, 1992.

an Abbey Wood car due in at 12.34am; the last New Cross tram was a 40 at 12.31am. The proceedings could not take place at Abbey Wood as the depot was adjacent to a residential street and there was limited space; this meant that the ceremony would have to be at New Cross and a way to achieve this was, surprisingly, easily achieved. Route 44 ran between Eltham and Woolwich and the 46 between Woolwich and Southwark; all 44s and some 46s were run by Abbey Wood depot with cars running to and from Woolwich in service. The plan devised was that all depot runs on 5th July to Abbey Wood on routes 44 and 46 (which were after 10.30pm) were cancelled; they would finish at Beresford Square from where they would be run out of service to 'Penhall Road cemetery.'

FIRST & LAST TRAMS On & after November 14, 1951

ROUTE 40 | Plumstead - Greenwich - Camberwell - Savoy St. | P.M. times are in heavy figures

Via Plumstead High St., Plumstead Rd., Beresford St., Woolwich High St., Woolwich Church St., Woolwich Rd., Trafalgar Rd., Romney Rd., Nelson St., London St., Greenwich Rd., Deptford Broadway, New Cross Rd., Queens Rd., Peckham High Rd., Peckham Rd., Camberwell Church St., Camberwell New Rd., Kennington Park Rd., Kennington Rd. Westminster Bridge Rd., Westminster Bridge, Victoria Embankment.

RAILWAY STATIONS SERVED: Plumstead, near Woolwich Arsenal, Charlton, Greenwich, New Cross, New Cross Gate, Queens Road *Peckham*, Oval, Lambeth North, near Waterloo, Westminster, Charing Cross

Service interval: MON. to FRI., Wickham Lane–Perrott Street, peak hours only 4-5 mins.; Perrott Street–New Cross, 10 minutes (peak hours 4-6 mins.); New Cross–Embankment 10 mins. (peak hours 4-6 mins., evening 12 mins.); SATURDAY, Wickham Lane–Perrott Street, peak hours only 5-8 mins., Perrott Street–Embankment 7-8 mins. (peak hours 5 mins., eve. 12 mins.), SUNDAY, Perrott Street–Embankment before 3 0 p.m. 12 mins., after 3 0 p.m. 9-10 mins.

	WEEKDAYS			First	MON.-FRI.	Last		SAT.	Last		First	* SUNDAY		Last	
PLUMSTEAD *Wickham Lane*	....	....	....	6 57	7 11	....	....	2 42	....	....	....	8 32	....	....	....
Woolwich *Perrott Street*	..	..	4 58	7 4	7 18	10 31	11 54	2 49	10 31	11 57	7 52	8 39	..	10 35	11 56
Woolwich *Beresford Square*	....	....	5 0	7 6	7 20	10 33	11 56	2 51	10 33	11 59	7 54	8 41	....	10 37	11 58
Woolwich Road *Blackwall Lane*	..	4 42	5 15	7 21	7 35	10 48	12 11	3 6	10 49	12 14	8 9	8 56	..	10 52	12 13
New Cross Gate	4 35	4 57	5 30	7 36	7 50	11 3	12 26	3 22	11 4	12 29	8 23	9 10	....	11 6	12 27
Camberwell Green	4 46	5 8	5 41	7 47	8 1	11 14	..	3 34	11 16	..	8 34	9 21	..	11 17	..
Kennington Gate	4 52	5 14	5 47	7 53	8 8	11 21	....	3 41	11 23	....	8 40	9 27	....	11 23	....
EMBANKMENT *Savoy St.*	5 5	5 27	6 0	8 6	8 23	11 35	..	3 58	11 37	..	8 52	9 39	..	11 35	..
EMBANKMENT *Savoy St.*	....	5 6	§5 43	¶5 54	5 56	10 48	11 36	1 26	10 49	11 38	*	8 24	..	10 52	11 36
Kennington Gate	..	5 19	§5 56	¶6 7	6 10	11 2	11 50	1 40	11 3	11 52	6 26	8 36	....	11 3	11 47
Camberwell Green	A	5 25	§6 2	¶6 13	6 17	11 9	11 57	1 47	11 10	11 59	6 32	8 42	..	11 10	11 54
New Cross Gate	4 22	5 36	6 13	¶6 24	6 29	11 20	12 8	1 59	11 22	12 11	6 43	8 53	....	11 21	12 5
Woolwich Road *Blackwall Lane*	4 37	5 51	6 28	¶6 39	6 45	11 35	..	2 15	11 37	..	6 57	9 7	..	11 35	..
Woolwich *Beresford Square*	4 52	6 6	6 43	¶6 54	7 0	11 50	....	2 30	11 53	....	7 12	9 22	....	11 50	....
Woolwich *Perrott Street*	4 54	6 8	6 45	¶6 56	7 2	11 52	..	2 32	11 58	..	7 14	9 24	..	11 52	..
PLUMSTEAD *Wickham Lane*	....	....	6 52	¶7 3	7 9	....	....	2 39	...	....	7 21	....	..	....	....

EARLIER JOURNEYS–SUNDAY

Perrott Street to Oval at 7 39 a.m.
Perrott Street to Camberwell Green at 7 27 a.m.
Blackwall Lanc to Camberwell Green at 6 36 a.m.
Blackwall Lane to Oval at 5 27, 6 17 a.m.
New Cross Gate to John Carpenter Street at 7 48, 8 1 a.m.
New Cross Gate to Savoy Street at 7 10 a.m.
New Cross Gate to Oval at 5 27, 6 7 a.m.
New Cross Gate to Camberwell Green at 4 46, 7 17, 7 30 a.m.
Wickham Lane to Greenwich *South St.* at 7 23 a.m.

Savoy Street to Perrott Street at 7 40 a.m.
Oval to Perrott Street at 6 49, 8 28 a.m.
Oval to Blackwall Lane at 5 45, 5 59 a.m.
Camberwell Green to Blackwall Lane at 4 58 a.m.
Camberwell Green to Perrott Street at 7 8, 7 30, 7 43, 8 12 a.m.
New Cross Gate to Perrott Street at 6 54 a.m.
Greenwich *South St.* to Wickham Lane at 7 55 a.m.

¶–Monday to Friday §–Saturday only.
*–Single journey. A–2 minutes later on Saturday.

Service to and from Plumstead *Wickham Lane* during the following periods only:–
From Savoy Street, MON. to FRI. 5 54 to 7 21 a.m., 2 50 to 5 56 p.m. SAT. 5 43 to 7 30 a.m., 10 45 a.m. to 1 26 p.m.
To Savoy Street, MON. to FRI. 6 57 to 8 31 a.m., 4 0 to 7 11 p.m. SAT. 6 57 to 8 46 a.m., 12 2 to 2 42 p.m.

FIRST AND LAST TRAMS On and after January 2, 1952

ROUTE 44 | Woolwich - Eltham | P.M. times are in heavy figures

Via New Road (return via Grand Depot Road), Woolwich Common, Academy Road, Well Hall Road, Eltham Hill.

RAILWAY STATIONS SERVED: Woolwich Arsenal, Eltham Well Hall.

Service interval: WEEKDAYS ONLY 5-8 mins. (Mon. to Fri. before 9 0 a.m. 10 mins.)

	MON. to FRI. First		Last		SATURDAY First		Last	
WOOLWICH *Beresford Square*	5 54	....	10 14	....	5 52	....	10 15	....
Eltham *Well Hall Circus*	6 6	..	10 26	..	6 4	..	10 27	..
Eltham *Church*	6 12	....	10 32	....	6 10	....	10 33	....
ELTHAM *Middle Park Avenue*	6 15	..	10 35	..	6 13	..	10 36	.

	MON to FRI. First		Last		SATURDAY First		Last
ELTHAM *Middle Park Avenue*	....	6 17	10 37	....	6 15	....	10 39
Eltham *Church*	..	6 20	10 40	..	6 18	..	10 42
Eltham *Well Hall Circus*	6 10	6 26	10 46	....	6 24	....	10 48
WOOLWICH *Beresford Square*	6 22	6 38	10 58	..	6 36	..	11 0

ROUTE 46 | Woolwich - Eltham - Lewisham - New Cross - City *Southwark* | P.M. times are in heavy figures

Via New Rd. (return via Grand Depot Rd.), Woolwich Common, Academy Rd., Well Hall Rd.. Eltham Hill. Eltham Rd., Lee Green, Lee High Rd., Loampit Vale, Loampit Hill, Lewisham Way, New Cross Rd., Old Kent Rd., Great Dover Street, Marshalsea Rd., Southwark Bridge Rd., Southwark Bridge

RAILWAY STATIONS SERVED: Woolwich Arsenal, Eltham Well Hall, Lewisham, St. Johns, New Cross Gate, Borough

Service interval: Woolwich–New Cross, MONDAY to FRIDAY 7½ minutes (peak hours 3-4 minutes), SATURDAY 3-4 minutes (before 9 0 a.m., 8 minutes, evening 6 minutes), SUNDAY morn. 5 minutes, afternoon and evening 4 minutes. New Cross–City, WEEKDAYS 6-8 minutes (Mon. to Fri. evening 15 minutes, Sat. evening 12 mins.), SUNDAY 10 minutes (afternoon and evening 8 minutes).

	WEEKDAYS First *			*	SO	MF	MON. to FRI. Last			SATURDAY Last			SUNDAY First				Last		
WOOLWICH *Beresford Square*	....	4 17	....	4 37	5 0	5 11	9 48	11 32	....	9 49	11 32	....	4 43	5 5	5 40	7 10	9 50	11 28	11 32
Eltham *Well Hall Circus*	..	4 29	..	4 49	5 12	5 23	10 0	11 44	..	10 1	11 44	..	4 55	5 17	5 52	7 22	10 2	11 40	11 44
Eltham *Church*	4 0	4 35	....	4 55	5 18	5 29	10 6	11 50	....	10 7	11 50	....	5 0	5 22	5 57	7 27	10 7	11 45	11 49
Eltham *Middle Park Avenue*	4 3	..	..	4 58	5 21	5 32	10 9	11 53	..	10 10	11 53	..	..	5 25	6 0	7 30	10 10	11 48	..
Lee Green *Tigers Head*	4 8	....	....	5 3	5 26	5 37	10 14	11 58	....	10 16	11 59	....	....	5 29	6 4	7 34	10 14	11 52	....
Lewisham *Clock Tower*	4 15	..	..	5 10	5 33	5 44	10 21	12 5	..	10 24	12 7	..	..	..	6 12	7 42	10 22	12 0	..
New Cross Gate	4 25	....	5 11	5 20	5 43	5 54	10 31	12 15	....	10 34	12 17	....	....	....	6 22	7 52	10 32	12 10	....
Old Kent Road *Bricklayers Arms*	4 36	..	5 22	5 31	5 54	6 5	10 42	..	..	10 45	..	..	..	..	..	8 3	10 43	..	..
CITY *Southwark*	4 46	....	5 32	5 41	6 4	6 15	10 51	....	....	10 54	....	....	....	....	....	8 12	10 52	....	....

	*	*			*	MF	SO	MON. to FRI. Last			SATURDAY Last			SUNDAY First				Last		
CITY *Southwark*	....	....	....	....	4 51	5 34	5 35	10 56	....	....	10 56	....	....	....	....	....	8 15	10 56	....	....
Old Kent Road *Bricklayers Arms*	..	..	..	..	5 1	5 44	5 45	11 5	..	..	11 5	..	..	..	..	..	8 24	11 5	..	..
New Cross Gate	3 33	3 42	....	5 5	5 12	5 55	5 56	11 16	11 32	....	11 16	11 32	....	....	....	5 32	8 35	11 16	11 32	....
Lewisham *Clock Tower*	3 43	3 52	..	5 15	5 22	6 5	6 6	11 26	11 42	..	11 26	11 42	..	..	..	5 42	8 45	11 26	11 42	..
Lee Green *Tigers Head*	3 50	3 59	....	5 22	5 29	6 12	6 13	11 34	11 50	....	11 34	11 50	....	....	5 34	5 50	8 53	11 33	11 50	....
Eltham *Middle Park Avenue*	3 55	4 4	..	5 27	5 34	6 17	6 18	11 38	11 54	..	11 40	11 56	..	..	5 38	5 54	8 57	11 38	11 54	..
Eltham *Church*	3 58	4 7	4 38	5 30	5 37	6 20	6 21	11 41	11 57	....	11 43	11 59	....	5 4	5 41	5 57	9 0	11 41	11 57	....
Eltham *Well Hall Circus*	..	4 13	4 44	5 36	5 43	6 26	6 27	11 47	12 3	..	11 49	12 5	..	5 9	5 46	6 2	9 5	11 46	12 2	..
WOOLWICH *Beresford Square*	....	4 25	4 56	5 48	5 55	6 38	6 39	11 59	12 15	....	12 1	12 17	....	5 21	5 58	6 14	9 17	11 58	12 14	....

MF–Monday to Friday only. SO–Saturday only. *–Special early journey.

EARLY AND LATE JOURNEYS: Abbey Wood to Woolwich, WEEKDAYS at 4 2, 4 22 a.m.; SUNDAY at 4 28, 4 50 a.m.
Woolwich to Abbey Wood, MON. to FRI. at 11 38, 11 45, 11 53, 11 59 p.m., 12 3, 12 7, 12 15 a.m.; SATURDAY at 4 56 a.m., 11 33, 11 39, 11 45, 11 51, 11 56 p.m., 12 1, 12 10, 12 17 a.m.; SUNDAY at 11 44, 11 48, 11 50, 11 53, 11 58 p.m., 12 4, 12 9, 12 11, 12 14 a.m.

Back a few months and on 17th March 1952, there is plenty of activity in New Cross depot. It is still very much a workaday depot and with almost four months of tramcar operation ahead of them, the maintenance staff work in tidy conditions. (D.W.K. Jones)

Not a view that London Transport can be proud of; it is now 21st June 1952 and with the end of the trams in sight, there is a general malaise amongst the staff at New Cross depot. The traverser pit is full of detritus and a car is dumped on the traverser. A number of ploughs await further use. (John Gillham)

This evocative view was taken on the Victoria Embankment in the last week of the trams; a sight that Londoners had seen for many years would disappear in a few days time. The photographer has asked an obliging driver to keep the tram motionless while he took this view; the driver of the motorbus behind has little choice but to follow suit. (Online Transport Archive)

In the run-up to the end of the trams, conditions at New Cross depot deteriorated by the day. Work on demolishing the buildings continues – only basic maintenance facilities are available. 2000 leaves the depot during Last Tram Week. (Bill Godwin)

The LTE started to make plans about the ceremony with the number of people suggested as invitees being extensive. Members of the Executive were mentioned first; they were followed by members of the British Transport Commission, the Minister of Transport, the Lord Mayor of London accompanied by the Town Clerk, the chairman of the LCC accompanied by his clerk, the mayors of seventeen London boroughs accompanied by their town clerks, and engineers and surveyors. Why though, did the Mayor of Stoke Newington get an invite? Also invited were Members of Parliament for constituencies served at the time by trams, the Commissioner of the City of London and Metropolitan Police, various trade union representatives, all of the Executive's chief officers and some understudies, the secretary of the Institute of Transport, press representatives and retired officers. It got to the point of who wasn't invited!

There was a lot of high level discussion about the closing ceremony; of the options that were suggested, most were rejected – namely: 1) That a special tram, which would be attended by London Transport's top brass and local dignitaries, should start at Aldwych station in the Kingsway

This book would not be complete without views of a change pit – this is the one at Woolwich. The left picture is taken from the top deck of a tram – note the pit from where ploughs can be removed. In the photograph below a fork guides a plough into the carrier. This was a job for 'light duty' men; their grade was 'plough shifter'. (D.W.K. Jones/John Gillham)

There was good publicity for London's last tram week and not only in the areas where the cars were still working. Posters were to be seen at many Underground stations. This one is at Liverpool Street Station. (Clarence Carter)

subway where refreshments would be served and speeches made, after which the party would proceed to Westminster. This was found to be impractical as to reopen the subway would have entailed considerable work and expense with regard to the track, conduits, electrical supply and cleaning. It was felt that the cost could not be justified for a ceremony which would last not more than an hour. 2) A procession of four cars from the Embankment to New Cross depot; the invitees would assemble at the Savoy Hotel where refreshments would be offered and valedictory speeches made. They would then travel on the trams from Waterloo Bridge to New Cross depot via Westminster Bridge, Elephant & Castle and Old Kent Road; this was rejected because it was felt that the trams would not arrive at New Cross Gate within a reasonable time. The journey normally took 30 minutes, but on an occasion of this description it would take considerably longer, owing to the local interest that would be aroused. It would have entailed extensive arrangements by the police to ensure the safe accomplishment of the journey. 3) A short ceremonial ride for the last half-mile to New Cross depot. This proposal envisaged the last trams to be brought from the depot at about midnight to an assembly point in Peckham or in the Old Kent Road, and to convey the invitees to the depot where refreshments would be served and speeches made; the idea was rejected on the grounds that it would have been difficult to carry out the programme in an orderly manner. An apt proposal made by the LTE was that some form of memorial stone to commemorate the passing of the tramways from the London scene be erected on a site on the Embankment. It was suggested that Lord Latham would unveil it near the date of the final changeover; the Chairman was favourably disposed to this but the idea eventually fell on stony ground.

London Transport was rightly concerned about the ceremony occurring in a safe and orderly manner. Although many of the chairman's colleagues had come up with a number of ingenious ideas and suggestions, these same gentlemen provided graphic details, and in some instances photographs, of the scenes that marked the changeover from trams to trolleybuses in the later stages of the north London changeover. This had culminated in the disintegration of the vehicle with panels being ripped off and seats thrown from windows. It was to be expected that the passage of the last tram of all in London would attract no less attention, but it was thought that there was a very real possibility of escaping the attentions of an extreme local element by the very virtue of the non-residential aspect of central London. Precautions needed to be made though, and every endeavour was to be afforded to keep matters under control. It was thought that a ceremonial ride through the streets south of the river to New Cross would be uncontrollable, and it was doubtful whether the vehicle would ever reach the end of its journey – if indeed there were any vehicles left to complete the journey!

Back to the drawing board – and the Executive decided that the ceremony should be to some extent just symbolic; with this in mind they drew up a plan for 250 guests to assemble in the banqueting hall of Sion College on the corner of the Embankment and John Carpenter Street at 10.30pm – refreshments would be offered and farewell speeches made. At about 11.40pm, after the passage of the last service tram, a convoy of three or four cars which would have been decorated with coloured lights earlier in the day, and which would have travelled in darkness to the Embankment, would arrive at Sion College. At the appropriate time and signal, the lights would be switched on and the guests would cross the road between a police guard and would board the trams by means of a pre-arranged system of coloured tickets. The cars would be driven and conducted by appropriately chosen long-service staff. All would need police officers on the front and rear platforms – there would be a mobile police escort for the convoy which would proceed non-stop along the Embankment to just short of Westminster bridge, where the trams would halt and the decorative lights on the cars (if there were any left) would be switched off; arrangements were to be made with the police for this. Passengers would alight to pick up their own motor cars which would have been parked in front of New Scotland Yard. Some would catch their trains from Westminster station and special buses might be run for the invitees; the convoy, still with police protection, would then proceed to

LONDON TRANSPORT EXECUTIVE

SOUTH LONDON CONVERSION

STAGES VIII & IX

MOVEMENT OF TRAMCARS PRIOR TO 6TH JULY, 1952

At the completion of the final stages of the South London Conversion programme scheduled for 6th July, 1952, all tramcars remaining at New Cross and Abbey Wood Depots will require to be moved to Penhall Road site.

The number of tramcars which will be moved on the afternoon and night of 5th July will depend on the available capacity at Penhall Road, which is dependent on the burning programme up to that date.

Should the burning programme be delayed for any reason, it may be necessary to retain up to 20 cars at Abbey Wood for a limited period, but in order that this possibility can be alleviated so far as possible, a gradual reduction in the number of Rolling Stock spares is envisaged as from mid June in order that scrapping can be maintained, in which event the full peak service will not be available on 5th July or possibly on the days immediately preceding.

The following list represents the existing allocation at New Cross and Abbey Wood Depots, but from the foregoing it will be apparent that this may be reduced - probably by some 17 cars - before the conversion day.

NEW CROSS

One Hundred and Twenty Six cars to be moved for scrapping to.......PENHALL ROAD SITE

168, 169, 173, 175, 176, 179, 180, 181, 184, 185, 186, 187, 188, 192,
196, 200, 1854, 1855, 1856, 1857, 1858, 1859, 1860, 1861, 1862, 1863, 1864, 1866,
1867, 1868, 1869, 1870, 1871, 1872, 1873, 1874, 1875, 1876, 1877, 1904, 1905, 1906,
1907, 1908, 1909, 1910, 1911, 1912, 1913, 1914, 1915, 1916, 1917, 1918, 1919, 1920,
1921, 1922, 1923, 1925, 1926, 1927, 1928, 1929, 1930, 1931, 1932, 1933, 1934, 1935,
1936, 1937, 1938, 1939, 1940, 1941, 1942, 1943, 1944, 1945, 1946, 1947, 1948, 1949,
1950, 1951, 1952, 1953, 1954, 1955, 1956, 1958, 1960, 1961, 1962, 1963, 1964, 1965,
1966, 1968, 1969, 1970, 1971, 1974, 1977, 1979, 1980, 1981, 1984, 1986, 1987, 1988,
1989, 1990, 1991, 1992, 1993, 1994, 1995, 1996, 1998, 1999, 2000, 2001, 2002, 2003.

ABBEY WOOD

Fifty Seven cars to be moved for scrapping to....................PENHALL ROAD SITE

2, 82, 83, 84, 85, 86, 87, 88, 89, 90, 91, 92, 93, 94, 95, 96, 97,
98, 99, 100, 162, 165, 166, 295, 297, 298, 299, 300, 302, 304, 305, 307, 309, 311,
312, 332, 334, 335, 336, 337, 338, 339, 340, 341, 342, 343, 344, 557, 559, 560, 577,
578, 592, 593, 598, 601, 565.

NOTES:

1. The transfer will be carried out by the Operating Department, who will move the cars either by diversion immediately on completion of service or from the Depot later, dependent on local conditions, and the usual close co-operation between Engineering and Operating staff will be necessary to ensure a satisfactory movement.

DIVISIONAL ENGINEER

22nd May, 1952.
C21/C/EEW.

FAREWELL TO LONDON'S TRAMS

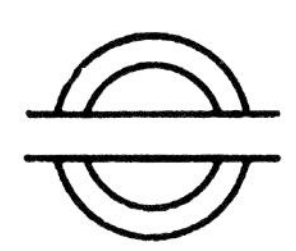

The Chairman and Members of the

LONDON TRANSPORT EXECUTIVE

request the pleasure of the company of

....

at 10.45 p.m. on Saturday, 5th July, 1952, at

CHARLTON WORKS

(*in Woolwich Road opposite Fairthorn Road near Westcombe Hill*)

to travel by special tram to New Cross Tram Depot

on completion of the work of converting

the Tramway System to Bus Operation.

R.S.V.P.
The Chief Public Relations Officer
London Transport, 55 Broadway, S.W.1

P.T.O.

New Cross. For this programme there was to be an invitation card, an admission card (four different colours for four different trams) and a souvenir brochure reviewing briefly the history of the tram system. No ladies were included amongst the suggested list of invitees as it was felt that if things became rowdy their presence would be inadvisable. It was thought that the cost would be £1000. This idea bore no fruit either.

It was felt by the operating department that some provision should be made for runs by decorated trams to both Abbey Wood and New Cross depots so that each locality could have the chance of seeing its own last tram. They could not be those used on the Embankment run as the vehicles could not be in several places at once. The same department suggested that local authorities such as the Chamber of Commerce sponsor the run of the last service tram to each depot where it would be received, and there would be feasting organised under local arrangements. It was also suggested that the Chairman and the Deputy Chairman and members of the LTE should

PROGRAMME

10.50 p.m. *Special tram leaves Charlton Works for New Cross Depot*

11.05 p.m. *Special tram arrives New Cross Depot*

11.10 p.m. *Refreshments served in the Traffic Office, New Cross Depot, and speeches by:*

The Rt. Hon. Lord Latham, J.P., F.A.C.C.A., *Chairman, London Transport Executive*

The Rt. Hon. The Chairman, London County Council (Mr. Edwin Bayliss, D.L., J.P.)

12.30 a.m. *Reception of last tram running into the Depot*

12.40 a.m. *National Anthem*

Guests will note that the arrival of the last tram will mark the end of the public transport service for the night until the resumption of traffic some hours later. They are, therefore, advised to make arrangements for their journeys home after the ceremony.

LONDON, FRIDAY, JUNE 20, 1952

Enjoy your London

Goodbye to the Trams

On Saturday, 5th July, London says a final goodbye to its trams. Next day the six remaining tram services will be replaced by buses. The coming fortnight, therefore, is the last chance you or your children will ever have of riding on a London tram. The services are: 36 and 38 from Victoria Embankment to Abbey Wood; 40 from Victoria Embankment to Plumstead; 44 from Woolwich to Eltham Green; 46 from Southwark Bridge to Woolwich; 72 from Victoria Embankment to Woolwich. Never again will you be able to ride on a London tram.

Thursday, June 26, 1952

From All Quarters

SOUVENIR LAST TRAM TICKETS

Souvenir tickets will be issued on London trams from next Monday to mark the last week before London's tram routes are finally scrapped at midnight on July 5. The tickets will have pictures of the first horse tram and the present day car.

About 180 trams on services 36, 38, 40, 72, 44 and 46 will take part in the finale. Their replacement by buses completes a £9 million post-war transport scheme.

The last tram, a route 40 car, will leave Woolwich on Saturday week, arriving at New Cross at 12.29 a.m. It will be driven part of the way by Mr. J. Cliff, deputy chairman of London Transport Executive.

proceed to New Cross and Abbey Wood and join in the farewells as may be appropriate. No financial allowance was made for these local celebrations; however, the LTE gratuitously agreed for the feastings to be charged against the department of the Chief Staff and Welfare Officer.

Another idea was for the 'special' to start from Abbey Wood depot some eight miles away and made on the assumption that their staff could have the opportunity of participating in the occasion; an undecorated tram would convey a party of fifty-seven people from Abbey Wood to New Cross depot before close of traffic. Owing to the undesirability of making the party any larger, and yet faced with the desirability of extending invitations to many who had an interest in the occasion, it was proposed to invite others, not exceeding a hundred, to proceed direct to New Cross, where on arrival of the tram party, there would be refreshments and speech-making in the traffic office. The ceremony would conclude with the reception by the Executive of the last tram to run in. Departure from Abbey Wood would be at 10.15pm and except for a stop at Woolwich changeover pit would run non-stop; the police would provide a special mobile escort to ensure a safe and uninterrupted journey. It was expected that the last tram would be received at 12.30am with the ceremony terminating at 12.40 – in reality there was no chance of it running to time. It was not proposed to invite any ladies but it was expected that one or two of the mayors would be female; no plans were made for conveying guests to their homes after the ceremony. The cost of all of this was thought to be roughly £500. The Abbey Wood and New Cross staff were to make their own arrangements as to any send-off they wanted; Abbey Wood arranged their own private function and declined any of LT's proposals. Maybe they were offended by the fact that 'last car of the night' should have been an Abbey Wood tram. With the removal of the primary reason for starting from Abbey Wood, the plan now envisaged a departure from Charlton Works as the place to start the journey; this would be at 10.45pm. This was deemed preferable to a start from Abbey Wood, as it cut the journey in half and obviated the need to negotiate the congested area of Woolwich just after licensed houses there had closed. At last, a decision had been made.

London Transport was aware that Londoners loved their trams. For many who travelled on 'the iron horses', they appreciated their enduring rattle and creak; many had been using them as a means of transport since the turn of the century, and for those in South London the trams had seen them through two world wars. The event was seen as an opportunity to make money without going to too much expense. LAST TRAM WEEK posters were fixed to the sides of all serviceable cars apart from the former West Ham trams whose advertisement panels prevented them from being so adorned. The task of fitting the adverts was so big that some were applied before 29th June. 'Last Tram Week' tickets were issued – a set cost four shillings and one penny. Record takings per duty were made on 5th July; it was estimated that three million tickets were sold since going on sale on Monday 30th June.

WOOLWICH, FRIDAY, JULY 4, 1952

MAKE YOUR LAST TRAM RIDE

A PROFITABLE JOURNEY AND VISIT

CUFFS SALE

STARTING TO-DAY (FRIDAY), JULY 4
at 9 a.m.

CUFFS OF WOOLWICH

Powis Street, S.E.18 **Phone: WOO. 2212**

SATURDAY 5th JULY 1952

Saturday 5th July dawned sunny and bright, but with not enough cars to go round some crews got paid for just hanging around. To give an idea of the shortage, only 93 were nominated on the New Cross 'cars for service' sheet that day. The problem was heightened by people wanting a last tram ride – a two-hour wait was not uncommon with the service being in total disarray in the evening owing to delays at the London end; few cars got through to Woolwich and Abbey Wood. The policy of sending cars to the scrapyard before their projected date was seen by many as a negative step, but provided people were prepared to wait, they would eventually get a ride. Revenue lost in 'real' terms was more than made up by extra riders – more could have been made if there had been a full complement of cars, but it was a drop in the ocean compared to the money saved by combining two stages of the conversion into one. The day was very busy for tram crews as crowds piled on to all available cars and souvenir hunters stripped everything that was easily removable. Route boards and service number plates were missing from most trams and many were in darkness – bulbs having been swiped too. Appropriately scrawled chalk slogans along the trams' flanks were comments such as 'Goodbye forever', 'Will ye no come back again', 'Shan't be rahnd termorrer', 'Do not worry, do not fuss, come and have your last ride with us.' etc. On the Victoria Embankment, queues of people waited patiently in the sunshine of the afternoon to make their sentimental journeys. As they waited they read the hastily chalked slogans on the sides of the trams as they passed by. The price of the specially printed souvenir tickets rocketed, so keen were the unlucky non-travellers to have a souvenir of the last run; maybe this was an early enterprise of Stan Flashman, a notorious ticket tout of old.

The tramcar had been forced to abdicate after a life that had lasted 91 years; it made a brave showing on Saturday, its last day of public usefulness. All day long, thousands of people made sentimental journeys on trams; the buses were almost neglected. For once the floors of the electric 'jam-jars' (rhymes with tramcars) were completely devoid of tickets for people were buying whole sets of them. On more than one occasion conductors were asked to autograph them. Small boys spent all their pocket money in buying a set of the coloured souvenir tickets which bore pictures of the first horse-drawn tram and the latest powered-model. Old and young alike, thousands of them, clambered and squeezed aboard whatever tram they came across which went rolling and rattling away down the lines. At the Elephant and Castle, an elderly woman with two grandchildren clutching her hands waited for almost two hours for a vacant seat. "One of my earliest recollections of London" she said "was a ride on one of the old horse trams at Camberwell, and I am determined to have one more ride just for old time's sake". Other trams packed to capacity rumbled past with hundreds of

Between Bostall Hill and Abbey Wood, trams and trolleybuses had their own separate overhead wires as exemplified on 'Last Tram Day' by former Leyton car 184. This view was taken at the junction of Dahlia Road with Mcleod Road, near Abbey Wood. 184 is on its way to Embankment with a large number of passengers on board; surprisingly, at 4.55pm it has no chalked farewell inscriptions. (Peter Mitchell)

New Cross depot run-out sheet Saturday 5th July 1952

LIST OF VEHICLES FOR SERVICE NEW X DEPOT/GARAGE 5th DAY JULY 1952

ROUTE No. 38-38

Running number	Vehicle number	Road number	Time due out
45	1933		
17	1943		
48	1916		
42	1923		
46	1948		
20	1922		
49	1987	16	
5	1955	21	
35	1953	17	
25	183	31	
7	1971	12	
9	1869	22	
29	1856	3	
14	1930	24	
33	179	19	
19	175	24	
22	184	21	
41	1938	21	
44	1932	5	
26	1907	3	
64	186	8	
53	1854	3	
67	1915	7	
54	1941	7	
69	1984	32	
62	1994	32	
68	1995	32	
23	1974	18	
65	1928	18	
27	196	29	
56	1871	29	
66	1937	29	

ROUTE No. 36-38

Running number	Vehicle number	Road number	Time due out
31	1873	7	
61	185	1	
66	1912	1	
38	1855	13	
43	1966	13	
47	1945	13	
2	1947	13	
SERVICE 46			
1	1925		
25	1929		
30	1993	23	
36	1910	3	
3	1979	19	
9	1862	8	
11	1991	21	
27	1877	21	
29	1942	9	
34	1970	16	
35	1940	9	
26	1918	9	
28	1864	9	
37	187	25	
33	2002	25	
13	1954	1A	
14	1980	31	

ROUTE NO. 72

Running number	Vehicle number	Road number	Time due out
9	176	23	
11	1961	5	
12	2003	29	
14	1950	19	
15	1914	1	
16	1858	19	
17	1861	23	
1	1863	23	
2	1996	31	
3	1905	1A	
4	1911	1A	
5	200	11	
6	1875	11	
7	1935	11	
8	1936	11	
10	1956	11	
13	1981	5	
18	181	13	
SERVICE 72X			
1X	1906	9	

ROUTE NO. 40

Running number	Vehicle number	Road number	Time due out
13	1962		
2	1904		
23	169		
3	1934		
5	1977	10	
19	1969	14	
20	1920	7	
24	2000	7	
21	1857	17	
10	1939	17	
22	1867	15	
12	1926	22	
1	168	27	
7	1999	27	
4	2001	27	
6	1964	12	
9	1872	27	
14	1913	1	

410/49 (2)
(2000/100 7.50-C16-Stock)

SIGNED............................

DO NOT USE THIS FORM IF THE SMALLER SIZE [410/49 (1)] WILL DO

others who had the same idea. On the final day, one of the old faithful trams clattering down the Old Kent Road claimed a few more precious minutes of life by getting its plough entangled with a piece of wood which was lying in the centre conduit; following trams were held up as it squatted in the roadway like a stubborn old hen. Many of the passengers, who were taking purely sentimental journeys, laughed and chatted as they tumbled out of the tram, unable to complete their joyride. Nearly twenty other trams were piled up in the queue before the broken down one got underway again, this time being pushed back ignominiously to its depot. When the breakdown gang came out, a passing bus driver called out to the crew who were sweating around the broken plough "Burn the thing".

It was a requirement that Metropolitan Stage Carriage licence plates be removed as soon as trams entered 'Penhall'.

JOURNEY'S END FOR LONDON TRAMS

A bye-law prevented artistry on London's trams. The children putting graffiti on this unidentified car at an unknown location would be unaware of this and, bearing in mind that it is Last Tram Day, nobody will discourage them. Maybe they were just copying what adults had been doing that day.

(14.5.52) 17

ALLOCATION OF SCHEDULED SERVICE TRAMS.

By DEPOTS.

Depot	Route No.	Monday—Friday			Saturday			Sunday	
		a.m. pk.	mid-day	p.m. pk.	a.m. pk.	p.m. pk.	p.m. nor.	a.m.	p.m.
Abbey Wood ... AW.	**36/38**	23	24	23	18	26	14	9	12
	44	6	7	9	5	9	10	—	—
	46	18	7	20	13	20	12	9	12
	46 Ex.	5	—	—	—	—	—	—	—
		52	38	52	36	55	36	18	24
New Cross ... NX.	**36-38**	36	23	35	32	43	33	15	19
	40	31	13	33	18	30	18	11	14
	46	19	11	19	12	22	17	13	16
	72	15	15	15	14	18	18	9	11
	72 Ex	8	—	8	1	2	—	—	—
		109	62	110	77	115	86	48	60
Total No. of Scheduled Trams		161	100	162	113	170	122	66	84
Max. No. of Vehicles Scheduled		162			170			84	

In the iconic film 'The Elephant Will Never Forget', mention is made of trams passing through Beresford Square; London Transport's three modes of road passenger transport are seen together at this location – three trolleybuses, three motorbuses and two trams. The tram on the right nudges past people patronising the market stalls on a busy market Saturday; it is on London Transport's shortest post-war route, the 44. This is an ex-West Ham car which has terminated here and is about to return to Middle Park Avenue. On three sides of the square a line of cobblestones cut across the pavement, indicating the boundary; this area was owned by the Market Traders Association and the track could not be lifted in the aftermath of the trams as they did not have enough money to carry out this work. The tracks could not be removed by Woolwich Borough Council as they were not allowed to lift them; they remained in-situ until 1984.

Seen at the 'Welcome Inn' in Well Hall Road on route 44 are 'East Ham' 90 and LT 593; the lower numbered car has a linen route blind while the higher numbered one uses a stencil. 90's destination blind shows a route 46 display for Beresford Square from where it has just come – the conductor is either rushed off his feet collecting fares or has forgotten to turn the blind. 593, emblazoned with chalk, heads for Beresford Square. There is an intriguing contrast between the tarmac and the cobbled part of roadway used by the trams. Crews working on route 44 on this, the last day, had an easy time compared to those serving Peckham, Camberwell and Central London. (Jack Wyse)

1926 is running late on route 40 on 5th July and has turned short at New Cross; it is in Lewisham Way, at the Marquis of Granby crossover, and therefore just off its line of route. It looks as if it is being curtailed again at Kennington rather than going to Embankment on its next trip. The less frequently used crossovers needed to be manually operated, and a lever (which was held in each tram and placed behind the controller) was inserted in a slot in the road; as seen here, the conductor pulled it over to set the points. Note the sandbags on 1926 – the cabs tended to leak in their final years and this was a preventative measure. RT 2917 is on route 36. (Jack Wyse)

Taken from Waterloo Bridge on the last day, this image shows the trolley booms of this unidentified car to good effect. Some of the passers-by give scant regard to a vehicle serving out its last day on the streets of London. (Jack Wyse)

Members of the Ian Allan Bus-spotters club wait for the two trams that they hired to pick them up. A number are photographing the rear of 1923 whose conductor waves at them with his ticket rack. Working on route 36 to Abbey Wood is E3 1947. (London Transport Museum U53452)

The Ian Allan Bus-spotters club hired 1909 and 1998 on 5th July 1952. Bus-spotters were considered to be youngsters, but many of those about to board are adults. It is an easy day for the crew – the driver does not have to stop and start all the time, while the conductor has not got to collect any fares. The two cars load up on the Embankment. (London Transport Museum U53453)

1908 and 1931 were hired by the LRTL on 5th July 1952; at Addington Street siding, cameras are pointed at 1931 which is having posters fitted to it. With the aid of chalk, LCC TRAMWAYS replaces the LONDON TRANSPORT fleetname; another phrase is: 'WAIT FOR THE FOG & SNOW!!!' At 3.35am the next morning, 1931 will be the last tram to enter Penhall Road scrapyard. (Jack Wyse)

1863 working on route 72 and 1908 on tour are seen at New Cross Gate; 1908 shows BLACKWALL TNL. In view are RT 2847 and RT 2849 (which have been in service for three months) which are on route 172 which replaced the 35 tram on 6th April 1952. (Jack Wyse)

Two 40s are in Peckham High Street; 1916 heads for SAVOY ST STRAND while the other is for New Cross Gate. Wartime bomb damage is in evidence. The pedestrians take little notice of the trams – to many it was just like any other day. (Jack Wyse)

From 10th November 1935 until 5th July 1952, trams and trolleybuses ran alongside each other between Woolwich and Abbey Wood; this was the longest period of simultaneous operation of these two modes of transport. Ex East Ham tram, and now London Transport 90 takes on passengers in what can only be described as a precarious situation. Adjacent is D2 class trolleybus 411 working on route 698; the conductor has not positioned the front blind very well as it shows part of a Woolwich Ferry display and part of a Bexleyheath display. 411 heads for Woolwich; 90 with no route blind, will soon start its journey to Embankment. From the commencement of tram services on 26th August 1903 until 5th July 1952, street transport at Abbey Wood was solely by electric-powered vehicles. (Online Transpoirt Archive)

The highest renumbered car in the former East Ham Corporation Tramway's fleet survived until London's Last Tram Day. As there is no rope attached to the trailing boom, 100 uses its leading boom, hence the askance angle. 100 is near Woolwich Ferry Power Station on the final afternoon. (Peter Mitchell)

593 was fitted with high horse power motors and therefore outlasted the slow motored members of the 552-601 class; it survived until the last day. It has been the centre of attention for slogan writers – the REST IN PEACE phrase is appropriate as this is Woolwich on 5th July. The last six tram routes all worked in Woolwich on Last Tram Day. (Peter Mitchell)

Clarence Carter's photographs have enriched many transport books; all views are meticulously recorded in an index which gives vehicle number, route number, location, time and camera speed. He has given his camera to a friend at 2.30pm on 5th July; a dapper Mr Carter stands to the right of 1948. An inspector and 1948's crew are engaged in conversation at Abbey Wood. Both trolley arms are on the overhead; the one nearest the camera will have to be pulled down before 1948 departs. (Clarence Carter)

New Cross Gate on the final afternoon. E3 1926 on route 40 and E3 1996 on route 72 both show NEW CROSS GATE; this was common as inspectors and crews were often working on an ad-hoc basis. Maybe 1926 is running in and 1996 has just run out of New Cross depot. To the right, an RT on route 69 hugs the pavement; adjacent to 1996 is a motorbike and sidecar. Jack Wyse took many of his photographs from the top deck of trams. (Jack Wyse)

339 is just north of Woolwich Arsenal Station at 2.39pm while working short to Lewisham on route 46 on 5th July; the LAST TRIP slogan is premature as 339 did not come out of service until 11.52pm. The advertisement panels on the former West Ham cars precluded the use of LAST TRAM WEEK posters. These cars were fitted with only one trolley arm, and therefore one retaining hook at each end. It was deemed safer to have two trolleys as crews did not have to walk in the roadway at termini; with one boom, they could find themselves in confrontation with motorists when 'walking' round a trolley boom. (Peter Mitchell)

Abbey Wood depot was the sole operator of route 44 which ran between Woolwich and Middle Park Avenue; this required 'lengthy depot runs' which ran in service. This view shows the single line of track in Bostall Hill (approaching Wickham Lane corner). Drivers worked on the 'line of sight' principle; only in foggy conditions were inspectors on hand to help cars through. It is 4.11pm on the last day and 90 (formerly East Ham Corporation Tramways property) is probably being driven uphill on top parallel notch. 90's trolley boom is on the positive overhead trolleybus wire. (Peter Mitchell)

The message did not get through in time for the first conversion and a number were burnt with them on. Panic struck the authorities and from then on they were meticulously removed; in fact so stringent was the rule applied that plates were chiselled off while trams were still on Woolwich Road and moving into the yard. With the mass arrival of trams late at night on the bigger conversions, some went in with their plates on but were removed at the earliest opportunity. The lowest numbered MSC plate 'live' on 5th July 1952 was oval plate 7N on ex-East Ham car 90; the highest numbered plate in use that day was 'oval' 11244N on ex West Ham car 343.

The traverser at Penhall Road experienced its heaviest day's workload on 5th July; however, it failed in the afternoon. Fortunately (many would say otherwise), it was put right before the evening's serious business began. Cars started to arrive in the early afternoon – now all tracks led to the tram graveyard.

On 5th July, 158 trams were available for service; 110 at New Cross and 48 at Abbey Wood. As anticipated, the full peak hour service was not provided: 162 were needed in Monday to Friday peak hours and 170 for the Saturday midday peak (115 at New Cross and 55 at Abbey Wood). The shortage was exacerbated by six cars

The afternoon and evening of 5th July saw trams entering the scrapyard 'thick and fast' – that is at regular intervals. All tracks now led to the tramatorium. It was common practice for cars running there to show SPECIAL. 1930 (left) operated in London for twenty years – its working life is now at an end. Its plough is being helped out of its carrier; the plough will go into the open pit where it will be taken out. 82 (below) has just had its plough removed at the entrance; the conductor is placing the trolley arm onto one of the two overhead wires used for incoming cars. (D.W.K. Jones)

A mock funeral at CRD saw a model tram placed in a coffin; it was later exhumed. A 'minister' took the ceremony; two youngsters lower the model into position. A poignant message is on a table; to some staff a tram was the best pal they ever had.

Two views of the last private hire tram, E3 1988, used by the Infantile Paralysis Fellowship. The first shot is at the start of the tour (Addington Street) where a number of people are dressed in pearly king and queen ceremonial outfits. In the second photo, 1988 is mobbed somewhere along its route – no wonder the trip had to be curtailed. (London Transport Museum U3515/Online Transport Archive)

set aside for private hire (at premium rates). In the daytime, 1909* and 1998 were used by the Ian Allan Bus Spotters' Club, 1908 and 1931* by the Light Railway Transport League, while 1946 was with the Omnibus Society. 1988 was used by the Infantile Paralysis Fellowship Association for an evening trip from Westminster to Woolwich; it was timed to leave at 7.57pm. At Westminster, comedienne Ethel Revnell broke a quart bottle of stout over its nose before it left; in front of it rode a police motorcycle escort. At the Elephant and Castle, Miss Revnell nearly left with a souvenir; accepting the conductor's duties for a while she had borrowed his MSC badge, 'LTE staff for the use of only'. Only at the last moment before she left did she remember to return the trinket. Such were the crowds that 1988 was severely delayed and running an hour late, the tour was curtailed and hundreds of people in Lewisham, who were expecting to see it, were disappointed at its absence. 1988 was followed by three gaily decorated veteran cars with the occupants dressed in Edwardian costumes; in one, Marie Lloyd songs were played on a gramophone. Driving 1988 was Bill Appleton of 6 Pitfield Road, Lee who had completed 36 years service; his conductor was his old pal, Mr F. Carter of Oakridge Road, Bromley who had 37 years service to his credit. Their first stop on the penny-showered route was at the Waterman Arms, Charlton where the licensee, Mr Pennington and his wife, laid on food and drinks for the weary travellers. South London's Pearly Kings and Queens left their donkeys in the stables and medical students made collections along the route (money was thrown from windows and collected from cafes). A number of other hostelries were visited – no wonder the tour was described

*it is possible that 1909 and 1931 were hand-picked; 1909 had been the last tram to be overhauled and returned to everyday service, while 1931 had received a depot repaint in New Cross in March 1952 – it had also been used in the opening of the enlarged Kingsway subway in the year 1931.

A non-standard car that survived until the end was number 2 which is seen in Well Hall Road at 8.27pm. Late running was the order of the evening on 5th July and 2 should have gone to Woolwich on route 46; to get it back on its scheduled time an inspector has curtailed it at Middle Park Avenue. (Peter Mitchell)

It is dusk on Saturday 5th July 1952 and soon only flashlight photographs will be able to be taken. 343 waits at Middle Park Avenue before setting off on a journey to Beresford Square on route 44. A pre-war East Kent Leyland Tiger TS8 with a Park Royal 32 seat body scoots round 343. Crowds of people are on the pavement; all have come out to see the last hours of the London tram. (Peter Mitchell)

1952 took civic dignitaries from Charlton Works to New Cross depot on the evening of 5th July. What is the conductor taking out of the bag to give to passengers? (London Transport Museum U3524)

Driver Alfred Jago of Abbey Wood depot is immaculately turned out for his duty on 5th July which was to drive 1952 from Charlton Works to New Cross depot. Sharing the controls was the deputy chairman John Cliff. (London Transport Museum U3523)

as the equivalent of a 'south London pub crawl'. The tram had its own humorous souvenir ticket designed by cartoonist and broadcaster Gerard Hoffnung. Also unavailable were 1951 in New Cross depot and 1952 in Charlton works – both were assigned to 'special duties' that evening.

A small replica of a London tramcar was buried in the grounds of the tram and trolleybus works at Charlton in the evening of 5th July. After the singing of 'Cock Robin' and similar sad ditties, a miniature tram carefully packed into an aluminium coffin was officially laid to rest. Later, the tram was exhumed and taken from its coffin in which it was interred. A mock funeral followed with Mr F. Chamberlain acting as the clergyman; it was watched by hundreds of tram workers, families and friends who had been entertained during the evening with an impromptu concert and sing-song. Nostalgic tunes, remindful of the passing of an old-timer, were in great demand. The coffin was draped with a trolleybus destination blind showing BARKING BROADWAY STRATFORD; it would have been more appropriate if a tram blind had been used.

There were bittersweet scenes along the Old Kent Road and the Embankment; nearly everybody had a cheer for a departing old friend. Others remained silent in their memories and passengers leaned out of the windows holding Roman candles. Extra police were called out to control the crowds, and all along the routes people jostled to get aboard for a last ride; there were those with

Metropolitan Public Carriage Act, 1869. (32 & 33 Vict., c. 115).
London Passenger Transport Act, 1933. (23 Geo. 5, c. 14).
Road Traffic Act, 1934. (24 & 25 Geo. 5, c. 50).

Licence No. T3/ 14190

Badge No. T.15000

LICENCE TO ACT AS DRIVER OF TRAMCARS

I, being the authority having power to grant licences under the Metropolitan Public Carriage Act, 1869, hereby license John CLIFF
residing at 4, Cholmeley Court, Southwood Lane, Highgate, N.6. **to act as Driver of Electric Tramcars.**

This licence is granted subject to the provisions of

(a) the Metropolitan Public Carriage Act, 1869, and any Order made thereunder by the Minister of Transport relating to drivers and conductors of tramcars, and

(b) the Acts relating to Metropolitan Stage Carriages in force at the time of the commencement of the Metropolitan Public Carriage Act, 1869, subject to any alteration of those Acts by any such Order as aforesaid.

This licence shall have effect as from 30 June, 1952 **and shall continue in force for three years from that date unless sooner revoked or suspended.**

Harold Scott

Commissioner of Police of the Metropolis.

Date of issue 30 June, 1952

Fee 3/-

John Cliff

Signature of Licensee.

NOTES

(1) The licensee must sign this licence in the space provided above immediately on receiving it; but must not write anything else on it.

(2) The licensee must notify the Commissioner of Police of any change of address within 7 days of such change.

M.P.-40489/20 Pads Aug./1949 W182

'Last Southwark' was 337, a former West Ham car. Driver Richardson and conductor Rhodes crew the car. When it gets to Beresford Square, they will run it to Penhall Road scrapyard after which a staff bus will take them to their home depot of Abbey Wood.
(London Transport Museum U53462)

Surprisingly, 1933 has arrived at Embankment with its front route plate and destination blind in-situ; it is unlikely that they will be there on arrival at New Cross depot. Driver H.J. Strode and conductor W. Partridge pose in front of 1933 prior to departure of the last 36 from Savoy Street. Spanning a large age range, people witness the end of the tram era in London. Amongst the well-wishers is a policeman; this event was good-natured and the strongest words he may have had to use that night were "Sorry sir, the tram's full up." The tram stop flag will soon be replaced by one for buses. Leather gloves were often worn by drivers to prevent the controller handle chafing their hands; Mr Strode will not need them on 6th July.
(London Transport Museum U53465)

1904 is one of the last cars to run on the Embankment; many have not come for a ride but to see the passing of a familiar sight. Centrepiece is E3 1904 which has 'lost' its destination blind (and probably its route plate). Prematurely, the bus stop shows the new services that will be running in a few hours time. A feature of tramway abandonments up and down the country was the placing of coins on tracks; flattened, they would be mementos to remind people of times gone by. A number of people participate in this practice, and 1904 will soon commit the offence of defacing the King's head. (London Transport Museum U53460/U53461)

trumpets and accordions but the biggest noise of all came from hundreds of rattles. Last car south over Blackfriars Bridge crept across at midnight without lights; all the bulbs had been taken by souvenir hunters who were ripping service number plates and blinds from any car they could. Regulations were forgotten; smoking was permitted on the lower deck as well as the top deck of the cars, people boarded at the front and crowded on the track in such a mass that every tram was behind schedule. As 1863 reversed at Savoy Street Strand for her last journey to New Cross, all the lights failed and, without headlamp or rear light, it departed; after she left Westminster, scores of people got down on their knees to collect any tickets dropped from 1863 and other trams.

A 'posh tram' was to carry VIPs, including the London Transport Chairman, on a journey from CRD to New Cross depot where a reception was to be held. 1952 stood ablaze with lights on in the darkened yard of Charlton LTE Works – the invitees assembled at 10.30pm for a 10.45 departure. 1952 was chosen to be the official last tram as it was the year 1952; however a defect rendered it unserviceable for passenger carrying duties and the mammoth task went to 1951. However, 1952 was still fit enough to carry out the VIP run from CRD to New Cross. Sleek glistening cars with mayors and mayoresses from a number of south-east London boroughs, driven by uniformed chauffeurs did not in any way detract from the glorious moment that 1952 was experiencing. The Rolls Royces were deserted as the official party clambered aboard to the accompaniment of cheers from crowds standing four deep outside on the pavement. Driver Alfred Jago (a local councillor) and conductor W. Bullimore, both long service men from Abbey Wood depot, were selected to man 1952 on this special run; Jago said that he had been driving trams for so long that he knew every cobble in the road. Old acquaintances were renewed as Jago, a tram driver for over 40 years and a former Mayor of Woolwich, shook hands with LTE deputy Chairman, John Cliff, a brother tram driver of times past who had started as a tram-man in Leeds 52 years earlier. Cliff was allocated the highest numbered driver's MSC badge – T15000; issued on 29th June 1952 it was valid for three years. Cliff had been given a notional driving course and considered adept for his tasks on the night of 5th/6th July. After this, T badges were still allocated to trolleybus staff; whoever ordered the badges just about got the number required right, for when it came round to issuing the last ones to new trolleybus drivers, the highest was T14898 in March 1962).

Jago and Cliff took turns at the controls; Cliff confided that he was perhaps a little rusty, but soon got into the swing of things. As the tram slowly and majestically left the yard it was followed, as in a funeral cortege, by a long procession of cars. "And for a change they did not try to pass us" said Councillor Jago. But the solemnity of the occasion was only short lived for there was soon some accompaniment – a cacophony of hooters and cheers from the crowds lining the route as 1952 rattled along Woolwich Road, Greenwich High Road and New Cross Road. Apparently, there were many who were under the impression that this was THE last tram of all. The crowds near New Cross depot were so dense that 1952, motor cars and coaches full of returning holiday-makers became involved in a colossal traffic jam; no-one seemed to mind though. After all, it only meant spending a few more moments in "Ole Faithful". For other road users, a heaven-sent opportunity to become identified with one of the most spontaneous expressions of the London public – they were sentimental and humorous at the passing of an old friend. News cameras whirred as the tram party, rather regretfully it seems, left one by one to go into the main traffic hall, transformed for the occasion into a large refreshment hall where toasts and speeches were made.

Local and national newspapers covered the last hours of the trams extensively and eloquently. The next few paragraphs are taken either verbatim from them or are a combination of reports.

"A carnival atmosphere gripped the trams' last working area; it increased and ripened as the day drew to a close. It was a wonderful funeral with their wake being held at many a hostelry – outside public houses as night drew in, customers cheered and lifted their glasses to every passing tram. During the evening, a 72 tram was halted outside 'The Rose of Lee' and pints of beer were handed to the driver and conductor. All day long, people flocked to ride on the cars but, all too soon, darkness came and the life of the London tram could now be counted in minutes rather than hours. One reporter stated that the Victoria Embankment was where tramps sleep, lovers walk and trams clang; now it acted as a magnet for the festivities and tram after tram was cheered, mobbed, stripped of boards and blinds, chalked on and sung on its way back across the Thames. The sadness of it though was that an hour or so after it left town, each and every one of these celebrities would be lifeless in a scrap metal merchant's yard. Many a penny, a sixpence, a florin and even a half-crown coin was flattened by the wheel of a tram that day with their owners being able to tell their grandchildren the reason for its odd shape in many a year's time. Last tram from town, a 40, was the 11.38 pm from Savoy Street. Driving it was 43 year-old Thomas George Monk of 161 Kingsground, Eltham; his conductor was Alfred Edward Harriss of 21 Swallands Road, Bellingham. It picked up an escort of cars, motorcycles and bicycles; the cars hooted and the tram was overloaded with singing passengers. Tolling its bell, it penetrated deeper into South London where the escort became larger and longer and the hooting, cheering and ringing of bells became louder. The loudspeaker volunteer in front became more lyrical, his voice breaking as he declared "This really is the last, the very last tram" (though it wasn't). When it arrived at New Cross, the pavements were packed solid, people sat on trees, on lamp posts and on garden walls. People danced in the streets and those who lived on the main road packed their front room windows; some were on top of advert hoardings and flat roofs to see the last trams pass through. Late night lorries caught in the crush gave up trying to escape and their drivers cheered and hooted with the rest. The crews of the last few trams took it all in their stride; the drivers could only pass through the crowds at New Cross on first notch – they had a smile on their face though. The trams were going and London was about to lose one of its most characteristic features; the crowd gave them the most uproarious, tumultuous farewell ever seen in the boroughs. No king or queen received greater acclaim in the streets of London than did the last of the 'Tin Terrors' – it was a scene never to be forgotten. At New Cross depot the crowds cheered and sang – they were accompanied by the blowing of motor horns, bugles and whistles. All evening, crowds in the street had cheered every tram, tied streamers to it, chalked slogans on its bull-nose and stripped it of whatever they could as souvenirs. There was no doubt about it – the London tram had been a faithful servant."

The trams did not go without taking their last toll. On the last day, eight year-old Christopher Heath of 83 Mayday Gardens, Blackheath was knocked down by a motorcycle while getting off a tram; he was taken to hospital with leg

John Cliff and Alfred Jago are on the platform of 1952; it is impossible to say which of them has his hand on the controller. Between the main road and the top of the slope to New Cross depot, 1952 has been relieved of its 'front' blind. (London Transport Museum U53483)

injuries. The day before, Private Mary Jones, aged 20 of the WRAC was knocked down by a pedal cycle in Academy Road, Woolwich while dismounting from a tram; she was taken to Herbert Hospital with cuts to face, injuries to the ribs, and shock. The honour of the final 'tram injury' went to eight year-old Derek Purser of 105 Glengall Road, Camberwell who was a victim of the crush outside New Cross depot on the night of 5th/6th July; he was pushed by the crowd into a stationary bicycle and injured his thigh. Even though the trams had last run in the early hours of 6th July, there was an incident on the following Saturday (12th July) when the front wheel of a bicycle caught in the tracks in Lee High Road and its rider, Mr George Horton, aged 22 of St Paul's Cray was taken to hospital with an eye injury.

Not all of the staff wanted to take trams to Penhall; they just wanted to get home. This meant that cars were parked in New Cross depot awaiting crews; consequently there tended to be long gaps between trams being shunted to Penhall as crews who were prepared to do more than one run, had to get back to New Cross – a number went straight to Penhall rather than enter the depot. There was no backlog at Abbey Wood as on arrival at Beresford Square, all cars went directly to the scrapyard.

Extensively delayed was 'Last Abbey Wood'; the crew had to get 309 to the eastern outpost of the system. For one thing, the conductor had to pay in the money he had taken that day – for another, the last vehicle to any destination on the London Transport network HAD to run if at all possible. 309 was full of boisterous well-wishers and received acclaim with

LONDON, SATURDAY, JULY 5, 1952

QUEUES FOR LAST TRAM RIDES

FAREWELL TO-NIGHT

Daily Telegraph Reporter

Business was brisk and a good time was being had by all, except the conductors, as hundreds of people took their last-day-but-one opportunity to travel in London's trams yesterday.

To-night the last tram of all, a No. 40, leaves Woolwich at 11.57, arriving at New Cross, via Charlton and Greenwich, at 12.29 a.m. A favourite trip yesterday was a spin along the Embankment between Blackfriars and Westminster. There were long queues at the main stopping places.

At 7.57 to-night the last hired tram will leave Westminster after a bottle of stout has been broken on its "bows." It has been chartered by the Infantile Paralysis Fellowship. A special ticket, measuring 50in by 10in, in the form of a legal document, has been designed and will cost a minimum of £1. Proceeds will go to help infantile paralysis research.

The last tram to leave Central London will be a No. 40 from the Embankment at 11.38 to-night arriving at New Cross at 12.11 a.m.

the local populace and London Transport staff; to say that it was 'running hot' was an apt description. The Maybloom Club at Plumstead had an extension until midnight, and a band turned out to play 309 off on the last part of its journey. Inscribed tankards were presented at the club to driver George Gray of 24 Park View Road, New Eltham and his conductor George Stevens of 17 Openshaw Road, Abbey Wood, who were in charge of the last 38. Each tankard had an inscription commemorating 33 years service. Mr Stevens' pewter mug was, however, wrongly inscribed; he had nearly 40 years' service with London Transport – Maybloom were to take the mug back and have the wording changed. Somewhere between Plumstead and Abbey Wood, enthusiastic youths took the pole of Mr Gray's tram off the overhead wires; it was plunged into darkness and began rolling back. Thankfully, the brake was hurriedly put on. At the Harrow Inn at Abbey Wood, another presentation should have been made but by the time the car arrived, everyone had gone home – the ceremony was to be made at a later date.

Last service tram from Abbey Wood was 1922 on route 38; running extremely late, the crew arrived and departed in double-quick time – it was one trolley down the other trolley up and away with all those on board not having to alight. The conductor had had such a busy day that he would not take any fares on the trip to New Cross. "Have it on me" he said. Pausing only to pick up the plough at Woolwich change pit and drop the trolley arm, the driver hurtled through the darkness giving those on board a high speed run. 309's crew were to later take it to Penhall; wanting to get home at a reasonable hour, 309 would have been taken through its paces on its journey to the 'tramatorium'.

London's official last tram was 1951; crewing it were driver Albert Fuller of 310 Queens Road, Peckham and conductor William Bedford of 14 St Lawrence Road, Brixton. Due to the crowds giving the trams a nostalgic send-off in the evening, it would be impossible for it to arrive at Woolwich for a 11.57pm departure from Perrott Street. Presumably Fuller and Bedford carried out the first part of their duty in the normal manner, but upon resumption after their relief were instructed to run 1951 'light' to Abbey Wood; it travelled via Lee to avoid the masses of people lining the more direct route through Greenwich. 1951 left Abbey Wood at 11.40pm for its last ride. Flares set up by cine-cameramen looked for a moment as though they might prove a little dangerous; they were soon put out and the tram moved off to the accompaniment of rattles, cheers and catcalls. At Plumstead Corner, travellers could see young "bloods" perched on top of advertisement hoardings, and further on people were standing on the flat roofed portico of the Labour Club. Still with its interior lights out, 1951 ran empty to Woolwich. She rattled down to the stop there – just another tram; one of the many hundreds that Londoners have been alternatively cursing and blessing for nearly a century. The waiting crowd raised a great cheer as she swayed to a halt.

1951 was nine minutes late departing Perrott Street. From then on it continued to lose time, but the fault was not in the tram's inner workings but the crowds who were loath to let it pass. As the journey proceeded the crowds got thicker and gradually a cloud of assorted vehicles began to form itself around it. From the open windows on the top of the tram, the lucky people who managed to get seats leant out in defiance of the printed instructions against the practice. The downstairs was filled with a BBC recording team who, with the press, had been allowed to board at Abbey Wood; they were interviewing people who were smoking away quite happily. The ultimate blaze of glory though surrounded 1951 on its final trip from Woolwich to New Cross; the crowd that turned out for it was larger than royalty could command. Despite the 'celebrations', there was a little sadness in the air and the police turned a blind eye to rules and regulations. As 1951's journey proceeded, the crowds got thicker. What a night it was with London loath to let its last tram past; 1951 had to fight every yard of the way and could only get a move on when the crowds thinned. Along the line of the route crowds hammered on the windows until some thought that they would break; one did. Many cars had chalked farewells scrawled on them: "No tears, no flowers, by request" and "Goodbye love with three kisses". The favourite songs of those who had managed to clamber on board were 'Auld Lang Syne', 'Now is the hour', 'Any old iron' and 'Show me the way to go home'. People waved flags and beat drums; some sung, some wept. On board, one reporter wrote: "The tram nosed its way through the crowds and only at Perrott Street were ordinary passengers from the seething mob outside taken on. Some had been drinking. Others – when the conductor wasn't looking – continued to drink. One reveller insisted on performing London's most advanced form of expression 'Knees up Mother Brown'. The tram was followed by a long column of cars, motorcycles and push bikes, with some weaving around the tram like tugs. Traffic coming in the opposite direction was stopped by the approaching horde."

SATURDAY, JULY 5, 1952

And in London to-night—

MIDNIGHT FAREWELL TO THE TRAMS

London's last tramcars will disappear from the streets shortly after midnight to-night.

Their disappearance marks the completion of London Transport's £9,000,000 post-war scheme to replace all remaining tramcar routes by buses.

To-night, Lord Latham, chairman of London Transport, is to welcome at New Cross tramcar depot the very last passenger tramcar to run in London.

From Woolwich

It will be car No. 1951, on Route 40, leaving Perrott Street, Woolwich, at 11.57 p.m. and arriving at New Cross, via Greenwich and Deptford, at 12.29 a.m.

At the controls of the last tramcar will be Mr. John Cliff, deputy chairman of London Transport, who himself started his 52 years' career in transport as a tramwayman in Leeds.

The last tramcar from the Embankment and Central London, will be a route 40 tramcar, leaving Savoy Street at 11.38 p.m. and arriving at New Cross at 12.11 a.m.

Several farewell tramcar rides will be made by parties who have hired special tramcars, during the afternoon and early evening to-day.

London's tramcars — which were first introduced by an American, George Francis Train, in 1861—when the American Civil War was being fought—have served London for 91 years. They were electrified in the early 1900's.

Driver Fuller, with a tinge of regret at the passing of the trams, said "I've never seen anything like this in my 31 years on them". Conductor Bedford was at first bewildered by it all, but then like a soldier in a moment of battle crisis, fell back on drill. He began to move up and down his tram as he had done for many years before, shouting "Fares please". This was an official service tram and everyone had to have tickets. Solemnly he asked everyone what they required - not that it was necessary for we were all going to New Cross depot or bust. He punched the long white and yellow 8d tickets exactly where they were meant to be punched. Some passengers asked for a couple of extra 2d tickets to take home to the kids. Robert Lee Macintyre said to conductor Bedford "I should like to buy a complete set of tickets you have in the holder so that I can give them to Dad" (a former permanent way engineer with 40 years service and who was unable to attend the event). Coming along Woolwich Road, there on the right was the Charlton tram graveyard; but it wasn't really like a graveyard - no black hats and sombre clothing. Instead there were wildly cheering mourners in paper hats and bright summer shirts and dresses. Behind them, standing in funeral order were the "dead trams" awaiting cremation. There were 72s and 46s and 38s; they had been taken off the road only that day and bore the familiar but now obsolete legend "On July 5 we say goodbye to London." They had already said their goodbyes. But our No. 40 still had a few more moments of glory to come; on we went with the crowds in front and the great procession behind seeming to increase with every furlong. At East Greenwich Fire Station the fire engines had been drawn up smartly in front of the great doors. Their yellow warning lights flashed in salute and their crews cheered; quite a gesture as fire engines and trams never quite saw eye-to-eye on the road. We were getting over our bewilderment now, sufficiently to study our fellow travellers. There was Harry Packham of 28 Amersham Vale, Deptford. He had jumped aboard when the tram was already full; an inspector tried to turn him off - Harry was not budging. An inspector and another transport official threatened him with awesome penalties. Harry was adamant and a big man; they let him get on. "Whew" he said as he grabbed

Conductor Bedford collects fares from those lucky enough to board 1951 at Woolwich. The only people who will be issued with a ticket after that will be those who vie for one as the car approaches New Cross depot. They were under the impression that they could obtain the last ticket paid for on a London tram – what they didn't know was that 187 is still in service and it will never be known to whom the last ticket was issued on a passenger carrying London tram.

1951 is on its way from Woolwich to New Cross; it is not known where this view was taken. A fog flare illuminates this picture. (Mrs A.E. Lidbetter)

for a strap. "That was a close one; thought they were going to get tough for a minute." Then he explained why he was so determined: "I am a Londoner by birth but have only just come back after 14 years. I thought I just had to come and get on the last of the trams I knew in my boyhood."

Boy most envied by the children along the route was eight year-old Stephen Potts; he was the only child on 1951. His mother, Mrs Janet Potts of Kingston, Ontario, Canada was a Londoner who married a Canadian during the war. "We came over for a holiday a week ago," she said. "Stephen had never seen a tram before; he's thrilled to bits". On past another vast multitude at Blackwall Lane, on for the last time, disturbing the royal serenity of the Naval College and Maritime Museum. At St Alfege Greenwich, it was the same story – people, people, people. Children were putting pennies on the track to be flattened by the wheels; it was illegal to deface coins of course, but nobody seemed to mind. All that was needed was a New York ticker-tape shower – and sure enough at Greenwich Town Hall, down came clusters of paper scraps. Hundreds of motorists followed 1951 on its final journey. There were charabancs and vintage cars waiting on the road between Woolwich and New Cross. By the time the tram reached the depot, cars were jammed behind it for three miles. People who had gathered to wave to the tram remained after it had passed and watched the car procession with astonishment. On the platform was a police constable, all he wanted to do was to get to Lambeth, but admitted that he was enjoying himself all the same. He was interested in the efforts of a speed cop who was riding along by the side of the car; this officer was good-humouredly and successfully keeping young cyclists at bay as the tram struggled to make up time. "Just trying to stop the lads from killing themselves" he called as he gently forced forward one young man and his cycle into the kerb. At the Marquis of Granby there was a new diversion; a man of about 35 jumped on the rear buffer and whipped quickly round to the other side. A transport inspector edged his way along the buffer in an attempt to make him leave his precarious perch, but he did not succeed – the man was still there when No. 1951 reached New Cross. Then he was swallowed up in the crowd – and one of the tram's driving mirrors vanished with him! Last passenger to buy a ticket was Mr Bert Stone, aged 74, of 92 Besson Street, New Cross. Bert, who used to drive a horse tram sells newspapers opposite the New Cross Depot. Inspectors invited him to have a ride on the last tram. "I shall miss the old things, guv," he said. "I've known 'em for so long I've got attached to 'em." Out in New Cross Road, the dwindling crowd watched the stripped and empty shells of trams in darkness making their way to the Charlton breaking yard; the London tram was making its farewell to the capital.

The mayor of Deptford, Alderman Fred Morris JP, had been a tram driver at one time and called in a favour from his 'contacts above', so that he could drive part of the way. Also sharing the driving was the LTE deputy chairman, John Cliff who had been whisked from New Cross after his 'spin on the handles' with 1952. Both men climbed aboard 1951 at Deptford Town Hall and drove part of the way; Cliff gave a police motor-cyclist a close shave and the crowd roared unkind applause. 1951 stopped outside the Miller Hospital at Greenwich where patients made their tribute to the car – they were disturbed by the familiar tram clatter for the last time. There was an anxious moment when Cliff and Morris were lost to view – had they been enveloped by the crowds and carried away? Out of the crowd though, they materialised and with kisses blown to them by cheering nightnurses, and patients waving and watching from upstairs windows they reached the tram steps, enabling 1951 to slowly continue its melancholy journey. 1951 rode the metals as she had ridden them for years and this time the three-quarter mile tailback of cars, vans, cycles, and motorcycles in a great cacophony of noise behind her, did not attempt to pass. Along the route of the last ride it was ordinary people making their last farewell. While still outside the 'Marquis of Granby', John Cliff took over. Although there was only a short way to go he had a difficult job as the crowd had swarmed into the road, some sitting on 1951's fender. The driving was under the advice and guidance of 53 year-old driver Fuller. Cliff and Morris had a difficult time driving the tram and it was testament to their skill that nobody inside noticed the difference. 1951 was nearing the end of the line now; New Cross had never known a traffic jam like this. As the tram topped the crest by New Cross Gate station it was realised that what had gone before was nothing; in front, the road, the pavement, the gardens, the walls, the doorways, the front windows were packed with thousands of people. Police had to use all their strength to push aside an avenue for the tram to move down the tracks towards the depot. A milk van, off to deliver the morning's milk, was stranded helpless in the seething mass; a car was stuck across the lines and couldn't drive off because the crowd were in the way – men seized the bumpers and lifted it so that the tram could proceed. Lord Latham, chairman of the London Transport Executive, who was to make a farewell speech, just had to wait.

There had not been a night like it since VJ night; some just wanted to touch the tram. Women with their hair in curlers and wearing coats over their night attire were among the crowd watching. Only a guess could be made at the number of people who thronged the road outside the depot; it might have been ten thousand, it might have been fifteen thousand. Having waited well over an hour, many were cheering, yelling, singing; expecting the tram to arrive at 12.29am (two minutes allowed to get into the depot for a 12.31 arrival). They had stuck themselves to all points north, south, east and west in the roadway, but 1951 did not roll along until 1.20. Eventually London let go and what everybody thought was the last representative of the tram fleet got to the depot approach, it was 50 minutes late. Here, a swathe of inspectors and police constables encouraged 1951's passengers to leave. This was achieved in a friendly manner and would supposedly allow John Cliff to drive the empty tram up the slope and into the depot where Lord Latham would receive it. However, the crowds prevented him from getting a clear run and 1951 got stuck on a 'dead' section of conduit at the entrance to the depot. All her lights went out – it was her protest, her epitaph. A London Transport man explained vaguely "we are on a dead part of the line". For tram number 1951, the last passenger tram in London was stuck, as helpless as a becalmed clipper – this was her last gesture. 1951 was completely encircled and the chances of it ever moving again seemed remote. People laughed as she 'missed the current' and laughed even louder when rescue came in the shape of tram number 1931 formerly of 46 route which shuffled and rumbled out of the depot. With a chain attached between the two, 1951 was pulled clear and to the strains of 'Auld Lang Syne' it followed its helper into the depot under its own power. Once 1951 started to move up the slope, people clambered on board again. It was like a nightmare – sweating there in that darkened tram with hordes of strange blurred faces peering in through the windows, shouting. They tried to rip off pieces of the tram; a group of particularly high-spirited young men tried to push the car over – it was

1951 moves up the slope into New Cross depot at about 1.20am on 6th July. Amazingly, the rear destination blind is still in situ; the correct display of NEW CROSS GATE was not shown on the front or back of the car on its trip from Woolwich. In the background the interior lights of 1931, which had pulled 1951 off a dead section of track, can just be discerned. Fog flares create an atmospheric image to the picture. (Clarence Carter)

Revellers aplenty cling to 1951 as it climbs the approach to New Cross depot. The bravehearts will be encouraged down by police, and London Transport officials. By now the destination blind has been removed.
(Online Transport Archive)

good to see the police though they just smiled and were 'blind' to it all. The number of people was so great that there was nothing that the authorities could do and when it came to a halt it was filled to capacity with well-wishers. Souvenir hunters began looting with deadly efficiency; screwdrivers and spanners appeared with bits and pieces of the tram being tossed to the crowd. The destination blinds were easy prey as were the saloon lights; men clambered on to the roof. As 1951 lurched into the depot about 8,000 people, who had waited outside for hours, sent up a resounding cheer. Several women fainted in the crush and were carried to safety over the heads of the excited crowd. All that was needed now was for the newsreel cameras to buzz and Lord Latham, who was to receive 1951, to make his speech from its platform (Latham represented London Transport while Edwin Bayliss as its chairman represented the LCC). When Latham had finished his oratory a verse of "Auld Lang Syne" was sung. Then tram number 1951, minus many of the parts with which it had set out, went to join its dead sisters at Charlton. Out in New Cross Road, the dwindling crowd watched the stripped and empty shells of trams in darkness making their way to the Charlton breaking yard. The London Tramway service was a thing of the past. Nine cars were still in the depot after Lord Latham's speech; when enough crews had been mustered they departed for Penhall Road. The last 'civvies' to travel on a London tram were Peter Mitchell and a colleague who had started to walk from New Cross to Penhall Road. Flagging down tram after tram without success, eventually one crew did stop for them and allowed them to travel.

On this highly-charged evening, a very late running 187 arrived at New Cross at 1.33am; it was out of sight of 1951 which was in the depot. This was embarrassing for the LT officials on duty – they did not want 187 climbing the incline into the depot just as Lord Latham was making his 'last tram' speech to the assembled crowd. Persuading 187's passengers to alight, the inspectors told the driver to reverse on the crossover outside the depot and take the car direct to Penhall Road; the crowds prevented this and 187 proceeded into Queens Road where an official placed a point iron into the

It is a general mêlée in New Cross depot at about 1.30 am on 6th July 1952; A 'LONDON'S LAST TRAM' board has been attached to 1951 whose destination blind has now disappeared. Lord Latham (with spectacles) has just said "In the name of Londoners and London Transport I say goodbye old tram." He alights from 1951; the gentleman next to him wearing a tram driver's badge is John Cliff. The service driver, Albert Fuller, is the man with glasses and black cap. A reveller perches precariously on the canopy of 1951. (London Transport Museum U22788)

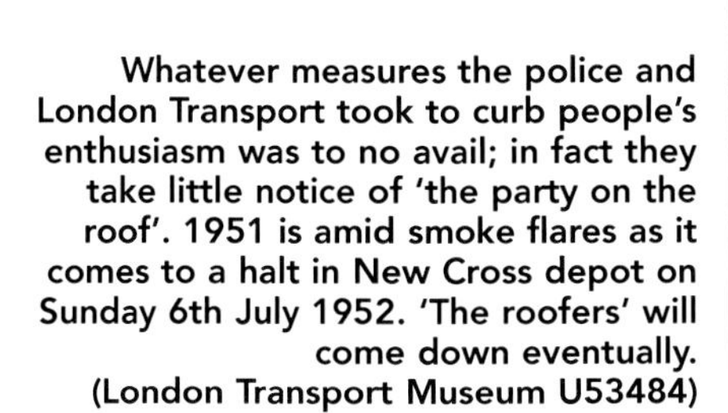

Whatever measures the police and London Transport took to curb people's enthusiasm was to no avail; in fact they take little notice of 'the party on the roof'. 1951 is amid smoke flares as it comes to a halt in New Cross depot on Sunday 6th July 1952. 'The roofers' will come down eventually. (London Transport Museum U53484)

'It's all over' as they say, and conductresses T18544, T17113, T17794 and T18787 pose for the camera at the last tram ceremony; the high numerals of their badges indicate that they have not been working on trams for long. Three use blue motorbus beret badges rather than red tram ones. The three clippies on the left are in their summer dustcoats; the conductress on the right is in her serge winter jacket. (London Transport Museum U53497)

Information for staff for South London Conversion Stages 8/9

```
5.      Three staff buses will be arranged by the Superintendent of District No.20
   from Rye Lane Garage to operate ex Penhall Road 11 p.m. to New Cross and Abbey
   Wood Depots via Tram Routes 36/38, on a 20 minute frequency until movement is
   complete.

9.      The Permanent Way and Electrical Distribution Divisional Engineers have
   been requested to defer track operations to avoid single line working during
   this movement.
```

Point 9 was irrelevant as track operations would not be taking place during the movement of trams to Penhall Road site on the afternoon and evening of 5th July.

blade of a crossover enabling 187 to reverse and access an irregularly used spur and move into New Cross Road. The point iron was used again to get 187 on to the correct track; the car now faced east. 187's same driving end had been used when arriving and leaving New Cross Gate. 187 did not get away until 1.48am – it had taken fifteen minutes to perform this procedure such were the crowds. Presumably, Lord Latham and John Cliff later found out what had happened. Having been outsmarted, this may have given rise to the belief that Lord Latham drove the last out-of-service car (1931) off the tracks and into Penhall scrapyard at 3.35am. Whoever drove it in made the final movement of a London Transport tramcar.

There is a tendency for the lower elements of society to take advantage of celebratory events and this occurred on last tram night. A number of affluent people from suburbs such as Eltham, Sidcup and Chislehurst who had come to see the event, parked their cars in the New Cross area; when they returned they found that their cars had been broken into and items removed. Similarly there were pickpockets working the crowds as the last cars came into New Cross depot.

Most of the attention that day was centred on New Cross depot, with Abbey Wood hardly having a look in. During the evening, their 592 suffered a fault; it took time to make it serviceable after which a crew needed to be found to take it from Abbey Wood to Penhall Road. This did not occur until about 2am – the plough shifter at Woolwich was aware of this and stayed until when he thought the last tram to require his services had gone. He had no idea that there was still a rogue tram roaming the tracks.

Many staff buses were laid on that night; most were to take home the crews who had been moving trams to Penhall Road well after the time that they should have finished. Noted at New Cross were STL 1409 as NX 6 on route 182 at 12.53am and RT98 as NX7 on route 177 at 1.50am; both routes were not operational yet but presumably were prepared for their next day's work.

Into the early hours of the morning the party at New Cross went on as old-timers and depot workers got together and over a drink swapped anecdotes and reminisced over the 91 year colourful history of the London tramcar. Those involved in the late night shunting of trams had not reached their beds before those starting their next day's duties were reporting for work. After all the goodbyes to the trams, the first replacement bus was a route 177 which left Peckham garage at 4.13am on Sunday 6th July. London was now tram-less and before long the rails would gain a film of rust. Monday saw the maintenance staff at Abbey Wood and New Cross clearing out redundant material, and Charlton Works would gradually divest itself of all tram orientated items.

The last day of trams in London saw excerpts shown in cinema newsreels in most of the West End and suburbs on 10th, 11th and 12th July. Gaumont, Pathe News, British Paramount News, British Movietone News, and Universal News were the companies showing the films. The *Daily Telegraph* considered that the occasion warranted their presence and on Monday 7th July, 1952 a photo of 1951's arrival at New Cross depot was illustrated. The picture was accompanied by an article entitled CROWDS CHEER LAST TRAM with a subtitle of 'Plates & blinds as souvenirs'. The text stated: "Thousands of Londoners lined the streets between Woolwich and New Cross to give a tumultuous farewell to the last tram on Saturday night. All day, the surviving trams had been crowded with cheering, singing people and at night there were extraordinary scenes. Regulations were ignored; people rode on the front and rear bumpers and smoked inside while souvenir hunters removed service number plates, blinds, used ticket boxes and bell-push signs. The last vehicles travelled in darkness, all the light bulbs having been taken. Some trams were garlanded with wreaths or decorated with streamers."

Keen to give credit where it was due, one local paper congratulated the teams of men who covered up tram stops on the final changeover. They considered that smart work and efficient organisation had been carried out on a matter which had passed almost unnoticed. 'When the last tram passed early on Sunday morning the tram stop signs were still in evidence. But by the time people were waiting to catch the new buses at breakfast time on Sunday the tram stop signs – hundreds of them – had been pasted over. It would have been reasonable for London Transport to assume that everyone knew the trams had ceased; a lot of trouble had been taken to cover the old signs up. As soon as the last tram had stopped, teams of bill-posters, riding either on motorcycle combinations or in light vans, and equipped with ladders, paste pot and paper, set out. At each tram stop the ladder was raised and the sign papered over; eventually the tram stop signs will be removed. New bus stop signs for the buses had been erected previously and hidden under metal covers. As the paste-pot men covered up the tram stop signs through the night, so they unveiled the bus stop signs'. The same report stated: 'It was noticeable on Sunday that some of the drivers of the new buses, who the day previously had been driving trams, were finding the gears a bit difficult, but within a day or two were driving them easily as they had the trams.

Little time was wasted in covering up the tramlines – by first light on Monday morning 7th July, a gang of men were covering in the lines at Lee Green with asphalt. This was one of the places where tram wires could be seen but where no tram lines existed. The trams had their opponents and nobody except a few sentimentalists seemed to be sorry at their passing; they had served their purpose well and must now give way in the face of ever increasing traffic conditions. But like the prickling that remains in the eye well after the grit has been removed, the tram tracks – those shining treacherous threads – remain to menace the cyclist, motorcyclist and even the motorist. Ask any motor cyclist his opinion of tram tracks – his answer, characteristic of his kind, will be short

THE ODD AFFECTION PEOPLE HAVE FOR TRAMS . . . . .

"If you saw Fred's Missus you'd understand him being in love with his tram."

and to the point. They are a constant threat, throwing his wheels this way and that, every time he uses a road that contains them. In wet weather that danger is doubled by the possibility of skids. One 'bicycle' anecdote is worth relating. A cyclist had got the wheels of his bicycle caught in a tramline on the approach to Purley depot; a tram had just entered and the conductor had not had enough time to re-set the points. The cyclist could not get out of this predicament and was forced to follow the tramlines, ending up on the track fan of the depot.

There was correspondence in the *Evening News* in 1950 of people expressing regret at the burning of the old trams – some suggested they might be used as dwellings. The response from Cohen's was that having purchased as many of the trams that London wanted to dispose of as scrap, they estimated that some 10,000 tons of ferrous scrap and 500 tons of non-ferrous metals would be salvaged. The burning of the bodies was undertaken after the removal of glass and seats – this was solely to get rid of decayed timber fittings and so forth which it would not pay to recover. If anybody wanted to buy an old tram without its fittings, Cohen's were prepared to supply one loaded on to a purchaser's vehicle at Charlton at a price approximating to its residual value. It was right to point out though that, owing to the unwieldy bulk of the thing, transport to a site would be very expensive and that local authorities might take a poor view of its use as a dwelling. This was a statement from Cyril Cohen, chairman and managing director of George Cohen & Sons Co. Ltd, Wood Lane, Shepherds Bush.

The passing of the London tram was reported not only in local and daily newspapers but also in magazines of the time. One article which was written by a Paul Jennings was particularly erudite and much of it is quoted verbatim:

> "For the last two years Londoners, who are sentimental people really, have been developing the same sort of feeling towards their groaning, nodding trams that a family might have towards an old dog that is going to be put to sleep. Never mind the time the poor old thing bit the postman, tore the blanket; here's some nice liver. Never mind about those traffic jams, those skids on the sunken lines; let us take a last sad ride to Lewisham. London's tram service, already mortally wounded, was in its death throes. It's sad. How many of you have ever seen the unique place at Woolwich where they changed the trams over to trolley working, from that system of getting current from underneath a third, middle rail? The tram came flying round a bend, but the middle rail went straight on, and the power pick-up, a kind of horseshoe thing, came whizzing out from underneath the tram, along this middle rail, to an ancient man who stopped it with a kind of fork. Well, you will never see it now. It was fascinating. But saddest of all, although in a way also the most glorious, is the 'tramatorium.' Seven stages have been completed and soon there will be nobody who can tell us what it is that drivers do with those mysterious handles. But stage eight ends on an awful piece of waste land in Charlton, SE7. The whole scheme, which began in 1950, has been strategically destined to fall back on this place where they burn trams to death. On a good day they burn five; a bad day is one when the wind is wrong. The first thing you see there is a windsock, and if the wind is blowing towards the neighbouring furniture factory they don't burn trams that day. They pick out all the copper and leather and other useful stuff, hollowing out a long line of trams waiting gloomily for the end. Then, when the wind is OK again, the next tram in line is brought forward on a platform; a tractor pushes it over. A man goes round with a sledgehammer, gloriously breaking windows ("to get a good draught"). When it's all over, the scrap metal is dragged away and sorted. There remains behind a kind of reddish, metallic dust, a final, useless deposit of the twentieth century. It makes you feel that nothing will grow here for a million years. Nor, when those photographs of early West Ham cars have rotted away will the people

in a million years be able to tell what epoch of public transport it was that ended on this Wagnerian funeral pyre – the Tram Age."

There were reports in many Sunday newspapers of the trams' final hours. A *Sunday Dispatch* reporter wrote: 'CROWDS STORM TO SAY FAREWELL TO LAST TRAM'. "Thousands of Londoners, some in paper hats, all of them in high spirits and all it seemed determined to make the passing of the last tram a great occasion, lined the old steel road through South London, arms linked, as The Very Last Tram screeched its way to the scrap yard at midnight last night. Hundreds of people made the mistake of picking the wrong tram". An hour before the last one was to leave town, a 72 crossing Westminster Bridge was held up by a crowd singing Auld Lang Syne – they mistakenly thought it was the last car. Every tram which rumbled through the streets of south London was besieged by crowds of men, women and children waving paper hats and forcing drivers to stop; conductors allowed people to squeeze into already crowded lower decks.

THE DRIVER'S FAREWELL TO HIS TRAM
(*Dedicated to the last remaining tramcars, now due to be replaced by buses.*)

News of the World, Sunday 6th July 1952. This is a Streetcar story of retire – the story of how London's trams passed out of sight for the last time. In many parts of London yesterday, many Londoners fondly and nostalgically took part as London Transport's scheme to replace trams by buses reached its final episode. Those blundering, noisy, rather nice old pieces of history were soon to disappear; what a fond farewell they were given by people, not only in the metropolis but from further afield who were taking "Just one more ride before they go".

Although Alfred Jago finished his tram life on 5th July, his final epitaph was made by his grandson, Bernard Everitt (12 years old), who gave a talk to members of his class at Bloomfield School. He told them the history of the tram from its earliest days and admitting his indebtedness to his grandfather in the matter, was awarded maximum marks for his speech. Another epitaph was that a foal born to Angela, a two year-old mare belonging to the Cuaco Sports Club, Eltham Road, Lee, soon after the last 46 tram passed there early on the Sunday morning of 6th July, was called 'Trameer'. There was no sentiment for what had been the official last tram (1951); the *Kentish Times* featured it being burnt on 14th July: this was despite its formal sale to Cohen's on 24th July 1952.

LAST DAY DRIVER

Vic Peters

London Transport carried out many major changeovers during the years they were responsible for the travelling public. Three examples were: trams replaced by trolleybuses between 1935 and 1940; trams replaced by motorbuses between 1950 and 1952; trolleybuses replaced by motorbuses between 1959 and 1962.

It was always considered that a job with London Transport was for life, and a lot of drivers and conductors had long service. This meant that many did the double changeover: trams to trolleybuses, then trolleybuses to motorbuses. I worked on all three types of vehicle but in an unusual way: trolleybuses to trams, then trams to motorbuses. How did I do it? Read on...

Because Hanwell depot needed more than the one hundred F1 class trolleybuses for service, a number of other vehicles were allocated to make up the numbers. P1 class 1706 was one and is seen at Shepherds Bush before making a journey to Hayes End Road on 29th April 1949. This was just before I started on the job but I probably worked on this vehicle on occasions. (Fred Ivey.)

Following demobilisation in 1948, I said to my wife Lily that I was getting fed up with machine work, which I'd been doing for some time, and would look for an alternative. Jobs on London Transport were available, but only in a limited capacity – this was because those who had served during the war and survived had returned to their driving and conducting jobs on the trams, trolleybuses and buses (women who had taken conductors' places were retained). However, notional recruitment was taking place and having seen an advert on a 607 trolleybus for conductors, I applied for a position and was given an interview at Chiswick Works. At the time, London Transport called the tune about who they employed and were very particular in knowing potential employees' work history. I had to supply details of my previous employers, giving them a contact name, an address, my grade and how much I was earning each week (just over £5). I submitted the completed form but someone came back to me, asking me to account for a two week gap; as a temporary measure I had worked as a milkman. Satisfied with my explanation, and that I was of good character, I was offered a job as a trolleybus conductor at Hanwell depot; I was living at Southall at the time so wouldn't have far to travel each day.

My first day of employment with London Transport was 11th July 1949 when I commenced my training at Chiswick Works – thirteen shillings and fourpence a day. Following classroom training and 'on bus' instruction at Hanwell, I was issued with conductor's badge T16687. I was let loose on 27th July; on my first trip a dewirement occurred. I was allocated a duty on route 607 which ran between Uxbridge and Shepherds Bush; the first journey was to 'The Bush'. At the Askew Arms in Acton Vale it was necessary for conductors on trolleybuses turning right into Askew Road to pull a frog handle – this device was a 'pull and leave job' whereby once operated the conductor could go back to the vehicle (a re-set skate returned the overhead line to its original position). As I was busy, a motorbus conductor who was travelling as a passenger said that he would pull the frog for me; I didn't know any better and said 'okay'. Next thing, bang, the poles are off – matey thought the frog needed to be pulled when it didn't. Having told him what happened, my driver rewired the vehicle. I remember another dewirement on a 607 at Shepherds Bush; it was pouring with rain and as we moved around the far side of 'The Green', one of the trolley arms slipped off the wires. I removed the bamboo pole from beneath our trolleybus but as I did so a 630 ran over the top of it – I tried to raise the pole but the top end of the bamboo just keeled over. I dumped it in the gutter as it was no good to

PHOTO: PREVIOUS PAGE

Another member of staff used my camera to take a photograph of myself, another driver and two conductresses; we are standing in front of 2003 which was the highest-numbered passenger tram in the fleet at the time. It is the morning of Saturday 5th July 1952 and the sun is out for the trams' last day. I am on the left and holding my camera case. The young lady in the middle looks very much like Raquel, the wife of 'Del Boy' in 'Only Fools and Horses'; she is Tessa Peak-Jones and I would be interested to know if this conductress is Tessa's mother. Curiously, the clippie on the right looks like a young Julia MacKenzie, the actress. The clippies' footwear is intriguing – these two ladies are going to have a very busy day. We are all wearing our summer dustcoats – my driving colleague has a pin-stripe suit under his dustcoat; maybe he's going on a 'jolly' after work. (Vic Peters)

On 8th August 1949 the only trolleybus in the fleet that had a four-wheel front drive, 1671, is about to pass Chiswick Works on its way to Hanwell Broadway on route 655. By now I am working for London Transport and recall working on this vehicle a number of times. (Alan Cross)

In conjunction with the 1951 Festival of Britain, new trackwork was laid on the south side of Westminster Bridge. First to test the new lines was 1877 which did so at 9.38am on Sunday 11th June 1950. Not only are a number of labourers watching the proceedings but there are also some smartly turned out gentlemen who probably represent London Transport and various authorities. Also in the view is an RT on route 12; Big Ben is in the background. (London Transport Museum H16610)

anybody now and went for the 630's pole – it hadn't got one! There were always plenty of trolleybuses at Shepherds Bush and it didn't take long for us to commandeer a bamboo; we'd lost a few minutes but went straight in and out of 'The Bush' and made our time up by the time we got to Hanwell Broadway.

The 607 was a busy road; in the peak hours, trolleybuses (nearly always full) were passing through Hanwell every minute or two. I soon learnt to be quick on the bell and it was counterproductive to wait for last-minute runners – there'd be another one along shortly. It tended to be easier once past Southall when going west. Much of the service only went as far as Hayes End – after that it was toe down all the way with the result that four 607s could be seen at Uxbridge together sometimes. Inspectors weren't bothered about us arriving a few minutes early – they were just glad to see us. Hanwell also worked the somewhat easier 655 which ran from Hanwell Broadway to Clapham Junction with a peak hour extension from Hanwell to Bromyard Avenue in Acton Vale. From Hanwell to Brentford the 655 was on its own but unlike the 607s there weren't huge volumes of passengers. Once we got to Brentford there were 657s and 667s between there and Chiswick and between Hammersmith and Wandsworth there were 626s, 628s and 630s. Tuck in behind one of them and it was an easy ride. I was put on the spare list, covering for conductors off sick or on leave; as staff tended to have long service, rota lines only came up occasionally and my whole time at Hanwell was spent as a 'spare' conductor.

The vehicles I worked on were mostly of one main class – F1s, numbered 654-753. We had the lot of them which were to a standard design of thirty seats downstairs, forty up. However, there were two odd trolleybuses at Hanwell that I worked on. There was one where two seats were positioned adjacent to the driver who sat in a half cab – all the others had a cab which stretched the width of the vehicle. I was able to speak to the driver on this vehicle as a glass partition on his left only went halfway across; this was number 445 which was an oddity in the fleet and was on loan from Hammersmith depot. Then there was the experimental 1671 which had recently been transferred to us from Fulwell. Although it had four wheels at the front (two at the back), our drivers didn't consider this to be an impediment; any new man coming to the depot had to be given a short familiarisation course on it.

Lily and I had now started a family and needed somewhere larger to live; a friend knew of a flat near New Cross station. Knowing that we needed somewhere bigger as soon as possible we jumped at the chance and I went to see my chief depot inspector who was very understanding; he set the wheels in motion for a transfer to another workplace. He said that as I worked for the tram and trolleybus department I would have to move within the same section; this was fortuitous for me as New Cross tram depot was very near to where I would be living. I was transferred there on 15th March 1950 with my trolleybus conductor's licence valid for trams. Before I started work at New Cross, I had to be familiarised with some tramcar procedures. I was given instruction on how to release the handbrake at each terminus: I had to knock the 'dog' out but it could give a bit of a clout if I didn't watch it: 'dog' was the nickname for the pawl. Although elementary, I was told to turn the swing-back passenger seats when necessary. When I was at Hanwell I had been manipulating two trolley arms with a bamboo pole – at New Cross I received instruction on how to deal with a tram's single trolley boom. A rope was used instead of a bamboo and care had to be taken to see that it was properly positioned between the 'pigtail' on the canopy and the cleat on the dash.

It was a different world working on trams than on trolleybuses; it was extremely busy and loads of charladies were carried on the very early morning shifts. When we arrived at Tooley Street at London Bridge, the quickest way to get all the passengers off was to open both exits. It could be difficult working on routes 68 and 70 – so many short riders. Money was thrust into my hands all the time and it was difficult to keep on top of the situation; many a time I had a handful of cash and would just punch off that amount in tickets. The 54 ran between Grove Park and Victoria and that too required conductors to move quickly; at Victoria as soon as the last passenger had alighted in the morning peak, we were away back south such was the speed of our turn-round. Similarly in the evening peak, we'd arrive to find a huge queue of people waiting; no sooner had the tram been brought to a halt than the driver would hurry through the saloon, put his controls in the 'on' position by which time the car would be

I do not recall the number of any trams used for my driver training – it might well have been 1669 which is seen in Kennington. A learner plate was fitted to the front and back of trams when trainee drivers were at the controls. (Fred Ivey)

loaded and we'd be away. It could get very congested at Victoria and often we would have to wait for trams to clear the shunt before we could get onto it.

The only time it was quiet was on the 'all-nighters' – routes 5 and 7. I had one week on the 7; it was so quiet that I spent most of the time with the driver chatting to him. It was here that I had my first go at tram driving as he said to me "Do you want to have a go?" and I did!

Arriving at New Cross, I soon became aware that the trams' time was limited and that a scrapping programme was to commence soon. Saturday rest days were few and far between; on the 36/38 roster there were only five Saturdays off in 141 weeks. Sunday rests were a bit erratic as it could be six on followed by five off. New Cross was a very large depot with about 250 cars.

When I joined London Transport there was a pay difference between those working on motorbuses and those employed on trams and trolleybuses – motorbus staff got a bit more than us and was a vestige of different pay rates from times long ago. Also, tram and trolleybus drivers and conductors had the same hourly rate while motorbus drivers got a bit more than conductors. When trams and trolleybusses were amalgamated with Central buses in 1950 there was parity in pay, though drivers and conductors had a different rate; this gave an increase of 1/6d a week for conductors and 5/6d a week for drivers. When I moved from tram conductor to tram driver I immediately got a 4/- increase. By 1951, a considerable number of staff were leaving the job as they could find more remunerative work elsewhere. This meant that there was plenty of overtime and rest day work available and I took advantage of the situation.

Being new on trams I was thrown in at the deep end about luggage – it hadn't been mentioned to me on my 'tram initiation' so it was a surprise to suddenly find people hoisting items on to the platform and then asking me for a tuppenny luggage ticket. There were side boards (which had to be changed at times) so that passengers knew when cheap fares were available and where each tram was going.

Trams were slow and a good job too, for I found that an enormous amount of transfer tickets were used (at Hanwell there were just a few but on trams it was a nightmare as there were so many). Many a time I punched a ticket in the wrong fare stage and a passenger gave it back to me as he knew it wouldn't be accepted on the next tram. I couldn't be bothered about going through all the rigmarole of filling in a form about a wrongly issued ticket, so on the occasions I punched a ticket in the wrong stage, I tore it up and made the money up myself. Some passengers knew more about transfer tickets than the staff, and they'd make things easy for me when they required one by saying "Elephant, change at Camberwell", even pointing to the ticket in the rack and showing me where to make the punch hole! The transfer tickets were the bane of my life; they needed to be punched inward and outward and caused total confusion – I wasn't the only one to echo this sentiment. Many of the seasoned conductors were professionals and knew everything about the intricacies of the transfers and workman's tickets; these all came to an end on September 30th 1950 and most conductors breathed a sigh of relief.

The chief depot inspector at New Cross was a strict disciplinarian; if anyone was late for work and a tram lost mileage it would be a roasting for that individual. Drivers who'd had a dewirement also got the rough end of his tongue, even though the pole might have come off the wire through no fault of their own. Due to the way that trams and trolleybuses were constructed, crews were in constant touch with each other. On trolleybuses, drivers and conductors could speak to each other through the window between the cab and saloon: on trams, conductors could come on to the platform and speak to the driver. There was close camaraderie all day. Unless a driver called a conductor round to speak with him, motorbuses staff only came together at termini.

Towards the end of 1950, I applied for a position of tram driver. At the time no-one under twenty-five could drive a London tram, trolleybus or bus, so I was just old enough to come into this remit. Having passed my medical on 28th November 1950, I started the tram driving course shortly afterwards. Instruction was thorough. There were minor differences between the classes of car; however, they all had the same basic features of eight power notches and seven brake notches. All of my training was done from New Cross; I was successful in passing first time on 18th January 1951 and given badge number T12831. Having passed my test I had to spend a few days with a regular driver. He stood next to me while I was in charge of the tram. When we got to the depot canteen he said he wanted a 'full English' for breakfast – I ordered the food for him but he was expecting me to pay. It seemed the done thing that novice drivers paid for all the refreshments. I only had enough money for myself so he was very disgruntled as he had to pay not only for his meal but

There were some very old cars at New Cross depot. One was 1005 which retains route light glasses above the destination box; the glasses had been painted over long ago. Only a few cars retained them until withdrawal. Word at the time was that these glasses were to be saved and given to high-ranking LT officials. Cohen's men did not get the message in time and as far as is known, none survived. Seen in Woolwich is E1 1005 working on route 38 to EMBANKMENT on 16th July 1950. (Clarence Carter)

also for his conductress. For a short while I was on a spare list but before long was given a service on the 46 and 72 roster.

Most of the trams at New Cross depot were very old; some had been built for the LCC as far back as 1907, and although many still had a fair turn of speed, they clanked along and were past their best. With the first stage of the tram to motorbus conversion programme, some newer cars arrived – as the changeover progressed, we got more and I found myself driving trams that had formerly been owned by Croydon and Walthamstow Corporations. New Cross participated in a never-ending change-about; older ones were replaced by newer ones as each stage kicked in. It has been calculated that about 570 different trams were in residence during my time there; I doubt if I worked on every single one, but probably most. New Cross' routes were: 36/38 Abbey Wood to Embankment, 40 Wickham Lane (peak hours) to Woolwich (other times) to Savoy Street, 46 Woolwich to Southwark, 52 Grove Park to Southwark, 54 Grove Park to Victoria, 66 Forest Hill to Victoria, 68 Greenwich Church to Waterloo, 70 Greenwich Church to London Bridge, 72 Woolwich to Savoy Street and 74 Grove Park to Blackfriars. There were also two night routes: 5 Downham to Blackfriars and 7 New Cross to Blackfriars.

I had an interesting experience on the way to Victoria one day. A car suddenly pulled out of a side turning and I had to put the brakes on hard. It caused all eight wheels of the tram to momentarily lock up, meaning that the wheels skidded on the rails; the tram was going bomp, bomp, bomp, bomp thereafter and I pointed this out to the inspector at Victoria. He said there were eight flats on the wheels and instructed me to run the tram back to the depot 'light'.

There was an emergency box which held many tools that could be used for problem solving. I avoided using it as I wasn't going to put on rubber gloves in the line of duty; electrical and mechanical problems were for support staff. Occasionally a tram would get stuck on a dead section or on points – the one behind would nudge up to it and push it clear. Sometimes a tram would become disabled in that the motor wouldn't function; one would couple up from the rear and push it back to the depot. The front tram would use its brake while the rear one would use its motors. It was also possible for one tram to pull another; whenever push and pull arrangements took place, there was an iron bar between the two trams.

In my first winter on the trams, I found that my hands were getting very cold operating 'the handles'. There was no heating on the driver's platform and there tended to be lots

1612 has been curtailed at Downham where a change pit was situated; the crossover was just before the pit. There were plenty of women working the trams in the post-war period and they did not shy away from manipulating trolley arms. This young lady and her driver are "ahead of the game", for the boom will be at the right end when they come back here and go to Grove Park which is on the overhead system. Some E1s had two trolley arms; others, like 1612, had just one.

There were a number of 'odd' cars at New Cross depot and I expect I worked on all of them. *Left*. One was 1444 which is in Peckham Road on its way to the peak hour terminus of route 40 – WICKHAM LANE PLUMSTEAD. 1444 had been modernised in the early '30s.

Below. Time's up for 1444 and it has reached what I called the graveyard. It is still complete apart from windscreen glass. It is next to works car 016 and the remains of two Felthams (2144 and 2162) which were burnt out in Brixton Hill depot. All are at 'the end of the road' (Fred Ivey)

I found myself driving trams that had been cascaded from other depots; this included those that had been with Croydon and Walthamstow municipalities. 'Croydon' 384 is seen below in Eltham on route 46 on 21st April 1951. When a trolley wheel touches the skate on the overhead here, it will indicate its presence to a nearby traffic light signal which will change in a tram's favour. (Clarence Carter)

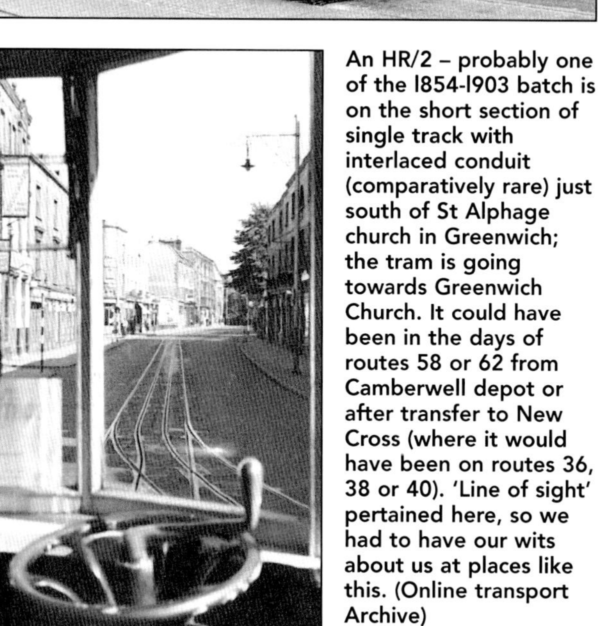

An HR/2 – probably one of the l854-l903 batch is on the short section of single track with interlaced conduit (comparatively rare) just south of St Alphage church in Greenwich; the tram is going towards Greenwich Church. It could have been in the days of routes 58 or 62 from Camberwell depot or after transfer to New Cross (where it would have been on routes 36, 38 or 40). 'Line of sight' pertained here, so we had to have our wits about us at places like this. (Online transport Archive)

of draughts as well. I hit on the idea of having some mittens for the 1951/2 winter and Lily made me up a pair; they were made out of wool and a pair of leather flying boots which had been surplus stock – all the fur was cut off the boots. I was the envy of a number of other drivers. However, the brass handles of the controller and brake handle made the mittens go green.

There is always a lot of banter and talk about old times in staff canteens; New Cross was no exception and the tales told by some of the long service staff were extraordinary. Some had worked on horse trams and many on open-front cars – how they got on driving in the coldest of weathers beggars belief. A tram was not held up so much in the fog as a bus; a tram could keep going, albeit slowly, on its rails.

One night, when travelling at normal speed, the plough broke when it hit a bolt in the conduit. The tram came to an immediate standstill and just wouldn't move as the plough and carrier were bent; I called out the breakdown gang who had no alternative but to dismantle the plough carrier. The service was held up but as it was late at night, not too much inconvenience was caused; an inspector came along and

Forest Hill tram terminus was a busy one; however only one tram could get on the terminal stub at a time so there had to be slick movements here. 1537 occupies the stub on 12th May 1951; despite it being a summer's day, all the pedestrians have their coats on. (Clarence Carter)

instituted one-way working – trams used crossovers either side of me. About thirty years after this when I was socialising, one of my friends mentioned to someone else there that I had been a tram driver. We got talking and I mentioned this incident; he said to me that he remembered it as he had been on the breakdown crew that came out to me.

It was tram and trolleybus culture for staff to own a billy can for their tea; in fact London Transport nominated a number of places where staff could replenish them. They weren't only used during the day, but also on the late shifts. I patronised the 'Cosy café' in Well Hall Road at night; when going up the slight slope here I would set the tram on half power and drink the tea with both hands round the can. At Westhorne Avenue roundabout, power was used to work the overhead frog and rail points; to operate them, I'd place the controller on second notch – the application of power changed the points and the frog in favour of the 'road' selected. Re-set equipment put the points back to their original setting. Now and again I put too much power through the motor and the circuit breaker would throw; without stopping I would turn the controller into the neutral position, turn around and bang the canopy switch back in (it was just behind and above the driver's head) – all this was done while the tram was still moving. Section insulators: on the overhead system it was obvious where they were, and it was necessary to 'shut off' when passing beneath one. On the conduit, I got to know where they were positioned. They were usually by plough hatches, and I would just bring the controller handle round to the 'off' position just before I got there; once past it I could notch up again.

One day a depot inspector asked if I'd like to be loaned to Camberwell depot for a few weeks as they had a temporary shortage of drivers during the summer of 1951; their men were on holiday or being trained as bus drivers. Camberwell operated route 35 through the Kingsway subway and no driver was allowed to work through there unless he had six months' service under his belt; although a few days short of the mark, London Transport bent the rule a bit such was the need. I'd receive travelling time between New Cross and Camberwell in both directions as well as my duty, so took up the offer. When I got to Camberwell I was told that, along with three others from New Cross, to go out and familiarise myself with the routes that the depot operated. Having done this we were told to report to Camberwell depot at a particular time one morning as an instructor was going to take us through the subway and on Dog Kennel Hill for 'road training'. We did a lot of trips between the Embankment and Bloomsbury, and some to Highgate – up and down Dog Kennel too. I was passed as qualified to drive on the Dulwich routes and Highgate route 35 on 5th July 1951 – a benefit of this was that when route 35 was transferred to New Cross depot in October 1951 I was able to work some extra shifts on it.

A fact emphasised on subway training was that we had to allow passengers to get off at the front end of the tram; this was because there were island platforms and people boarded and alighted on the right. I couldn't get used to this and kept forgetting to let the steps down; passengers were clambering over them to get on – some were saying "steps are high" (most trams had either folding or lifting steps to deter passengers from trying to get on or off at the 'wrong' end of the car). Eventually someone complained and a subway inspector had a quiet word with me. It was alright getting in and out of the subway at Westminster as a light duty man oversaw movements there. Special light signals applied for the subway and drivers entering and leaving it at the Bloomsbury end had to conform to diagonal and horizontal white lights. The horizontal ones indicated stop and I had to wait until they changed; the diagonal ones allowed me to proceed. Should it be necessary to call for the diagonal lights, indicating the right of way, the conductor had to press a push button fixed in the subway wall. Green and red lights at Holborn station prevented more than one tram being in the Holborn to Bloomsbury section at a time. I soon cottoned on to the fact that it was better to give the tram a few notches of power so that it would crawl up the ramp; when the white lights changed in my favour I'd move the handle on to a higher notch and get round quickly. This didn't always happen and at the last minute I would have to put the brakes on; I'd also put the handbrake on hard to stop it from rolling back. Conductors were required to place the chain across the platform when passing through the subway. On the occasions that HR2 trams were used on the 35s, they made loud echoing noises in the subway.

There were four tracks on Dog Kennel Hill – two up, two down; this was a safety feature and allowed two trams to move up and two trams to move down the hill (this meant that there could be four cars on the hill at the same time). Rigorous instructions had to be observed on Dog Kennel Hill routes on which only HR2 trams could be used – these cars

An individualistic car at New Cross depot was No. 2 which is seen on route 54 in Downham Way on 8th September 1951. It was transferred to Abbey Wood depot in January 1952; that meant that it continued to run through New Cross until 'Last Tram Day'. (Peter Mitchell)

had an additional mechanical track brake fitted. On the handbrake column there was a wheel that was turned clockwise at the compulsory stop at the top of the hill; this wound down the 'magnets' and brought the brake blocks closer to the rails – I'd wind it down until I felt it bite the rails. A 10mph speed restriction applied on the descent (but not the ascent) of the hill where the most scrupulous rules were in force; when going down (from London) I had to wind the brake round and put the track brake on too. I was sternly told that no two trams were allowed to follow each other up or down the same track and that if one was proceeding down number one track (the left-hand one), then the second descending tram could not access track two until the first had left the compulsory stop half-way down. The magnetic brake had to be tested upon leaving Camberwell Green; if defective, the tram was not to proceed beyond Denmark Hill station. The mechanical track brake had to be applied and released at a number of places (e.g. when travelling towards London, at Horniman's museum it was released at the pillar box beyond Lordship Lane station); there were also various compulsory stops where trams had to be brought to a standstill. At Camberwell I was paired with a conductor who was built like Charles Atlas; he was really strong and when we got to the end of the 58 route he put the rear handbrake on so hard one day that when it was time to leave neither of us could get the 'dog' out – not even the pair of us trying together. We had to get a breakdown wagon to come to the rescue, which they weren't too happy about. This conductor thought nothing of finding a reason to get his tram off the road and into the depot, missing out part of a journey. On one occasion he pushed on an upstairs window causing it to fall in the roadway; another time he bent a stair-rail in such a way that

When I was loaned to Camberwell depot, I completed some duties on route 35; this meant ascending and descending the northern ramp of the Kingsway subway at Bloomsbury. 196 heads into the darkness of the tunnel while working on route 35. The alcove in the wall enables track maintenance staff to step out of the way when trams pass by. (Peter Mitchell)

The two men posing for my picture have been on trams for a long time. 186 is about to run out of New Cross depot on the morning of 5th July. The photograph taken, the conductor, Mr Windebank will join me for a hard day's graft. (Vic Peters)

Drivers had to know what they were doing at the Westhorne Avenue roundabouts as both had complex track and overhead layouts; this view, taken on the last day at the southern one, is by the 'Yorkshire Grey'. Although 1964 shows NEW CROSS GATE it is going to Woolwich. (Jack Wyse)

it sprung out of its cup and away from the staircase – he blamed a passenger for this. On both occasions I had to run the tram into the depot and had to wait until they found a replacement.

When I was off duty one day, one of my colleagues waved to me saying "Look I'm on fire". He'd inadvertently placed the trolley/conduit changeover switch halfway between the two; the switch was under the stairs with the controller key being the means of changing from trolley to conduit and vice-versa. This caused a lot of smoke and he ran the tram into the depot.

I did a few duties on the 68s and 70s which mainly had cars with 42 horse power motors; if a tram which had 60hp motors was put on, it quickly caught up the slower ones. When inspectors knew this was happening they would hold the higher powered tram back a couple of minutes so as to give a regular service. These routes changed to motorbuses in July 1951. Spare space was only available in New Cross for a short time as Camberwell's 35 was allocated to us in the October; not only did the trams come across but also its crews. When the 68/70 came off, most of the crews went on to buses which were to be worked by Peckham Garage; this was considered to be a compulsory transfer for which a 'disturbance' allowance was given (a one-off payment). In January 1952 more of our routes disappeared from the London scene and again many staff had to move away from New Cross; this time they went to a new garage at Rye Lane, Peckham as did those when the 35 service was converted in April 1952. Even with the loss of the 35, there were still over a hundred trams left in what had been the largest tram depot in the fleet. It was policy that staff on the tram routes being converted went on to the replacing bus routes, but there was some flexibility between staff and management if someone really wanted to stay near to their home.

Although there was great affection and nostalgia afforded to the trams by Londoners, it was time for them to move on. They didn't fit in with the ever increasing road traffic and passengers were risking life and limb making their way across roads to board and alight from one. Most staff were glad to see the back of them; it was hard work driving trams and bus driving was deemed an easier life. However, for 'Last Tram Day' most staff (including myself) entered into the spirit of things. The trams were very busy and there were long gaps in the service as the trams attempted to deal with the crowds; some waited two hours to board one. All day people lined the streets – it was as if they were saluting an old friend. People from all walks of life had used the trams, and artisans held their own against the toffs.

In April 1952, it was announced that the last two stages of the conversion programme would be combined into one and instead of lasting until October the trams would finish on 5th July 1952. As the last week progressed, more and more people came out for a last ride and even at the quieter times of the day, we were carrying good loads. So many people were collecting the special tickets that the floors of trams were devoid of tickets (this pleased the cleaners). Early in the week a depot inspector said to me "Do you want to do six hours overtime on Saturday, shunting trams to Penhall?" I immediately said "Yes" as this was going to be easy money. At the time, tram and trolleybus staff could work a maximum of sixteen hours on duty; I said to the DI that I would be working over my allowed hours. He said "Don't worry about that". As it happened, I was resting on the Sunday so it wouldn't matter – London Transport wanted all the trams in the graveyard that night come what may. Saturday was bedlam. For the day, I was paired with conductor Windebank (pronounced Windybank) working on the 72 route. 1935 was the tram allocated to us for the first part of our duty. We just couldn't cope with the number of people who wanted a ride. Regular passengers, particularly shoppers, had to wait ages to get home; I'd never seen anything like it. The permanent way gangs were being disbanded that day but it didn't stop the paviours working on the tracks in the morning. Mr Windebank was weighed down with coppers when we came off for our break. The second part of the duty was on 1861.

Right, last run. We got to Savoy Street on our 72 and asked everybody to get off; many wanted to stay on 1861 for another trip, but we thought it fair for passengers waiting for a tram on the other side of the road to have their ride. Windebank changed the destination screens and moved the swing-back seats over while I took the controller key from one end of the tram to the other. At Savoy Street the points are set in favour of those returning towards Westminster so as soon as we had both done what we had to do, I set 1861 in motion and we clanked over the points to pull up at the stop. Putting the handbrake on, I got out of 1861 and took a picture of 'my last tram' – I was an amateur photographer and was pleased with the photos that accompany these memoirs. We took on a 'full house' – that's every seat taken with a few

Saturday 5th July was the opportunity for staff to have a bit of fun; one of my New Cross colleagues has acquired a top hat to wear while driving tram 1922. The top of the conductor's ticket box will not close – maybe he's been issued with an extra amount of tickets for the day. (Jim Wyndham)

SHAN'T BE ROUND TOMORROW was a slogan seen during the conversion programme; GEE UP MIKE is an encouragement for 1856's driver to get a move on. A joker has hung a sock on the headlight. (Jim Wyndham)

This is what conductor Windebank and myself were faced with all day long; crowds queuing with little chance of boarding the first tram that came along. These views were taken from the top deck of 1931 which is on an enthusiast's tour. In the top picture, two officials are on hand to control would-be riders. In the bottom shot someone has turned the 40 route plate on 1908 around the wrong way; co-ordination by the tour participants is lacking because Victoria has been wound up on the blind. Two motorbuses are on tram replacement services. (Jack Wyse)

Typifying 5th July, this view of 1927 illustrates how full the trams were that day. It was not just the men who came out for a last day ride, the ladies wanted to experience the rattle, clang and noise for one last time too. A couple of young boys are on board and a mother with 'child in arms' looks vainly down the car to see if there's anywhere she can sit down. In the fare chart holder, a poster encourages people to have a last chance to give themselves and their children a ride on a London tram. Underneath the left-hand border of the poster it states that 10,000 of these were printed; with only 150 or so trams for them to be placed on, where did the majority go? (Jack Wyse)

LONDON'S LAST TRAM WEEK

On Saturday 5 July London says a final goodbye to its trams. Next day the six remaining tram services will be replaced by buses. Here are the routes on which the last trams are running:—

36 & 38 Victoria Embankment to Abbey Wood *(Over Blackfriars and Westminster bridges)*

40 Victoria Embankment to Plumstead *(Over Westminster Bridge)*

44 Woolwich to Eltham Gn.

46 City (Southwark) to Woolwich *(Over Southwark Bridge)*

72 Victoria Embankment to Woolwich *(Over Westminster Bridge)*

You have a last chance to give yourself and your children a ride on a London tram.

DURING LAST TRAM WEEK SPECIAL SOUVENIR TICKETS WILL BE ISSUED ON LONDON TRANSPORT'S REMAINING TRAMS

A chance photograph taken from the top deck of a tram at Camberwell Green sees me driving 1861 towards the Embankment on route 72. Going the other way is 1926 which is only going as far as New Cross Gate on route 40. Sandbags were often placed over the drivers screen; this helped to cut down leaks. (Jack Wyse)

standing as well. Windebank gave me three bells which means 'don't stop'. I put the tram on to first notch but she hardly moved because of the weight; I moved the controller on a bit more and then a bit more and she did start to pick up speed. An experienced driver, whether it be bus, tram or trolleybus, notices the difference between a light load and a heavy load – this was a really heavy load on 1861. On this trip, there were people putting their arms out along the Embankment but I just waved my hand, implying that they couldn't get on. Left on to Westminster Bridge where trams coming into London were on the wrong side of the road to other traffic, then over the River Thames on a tram for the last time. Slowly negotiating the tracks around Addington Street, which had been put in for the Festival of Britain, I continued along Westminster Bridge Road until I got to its junction with Kennington Road. Past the Oval and into Camberwell New Road where I am able to get 1861 on to the higher notches as I had a clear run to Camberwell Green; this used to be a major tram junction but with only the 40 and 72 here now it's a lot easier to negotiate. All along Peckham Road there are people on each side of the road taking photos and looking at the trams that have been there since their childhood. Passing through Peckham and into New Cross Gate, I join up with trams that had come down the Old Kent Road. There were a lot of people milling about the entrance to the depot; enthusiasts, crews and inspectors. Since Savoy Street I have been losing time so we arrive at the relief point late; the new crew for 1861 take us off and we exchange a few words. Poor old Windebank was run off his tired legs and he said "Vic I've never been so busy in all the years I've worked on trams." I said that I'd put in an overtime docket for a late finish. He replied "Too right, what with all the money I've taken today."

We came off outside the depot at about 5pm; I walked into the traffic office and asked what time they wanted me back for shunting; "about eight o'clock" was the reply. Many crews were availing themselves of the opportunity to earn extra money and as it turned out I only had to work one tram down to the graveyard. Another man acted as driver while I stood on the back with the chain across the platform to prevent anybody boarding on what was a long trip. When we got to Penhall Road, my driver changed ends, I put the trolley on the wire and we moved slowly down the slope into the 'place

The last tram I drove on the King's Highway was 1861. I have just moved over the crossover at Savoy Street and put the handbrake on. Removing the controller key I left the tram and photographed her taking on passengers. On the back of the photo I wrote: 'Cramming them in, Saturday 5 July 1952'. Somebody has chalked OLD TRAMS NEVER DIE on 1861's dash – but they did! Going the other way is 1971; this will also turn at Savoy Street and go back to New Cross Gate. (Vic Peters)

Marooned in the safety of New Cross depot are a number of cars waiting to be taken to Penhall Road. I was shunting trams here for the British Transport Commission film unit into the small hours. The car on the far right, 1931 will be the last off the tracks a short while later. (D.W.K. Jones)

Using arc lights of the B.T.C. film unit on a time exposure on his camera, the photographer captures a couple of trams that have just one more trip to make – to the scrapyard; that will have to wait until filming is finished though. "I was one of the drivers moving trams and arc lights for the BTC film unit," says Vic. (John Gillham)

Motorbuses on tram replacement routes were allowed to use the westbound tram tracks on the Victoria Embankment not only during the conversion programme, but also until shortly before they were taken up. Eastbound buses used the ordinary carriageway. RT 11 is working from Peckham garage on route 177 which took over tram routes 36 and 38. (Ron Wellings)

of no return'. The plough slid out of the tram. The place was full of trams; it was like a massive marshalling yard or an open air tram depot. By now it was dark and we were told to leave the car on one of the receiving tracks. I tried to get hold of the controller key but one of the men said I couldn't have it; if I'd thought about it I could have had a destination blind and a fare chart which would now be collectors' items. We made our way back to New Cross on a tram still running; on arrival we were told that there weren't any others that needed to be moved for the moment but that there would be later on. Much of the time was spent hanging around and when the official last tram arrived I went out to see the ceremony; it was completely full of people milling around the place. Most were members of the public – I was there on business. Lord Latham made a speech, part of which I remember being "In the name of Londoners and London Transport, I say Goodbye old tram". When the crowds had dispersed there were still a number of trams ensconced in the safety of the depot. A British Transport Film unit wanted to film the last ones left; a few of us moved their floodlights around and their aim was for the lights to dim on the last few trams – this was to emphasise the dying out of the tramcar era in London. I had to shunt some for them but at 2am, I just wanted to get home. I went to the canteen to get an inspector

This was the class of bus that I first drove for London Transport and I would have driven STL1691 which is running into NX as it shows NEW CROSS GATE ONLY. It was a bit of a come-down having these 'old bangers' on the 163 and 182 when brand new RTs/RTLs were being put into service in the area; the STLs were not much newer than the trams they replaced. To 'save face', the STLs were 'dressed to the nines' and had full blind displays and a route number stencil on the offside. It is 12th July 1952, a week after Last Tram Day. (Clarence Carter)

to sign my overtime docket; they were totally sloshed but I did get it signed. Although I was told that the power was going to be shut off at this time, it did not and the last trams left at about 3am.

I had to undergo a two week bus driving course which was carried out on an RT bus: I passed my test first time – on 13th March 1952. I was given badge N19605 which had been previously issued to another man (both of my T badges were brand new). With my Public Service Vehicle licence came a council driving licence too – this was an anomaly but a welcome one. Until this time, the only vehicle I had driven on the King's highway was a tramcar. On Monday 7th July I started my bus driving career; that day, my conductor and I had to pick our way through building work at New Cross garage to get to our bus which was an old STL; a number had been roped in as there weren't enough new buses for 6th July. They were cold and old and I worked on these 'old bangers' for a few months. The brakes were like lead, there was a pump hooter and no cab door; they were difficult to drive as they had very heavy steering. I'd had some 'type training' on an STL, driving around local streets for a short while. I was on the 182s which ran between Woolwich and Cannon Street and replaced the 46 tram – crews went with their routes. It has to be borne in mind that I hadn't been in the cab of a bus since passing my PSV test in March; I'd been driving trams for eighteen months and had been in the middle of the road since January 1951 so it was a culture shock that day. It took a few days to acclimatise to my new role; by the middle of the month though, I'd taken to the job like a duck to water. The tram replacement buses had new Central London termini; route learning was required which was done on overtime.

New Cross depot was rebuilt so that motorbuses could operate from a brand new garage – it had the code NX and metal plates to that effect were placed in holders on each side of the bus. Work on the garage started in January 1951; with the withdrawal of the routes at stages four, six, seven and eight, contractors could work piecemeal. Gradually parts of the depot were torn down and the place was transformed from one of antiquity to one of modernity; there was a new canteen and a new operating and welfare block which were opened on 14th July 1952. The new complex bore no resemblance to the old one – the tram sheds and their pits disappeared. Come 5th July 1952, there was still a lot of work to be done and most of the crews there at this time were temporarily sent to Rye Lane, Camberwell and Peckham garages. This didn't happen to me as I was on the 182 rota, the only route to stay at NX – this was handy for me as I lived locally. Buses were unable to use the tram slope and had to enter and exit via Pepys Road where a back entrance had been made to the garage. By the end of the year, brand new RTs replaced the STLs; this happened at about the time that work and staff came back to New Cross. When NX was fully operational as a bus garage, it operated a far smaller number of buses than it had done trams, similarly, the last stage of the tram conversion was achieved with the use of about fifty less buses than trams over the same roads.

There was a stark contrast between driving a bus and driving a tram, the most obvious feature was that the tram used rails while the bus ran on tyres. Everything about a tram was electrical and I worked with hand operated controls. On buses all was motorised and both hands were on the steering wheel; for the first time I used my legs on a regular basis in that I had to operate an accelerator, brake and gear change pedal. Mind you, there was a lot more room driving a tram as a bus had a cramped cab. On the old tram I stood up all day long – not that it bothered me; on a bus I was sitting down virtually during my whole time at work. If I wanted to announce my presence with a bus, I would touch the horn – on a tram I operated a pedal on the floor which sounded a gong. Another aspect lost with the changeover was the need of sand; before leaving the depot it was necessary to check that there was plenty of it in the hoppers (these were under the longitudinal seats). If I reckoned more was needed I would grab a bag of it and empty it into the hopper; the sand was used for adhesion on wet rails – a pedal operated the hopper. I was a lightweight and I had to leap up in the air and then jump on the pedal to get a good flow of sand; the heavyweight drivers had no problem with this. It was one foot for the gong, the other for sand. Trams had a spring-loaded mirror on the nearside but seemed to be fair game for lorry drivers as there were many instances of them taking a tram mirror off; experienced drivers counteracted this by propping the point iron into the stalk of the mirror – the other end of the point iron was wedged firmly against the body of the tram. With the change to buses, I had a driving mirror on both sides of the vehicle. Another place where caution was needed was at a tram pinch – vehicles would try to nip in front of an ever-decreasing amount of roadway. A tram had what we called a 'cowcatcher' at each end; its official terminology was 'lifeguard'. It could trip if we went over a bump a bit too quickly; its function was to scoop up anybody who fell beneath a tram. On a bus there was a lifeguard each side, though it was only cosmetic. With a tram I just had to follow the rails; on a bus I had to make my own path through the traffic. On trams, the destination blinds were changed by the conductor; on buses the driver changed the front one.

It didn't take long before the tram tracks started to be lifted; this was done in daylight so that workers could see what they were doing. There was little room between the kerb and the lifting area so great care had to be taken when passing through. In Greenwich, one very foggy night, one of our drivers misjudged matters and put an almost brand new RT down one of the holes that had been created by the removal of the tracks. After a time, an inspector turned up and led a few buses through the affected area of about a hundred yards – buses used the carriageway on the other side of the road; he then got some buses to come the other way. He walked to and fro and at some stage, without telling us, went home. A lot of buses were banked up and we sat there for ages like a bunch of lemons. I was in one of those near the end of the queue; we didn't have much idea of what was going on so half a dozen of us got down to playing cards! Eventually a policeman turned up and asked what we were doing; "playing cards" was the reply! We told him that an inspector had taken charge of the situation but we hadn't seen him for quite a time. The policeman took over and waved us all through; I got back to New Cross very late that night, the only consolation being that I was paid overtime for my late finish.

With the coming of the motorbuses there were some changes in working practices. Trams and trolleybuses only used one timecard; when we changed to buses, two were issued – one for each crew member. Inspectors could move trams between routes; on buses this was not allowed. It was rigidly enforced and if a bus was allocated to the 177 then it couldn't be used on another route. With the changeover, there was a reduction in service levels and this allowed more frequent weekend rest days.

One final connection with trams. The Coronation of Queen Elizabeth II took place on Tuesday 2nd June 1953 and big celebrations occurred in central London; there was a Coronation route which was lined with flags and bunting and London Transport seized upon the opportunity for the public

One route I worked on at Edgware was the 52A which had an Express service in peak hours. Picking up at nominated stops in Borehamwood it was then non-stop all the way to Burnt Oak Station – lovely! The next and final stop was Colindale trolleybus depot where a cup of char could be had in the canteen above the operating block. From the canteen there was a vast complex of overhead in front of me and I could not quite get away from trolleybuses until January 1962 when stage thirteen of the trolleybus conversion programme took place. At the time this photograph was taken, the Borehamwood housing estate was still being built; the terminus was at Brook Road from where RT 2411 has just departed. The route would later be extended deeper into the estate, to Rossington Avenue. A slipboard (by the bonnet) informed passengers at which stops they can board; the background on all blinds was blue rather than the standard black. The express section worked in both directions. (Peter Mitchell)

to view them by running 'Coronation route tours' in the days preceding and following the event. A lot of garages participated in these tours with NX being one; they were manned by volunteer crews and I was booked up to work one of the two duties allocated to NX on one of my rest days. This was tour 73 with departures from New Cross Gate at 8 and 9.30pm. Aware that there would be a lot of traffic and many people milling around, London Transport erred on the side of caution with the duty being just one journey; I thought this would be an easy number – how wrong I was! I was given a map and instructions for the evening; as soon as we were on the Coronation route my conductor turned the saloon lights of the RT out so that the punters got a better view of the decorations. I had a good idea of where to go for the first part of the trip, but when I got into central London it was pointless trying to read the map as the police were diverting traffic away from the roads I was supposed to use. They kept saying "Left here, left there, left everywhere". There was so much traffic and the whole thing turned into chaos. Eventually, another bus pulled up on my nearside at a set of traffic lights; I opened my nearside cab window and said "Any idea how I can get to a bridge over the Thames?" He gave me some directions and eventually I went across one of the bridges and found myself back on one of my old tram routes; New Cross was eventually reached. All bus services had packed up by now. I left my remaining passengers with an inspector who told them that they would have to walk the rest of their way home. I transferred to Cricklewood garage in 1953 and thence to Edgware garage. My last day of service was 21st August 1990, thirty-eight years after 5th July 1952. I may have been the last employee on London Transport's books who had worked on trams.

The back end of 1953 saw me working in trolleybus territory again and I often competed with the 645 when I was working on route 142 at Edgware Garage. Sometimes a trolley would follow me from Edgware to Cricklewood; other times I would follow a 645 over this section. 1456 heads for Barnet and is outside Edgware Infants School. See Author's Note. (Ron Wellings)

DATE OF BIRTH:- 21-8-25 DATE ENTERRED SERVICE:- II JULY 1949
SENIORITY DATE:- 11 JULY 1949 GRADE:- CONDUCTOR

Victor Peters RATE OF PAY, POSITION & CHANGES

DATE	LOCATION	NUMBER	GRADE	RATE OF PAY	REASON FOR CHANGE
11.7.49	CHISWICK		TRAINEE	13/4d PERDAY	
27.7.49	HANWELL T.B.	16687	CONDUCTOR	AS PER UNION AGREEMENT	NEW APPOINTMENT
15.3.50	NEW CROSS	16687	CONDUCTOR	"	OWN REQUEST
18.1.51	NEW CROSS	12831	DRIVER (TRAM)	"	
6.7.52	NEW CROSS	19605	BUS DRIVER	"	CONVERSION
16.12.53	CRICKLEWOOD	"	" "	"	VOLUNTARY TRANS
17.3.54	EDGWARE	"	" "	"	" "
14.7.70	"	"	DRIVER OP	"	O.M.O.
21.8.90	"	"	RETIRED FROM SERVICE		NO OPTION!!

Vic Peters' Service Record.

CONDUCTOR, DRIVER AND REGULATOR

George Cook

George Cook was born in 1913. His first recollection of trams was at Brockley Rise in about 1925 when on a foggy night one caught fire; it had probably been driven continually on low notches, causing the resistors to overheat. In the years leading up to the Second World War, it was difficult to obtain employment with London Transport, but in 1936, George wanted a change of scenery and his father wrote to the LPTB, asking if there were vacancies for conductors. Although a cursory reply was received, it was not until 1938 that George was invited for an interview as a tram conductor; this was at Manor House which was a long journey from his Forest Hill home. He was successful in his application, and having gone through training, was allocated to New Cross depot which had many routes. Being a junior conductor, he was put on the spare list which meant that he had to cover for conductors who were sick, on holiday and the like; some duties were 'six o'clock show-up' which meant that he had to be there at 6am to cover for anyone who did not turn up. Being such a big depot meant that there was always work to be covered; however, the large number of staff meant that there was little opportunity to get on the regular roster. In fact by the time George was called up for the army in 1940 he was still a spare man. One wartime incident concerned a conductress on route 54; a bomb landed in Lewisham, her tram was damaged and she was thrown out of it on to the street. A short stay in hospital followed. When she got back to the depot, rather than ask how she was, an official asked where the money was that she had taken that day. Her reply was "On the streets of Lewisham".

Three anecdotes: 1) George was sent to Camberwell depot for a week when they needed cover; the man allocating the duties was an affable character and asked if he knew the 35 and 66 routes. George said he knew the 66 and the inspector said he'd try to keep him on that route. The first three days were on the 66s but on the fourth day he had to work a 35 which ran between Forest Hill and Highgate, traversing the Kingsway subway in the process. The 3d and 4d tickets were odd; northbound tickets had a capital A printed on them with southbound tickets having a capital B; George had not been given any instruction about these and had no idea of what he issued. Some passengers who travelled north had southbound tickets with some going south received north-bound ones – he was all over the place with his tickets that day. 2) It was very important that every ticket was punched correctly, though this could be very difficult when loadings were heavy. One day he was called into the guvn'rs office as a passenger had complained that he had been refused a return journey one evening, and had to pay another fare. George had inadvertently punched a transfer ticket for the outward journey rather than the inward one – this gave the impression to the second conductor that the ticket had already been used. Chastisement followed! 3) It was compulsory for conductors and drivers to wear a cap with a white cover from 1st April to 31st October. Inspectors were allocated to 'sections' with Inspector Reed being responsible for the Lee area. One very hot day, George had discarded his cap and put it under the stairs. At Lee Green change pit, Mr Reed noticed that George was not wearing his cap and told him to put it on. "Yes, guv'nr" he said, but as soon as he was out of sight put it back under the staircase. On arrival at Woolwich later on, inspector Reed saw him without the cap and booked him for the offence. Again he had to go and see the New Cross guv'nr who said "Why do we give you uniform?" "To wear, sir" he replied. "Okay laddie" was the response, "I don't

With the hump of New Cross Gate railway bridge in the background, about thirty trams have banked up outside New Cross depot on 30th September 1950, the date of stage one of the conversion programme. What the hold-up is all about will never be known but the professionalism of the inspectors will come into play to get the services back to normal as soon as possible. (London Transport Museum U1757)

want another report like this as there's lots more people after your job". Suitably rebuked, George made sure he wore his cap thereafter.

During George's conducting days most people paid their fares with threepenny bits, pennies, halfpennies and farthings. This meant that there was often a lot of weight in his cash bag so he would regularly put these coins in the bags London Transport provided; he would then put them in the locker which was under the stairs in the knowledge that they would be safe and sound there. Unfortunately somebody had a budget key and opened the locker while he was upstairs one day; the £5 that he had bagged up had gone. George had to make the money up; at the time his wages were £3 10s 6d so it was a hard lesson that was learnt. He took steps to prevent this re-occurring. During the summer he would lift the relevant seat and put the bagged coins in one of the sand hoppers; in the winter he would give them to his driver who would put them in the pockets of his winter great coat.

Following war service, George returned to his old job at New Cross depot – on paper he had now made it on to the roster, but had been left off as there was no guarantee of him returning! He soon went on the rota and although he had been previously turned down for driving because he was a tad too short, times had changed and he was told that he would now be accepted; training was from Clapham depot; after that there was 'on-road' training with an experienced driver. After he had been driving for two years he was given the opportunity, in 1950, to become an acting regulator. No training was given for this as it was felt that staff should have picked up the job and know what to do. He might start his duty driving a tram but on the second part of his shift, be regulating at 'Marquis of Granby' at New Cross. While he was an acting regulator he never booked a member of the tram staff; it would have been counter-productive because he might have to work with a rule-breaker the following day. Eventually a full-time position became available, but it was covering for other inspectors. One day he was sent down to Woolwich where a colleague had gone sick on duty. This was an important point to control and there had been no opportunity for the inspector's timesheets to be handed to him; all George knew was that it was at the tea stall where the owner was looking after it. He'd only been there a few minutes when a call came through that the trolleybus wires were down in Beresford Square. He hurried down there and got single line working in operation for the trams – trolleybuses got through on their batteries. On returning to Parsons Hill another incident occurred; a conductor had forgotten to pull down the trolley after a tram had picked up its plough. It was only realised that something was wrong when the driver saw the trolleybus wires bouncing around all over the place.

Tram Seats Were His Stumps

Albert George Marks, 47, a tram inspector, of Owenite-road, Abbey Wood, S.E., was given an absolute discharge on payment of 40s costs at Woolwich yesterday, for stealing two tram seats. His solicitor said Marks, a former tram driver, thought the tram was out of service and had acted like a cricketer at the end of a Test Match, "who is entitled to take the stumps as a souvenir."

OCTOBER 26, 1951.

THEFTS FROM TRAM "GRAVEYARD."

Gordon William Woods (39), lorry driver, Rokeby-road, Brockley, admitted stealing 2 cwt. of copper coils, value £16, the property of George Cohen and Co., Ltd., from the tram depot at Penhall-road, Charlton, on October 11.

Det. Showell said the firm were engaged on breaking up trams withdrawn from service. As a result of losses enquiries were made and it was ascertained that Woods' car had been parked near the shed from which the property was missing. Witness searched his address on a warrant and in the garden he found accessories belonging to a tram trolley box and small electrical parts. All the copper had been stripped and taken away. Woods admitted the thefts.

In a statement to the police defendant said he sold the property to two general dealers for £12.

Woods asked for another offence to be taken into account. This was one of receiving copper to the value of £1 belonging to the same firm, knowing it to have been stolen He had three previous convictions.

He was fined £25, or three months' imprisonment in default, and was given 28 days to pay.

Each day, drivers, conductors, inspectors and pointsmen carried out well practised scenarios. However, there were aberrations from time to time and on one occasion the pointsman at the Elephant and Castle junction inadvertently diverted George's 36 on to the wrong track. Initiative immediately sprung to the fore; George stopped the tram at the next crossover, changed ends and drove back to St George's Church; by using Great Dover Street he picked up his line of route at the Bricklayer's Arms.

150 trams an hour passed between New Cross Gate and the Marquis of Granby; there could be long queues outside the depot and controlling them needed good management. This was achieved by having spare route numbers (known now as running numbers) and access to crew timecards. Trams were continually coming up late and out of order and the only way to get on top of the situation was to change running numbers with the spare ones. Every attempt was made to do this on the same route and it was only occasionally that trams were changed from one service to another; when this happened, the number plates at the front and rear were taken out and a blank display shown. At New Cross, one man controlled the Peckham side of operations while the other dealt with the Old Kent Road services; sometimes it was not until 10pm that regular intervals were resumed. Then there was the noise: the local populace and the tram staff became used to all the crashing and banging of trams going over pointwork; when the trams disappeared from London there was a relative quietness to the scene.

Controlling trams in fog was a nightmare but it was far better than dealing with motorbuses whose staff could not safely continue in the London pea-soupers of old. Trams could keep going as they were on rails – eventually though, even the most dedicated of crews would call it a day and the trams would drift into the depot one by one. Snow could be dealt with up to a point as there were snowbrooms that came out to clear the tracks; tramway staff armed with shovels also assisted to keep the services going. It was the winter of 1947 when the conduit system really suffered. Snow built up in the conduit pits below ground and prevented good contact with the ploughs; this caused extensive delays until they were cleared. In everyday working, ploughs easily jammed which often resulted in a broken plough carrier; hold-ups of as many as twenty trams could occur until a disabled car was pushed to a plough hatch where the offending plough could be removed.

With the scrapping programme in full swing, one of George's responsibilities for a time was to open up Penhall depot which was locked and secured each night. He had to be there at 6am to open the gates for cars that were using it temporarily while Abbey Wood and New Cross depots were being rebuilt as bus garages. Local residents did not object to the breaking of trams near their homes; as compensation panes of glass and sundry fittings made their way between the two locations at night! Special precautions to combat tram souvenir hunters were taken at what was referred to as Charlton Tram Depot; attempts to steal articles from the yard had been discovered and London Transport had a detective permanently on duty there. This did not deter a well-dressed enthusiast in a dark brown suit who would regularly walk into Penhall Road and announce himself with a posh name to one of the workers, implying that he was in a position of authority with London Transport. He had spanners concealed upon his person, and would remove a number of trolley heads - these were then wrapped in a copy of the *'Evening News'* and he would walk out of the yard with his contraband. Another theft that took place when track was being lifted concerned wood blocks which were placed in piles ready to be taken away; these were seen as ideal for open fires and disappeared overnight. More substantial was the theft of tram lines which were similarly stacked.

It was accepted that conductors would occasionally make mistakes in the adding up of their day's takings. One was so good (he never ever made an error) that he attracted suspicion and plain clothes inspectors went out and checked him on a number of occasions to see if everything was as it should be - and it was. However, he was one of those few individuals who were dishonest and he was caught out perchance by an off-duty inspector. As the inspector came to the top of the stairs, he saw the conductor clicking his heels together as he punched tickets. The conductor had fixed a bicycle bell to one of his ankles and by pressing

Trams are packed in like sardines in a can in Penhall scrapyard. This unusual view shows trolley wheels and pigtails to good effect. All of these trams are unidentifiable and they wait silently for the end.

The sharp end of scrapping London's post war tram fleet. The four cars in view will soon be broken up – there is no hope, and the oxyacetylene pipes in the first car is a very ominous sign.

one to the other, made the bell ring, implying that the punch had made the noise. He was using discarded tickets and pocketing the fares – he was summarily dismissed.

On Last Tram Day, George was on early turn in Peckham where routes 40 and 72 passed through. This was a busy area, with a lot of shoppers wanting to get there and back with their Saturday shopping – with so many people having a last tram ride the regular passengers could not get on. Often, George had to go to the assistance of conductors and tell people that they would have to wait until a tram with spare seats came up; it was a long wait with some shoppers having to walk home. Upon retirement, George had three remaining items of London Tramway property in his possession. (1) A seven-a-side ticket rack – for protection, some conductors cut away a part of its wooden base and inserted a piece of iron. If things got nasty, they would whack any miscreant over the head with it. (2) A tram and trolleybus rule book which, over the years, has seen its red colour change to orange. (3) A tram conductor's whistle, which has LCCT engraved on it; it had been made for the London County Council Tramways and had no doubt been in many a conductor's possession before being issued to him.

The site where the trams were scrapped was sometimes known as 'Penhall Depot'; the use of the word 'depot' implies that cars are parked overnight – they were for a time here. This was when New Cross and Abbey Wood depots were being converted to bus garages and there was not enough room to stable all cars overnight there; crews were paid extra for taking them from Penhall in the morning and back in the evening. Parked up during this time are Abbey Wood's 334 and New Cross's 1965 and 205.

Although I spent most of my time as a regulator in the southern division, there were occasions when I entered the Central area where I saw remnants of my former work. Tram lines and conduit are being taken out on the Victoria Embankment, and replacement buses are using the ordinary roadway now. This view was taken on 26th September 1953, well over a year since the tracks were last used. An RT on route 177 takes on passengers at a dolly stop. (Clarence Carter)

187's LAST JOURNEY

Ken Blacker

"My first staff pass allowed me to travel on buses, trams and trolleybuses; living on the north side of the London Transport network, I used the 33 tram and 38 bus from time to time." Seen at the junction of Rosebery Avenue and Clerkenwell Road on 18th November 1951 are former Leyton car 185 working on route 33 to West Norwood, and RT2031 on the 38 to Victoria Station. Many trolleybus services operated in this vicinity. (Peter Mitchell)

When I set out from home with the express purpose of riding on London's last tram, it was as a semi-seasoned 'last nighter'. I had participated in a number of previous last nights and this was to be the climax of them all. Trams had been part of my life since my earliest years. I well remember, when travelling home on the upstairs of a tram, my father pointing out as we climbed the hill past Wood Green depot, "Those are the new electric buses in there". Trolleybuses were due to take to the road on 8th May 1938 and I would have been aged just three. Later, as children, a much favoured cheap day out could be had by catching a 33 tram from Manor House to the Embankment, knowing that the climax of the journey would be a thrilling plunge into the dark depths of the Kingsway Subway. Today it would be inconceivable that parents would allow children of nine or ten to explore such distances unaccompanied through dire fear of what might befall them; we took freedom to roam for granted then.

The post war tram conversion programme was part way through when I decided that, upon reaching the advanced age of sixteen and having just been taken on as a junior clerk by London Transport, I would take an active part in the remaining conversion stages. This meant deducing from the 'Red Book' – London Transport's internal working timetable – the last scheduled car on each conversion and travelling on it, followed by a few hours hanging around the streets before catching the first replacement bus en route to home. I missed the first few stages, but joined in at stage five on the Saturday night of 6th October 1951 when I and a few other last night 'regulars', some of whom are still on the enthusiast scene today, comprised the majority of passengers on the otherwise almost empty last tram through East Dulwich and up the steep, four track Dog Kennel Hill. The last car from Grove Park at stage six on 6th January 1952 was similarly sparsely attended, but in stark contrast, the final run through the Kingsway Subway on 5th April 1952 was jam packed. A trivial memory of that night was that the last car, E3 no. 185, had a pronounced 'flat' on one of its wheels which meant that you could recognise its approach from some distance away.

Kingsway Subway was the penultimate conversion and it left only the network of routes based on New Cross and Abbey Wood depots still to fall. At the time I was ambivalent as to whether the conversion to buses was a good thing or not. Without doubt the remaining trams were horribly outdated. In terms of passenger comfort they ranked far below the LT and ST motor buses that I had grown used to travelling on to school each day (and which had all but vanished by the end of 1949), and in terms of accessibility their difficult platform steps and ridiculous staircases were

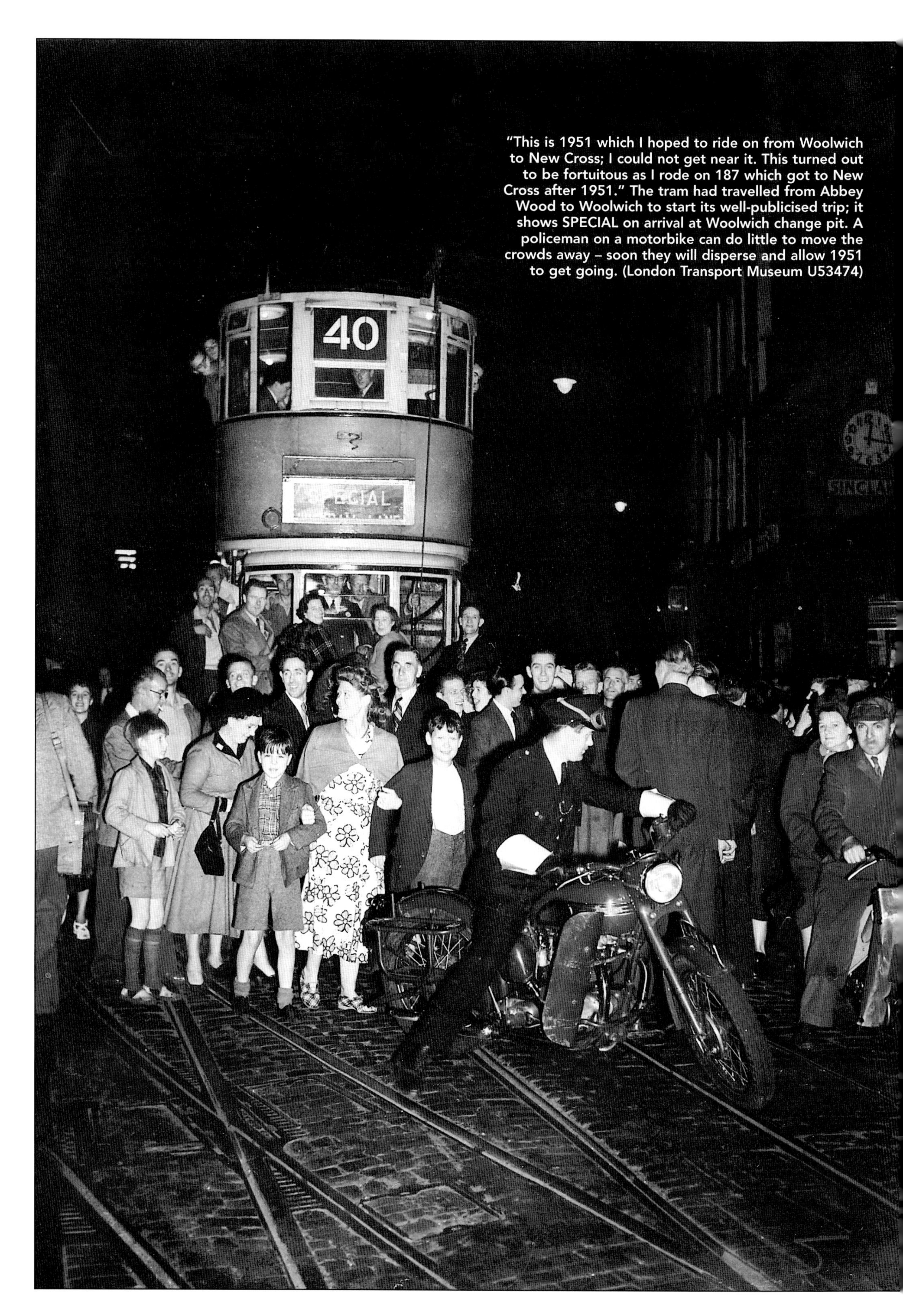

"This is 1951 which I hoped to ride on from Woolwich to New Cross; I could not get near it. This turned out to be fortuitous as I rode on 187 which got to New Cross after 1951." The tram had travelled from Abbey Wood to Woolwich to start its well-publicised trip; it shows SPECIAL on arrival at Woolwich change pit. A policeman on a motorbike can do little to move the crowds away – soon they will disperse and allow 1951 to get going. (London Transport Museum U53474)

an indictment of the London County Council's retrograde design policy of the early nineteen-thirties. On the other hand, I had seen in the Underground Group's splendid Feltham cars the sheer untapped potential of what a modern tram could embody, and to this day I still believe that these were the most advanced passenger road vehicles for their time ever to enter London service. However the Felthams had all gone to pastures new in Leeds by the time I began my last night jaunts, and apart from the ornately decorated, highly varnished wooden lower deck ceilings on some of the ex-municipal cars at Abbey Wood depot, there was not much to be recommended about the remaining London tram fleet.

And so we came to the last day, and then the last night. After several hours of final joy riding by tram our little group of last-nighters rode out to Woolwich to get favourably positioned for our last 'last ride' by London tram, all of us knowing that this would be a more special occasion than any of the others.

Very many years have passed since then and I have been on many 'lasts' in many places. The feeling has always been the same, a strange mixture of excitement at participating in the making of transport history, and of inevitable sadness – disbelief almost – that a feature of life I had taken for granted over the years would be gone for ever. There is nothing more final than riding along on a tram, trolleybus or whatever, knowing that another one will never pass that way again. But the end of Britain's greatest tramway network on 5th July 1952 was something extra special, and I was aware of this as I positioned myself at the head of the queue at Perrott Street Woolwich, for the route 40 tram departure scheduled at 11.57pm to New Cross depot where a big closing ceremony was planned when it arrived there at 12.31am.

Perrott Street is one of those undistinguished side turnings that you would never notice in normal times, and it only came to fame because of the crossing here, in Plumstead Road, that marked the off-peak outer terminus of route 40. We arrived there with almost two hours to spare, and in plenty of time to observe the comings and goings on routes 36/38 and 40. In normal times we would also have seen the running-in journeys on routes 44 and 46 to Abbey Wood depot but tonight they were absent, having been diverted from their terminus at Beresford Square direct to the scrapyard. A substantial queue built up behind us, well in excess of what any 74-seat E3 could ever hope to accommodate. The evening drew on, and the last 36/38 came up from Abbey Wood, to the best of my recollection more or less on schedule at 11.43pm. And then it was time for the last car of all.

No. 1951 duly turned up to start its final run to New Cross, and to my surprise the lower deck already appeared to be half full of what I took to be BBC sound recordists and their gear. Space for ordinary passengers was obviously going to be more restricted than I had originally imagined. Worse still, the driver overshot the Perrott Street stop by a considerable distance, which meant that everyone at the back of the queue boarded first in what became a veritable scrum. The others in our little group managed to elbow their way on, but I obviously didn't push hard enough as I was left stranded on the pavement at Perrott Street as the car pulled away. In a mild degree of panic I ran as fast as I could behind it hoping that, if I could catch it up at Beresford Square – two minutes' journey time away – it was likely to be delayed there and I might be able to get on. It was, indeed, delayed for quite a while at Beresford Square, but so huge was the crowd that I was unable to get anywhere near it.

Just as I was becoming gripped by despair at missing London's last tram despite all my best efforts, the totally unexpected happened. From the direction of Grand Depot Road came a number 72 tram which circled the Beresford Square loop and parked up at the normal 72 departure stop in New Road with its destination blinds clearly showing 'New Cross Gate'. At first few people seemed to notice it, the great majority being preoccupied with No. 1951. I had no idea why it was here, for the last 72 was scheduled to depart at 11.31 for a 12.12 arrival at New Cross. Therefore I immediately seized the opportunity and was one of the first to board no. 187, claiming a premium seat upstairs at the front. The tram filled, gradually at first and then more rapidly almost to overflowing, but the crew seemed to be in no hurry to depart. As we sat motionless at the stop, 1951 made its way out of Beresford Square at about ten minutes after midnight and I knew, there and then, that we would inevitably get to New Cross Gate after the official last tram. Even if we had departed immediately and maintained a good road speed, the circuitous 72 routeing via Lee and Lewisham required ten minutes more running time that the direct, 'lower' road through Charlton and Greenwich. The crew of 187 would have known this too, but they were obviously pursuing their own last tram night agenda, and when we finally set off no attempt was made to correct the late running and much of the journey was at little more than ambling pace.

Of the journey itself, there is nothing much to report. The car gradually emptied as passengers alighted, but not before a collecting hat had been passed around for the crew, to which I very gladly contributed. No trams passed going the other way and as far as I was aware we were the only tramcar still on this lengthy section of track. A few bystanders waved as we went past, notably from the houses along Westhorne Avenue, whilst on the tram itself, souvenir hunters began removing bits and pieces which I didn't really approve of, illogically really since 187 was destined to go for scrap anyway. Although what possible use tramcar light bulbs would have been to anybody is hard to imagine! For the last time I witnessed a change pit in action as we moved from the overhead supply to the conduit at Lee Green. The centre of Lewisham – which I had already visited twice late at night in recent months for the last 58 and then the last 54 – was largely deserted. For some reason, it struck me as particularly strange to think that, though the rails were still glistening, there would be no trams in Lewisham anymore. Finally, as we drifted down Lewisham Way towards New Cross, we began to pass little groups of people walking the other way, who I assumed were making their way home after witnessing the arrival of 1951. I wonder what they made of it all as our tram passed by.

To the best of my recollection we reached journey's end at New Cross Gate at about 1.30am where we found a sizeable number of bystanders still milling around. Lord Latham had already given his famous "Farewell Old Tram" oration on the slope up to the depot, and I had missed all of that. I presumed that many in the crowd were hanging about in the hope of seeing New Cross depot empty as the last few cars departed, out of service, for the tram graveyard at Penhall Road. I was the last passenger to alight from 187 and for me this truly marked the end of an era. And from a purely personal perspective, the fact that my last ride had been on an E3 was a particular bonus, as throughout my life this was the class of car that I had known best of all. 187 didn't go into New Cross depot, but reversed outside and was taken straight away unceremoniously to the scrapyard. I watched it go, and never saw it again.

I'll never forget the day...

I drove the last tram in London

by Albert Fuller

Lord Latham, then chairman of London Transport, makes a farewell speech from the step of London's last tram at New Cross – the end of its final run.

ALTHOUGH I had driven trams for more than thirty years, I never expected the crowds that turned out to see London's last tram run from Woolwich to the New Cross depot just before midnight on July 5, 1952.

Earlier that evening I helped the television people, who had come along to New Cross to put our last tram on the screen. Then I broadcast in In Town Tonight, and soon after eleven o'clock I went down to Woolwich where No. 1951, a veteran of Route 40, was waiting.

The tram's bottom deck was almost completely filled by broadcasters of all nationalities, who described and recorded the scenes along the route to New Cross. On the top deck were some ordinary passengers - those who had been lucky in the big competition to get tickets for the last ride - and a number of official guests. These included John Cliff, the deputy chairman of London Transport; George Utting, who joined the tramways in 1893, and who was then eighty-one; and George Harvey, who had helped to clip the tickets during the ceremonial drive of London's first electric tram in 1903.

As soon as we left the Woolwich depot at 11.57 p.m. I saw what I was in for. Thousands of people swarmed across the tracks all the way. Hundreds of those who had failed to get tickets for the ride laid money on the rails and then, after the tram had passed over, picked up the twisted coins for souvenirs.

The rumour – it's on fire

From Woolwich, through Charlton and Greenwich, the crowds surged round the tram. Some clung to the sides and some managed to get on the roof. I could not travel at more than a couple of miles an hour most of the way, and at one time I feared the tram's controls would burn out, as I was driving at the equivalent of bottom gear all the time. Hundreds of cars followed the tram, including a 1909 vintage Darracq. All round us were people in fancy dress, cheering and singing.

At one point, flares were lit to help the cameramen film the last journey. They were so effective that word went round that the last tram had been set on fire. Someone called the Charlton fire brigade and out the engines came, although they had almost as much trouble as I had in getting through the crowds.

When we reached Deptford the mayor, ex-tram driver Mr. F. J. Morris, came aboard, and for a short distance he took over the controls. All the time I was being asked for my autograph; the journey was taking about twice as long as usual.

We reached New Cross with the crowds as large as, ever. Then we came to the sharp right-angled turn-in to the depot itself. There is a slight pull up-hill there, and as the tram took the corner she stopped. Hundreds must have thought at the time that she had broken down, and some of the papers said so afterwards.

But nothing of the sort had happened. It is a particularly sharp corner and that, coupled with the slight gradient, meant that the speed of the tram had dropped so that it was not carried on from one set of contacts to the next. Although another tram finally towed No. 1951 into the garage, she had not broken down.

Before she completed her journey into the depot, however, the last unofficial passengers had to be induced to get down. The passengers with tickets came off as well - some of them with souvenirs - and we rolled in. London's last tram had finished her last journey.

At Perrott Street, driver Fuller shakes hands with conductor Bedford. A number of boys have been brought out to see the spectacle; in years to come they will be able to say that they were there to see off what had been 'billed' as London's last tram. It was the intention that 1951, a former London County Council Tramways car, should be 'last in service'. London Transport's well laid plans came to naught though, as two others were still out on the tracks after 1951's arrival at New Cross. Both were from former municipally owned tramway operators – one car from Leyton, the other from East Ham.

"I used the Kingsway Subway trams on many occasions. One car that I may have travelled on would have been 187". It had been formerly owned by Leyton Corporation and worked on route 61 regularly. Seen in pre-war days at Stratford Broadway, 187 heads for Aldgate.

187 arrives at New Cross where it was quickly hurried away by inspectors. People looking out of their windows have seen two last trams arrive within minutes of each other! 187 is empty; the flap of the destination blind box hangs down, its contents now on its way to a reveller's home. (Clarence Carter)

Former LCC car No 1 was popular with enthusiasts. Its last day of use in London was 7th April 1951 when the LRTL used it for a tour which saw it operate in North London for the first time since 15th May 1938 when it made a marathon trip from Waltham Cross to Purley. It is seen on 7th April at Archway Tavern.

The three trams used by Cohen's staff for miscellaneous purposes are seen in this view; the front car, 1727, is the canteen. The middle one is 1768, the third car being 1730; they are cloakrooms and to give some privacy, the lower deck windows are boarded up. In the background a Feltham can be seen on one of the stabling tracks.

Above and Left. As 2079 is parked on the scrapping area of Penhall Road it would appear that it will shortly have the attention of Cohen's workers – this of course will not happen and it is unlikely that the reason for it being parked in this position will ever be known. At some stage it will be pushed back into the safe area of Penhall depot – its next move will be to Charlton Works for modifications before it is sent to Leeds. Note the LTE traverser in the foreground.

1398 served Londoners for more than forty years; no doubt there are a number of photographs taken of her during this time – this is the last one. Probably still serviceable, she has been pushed onto Cohen's side of Penhall Road scrapyard where workers will attack her with a vengeance. Soon 1398 will be turned on her side and burnt. This view, in April 1951, shows the finality of it all. In the background are four E1 'spark shields'.

581 is working on route 70 and is seen at Creek Road, Greenwich. This is an excellent view of back street London in the early 1950s.

Presumably this photograph taken at the temporary Deptford Creek bridge was taken on the same day as the lower view opposite. 581 on route 70 heads for Tooley Street; 600 on the 68 makes for Greenwich.

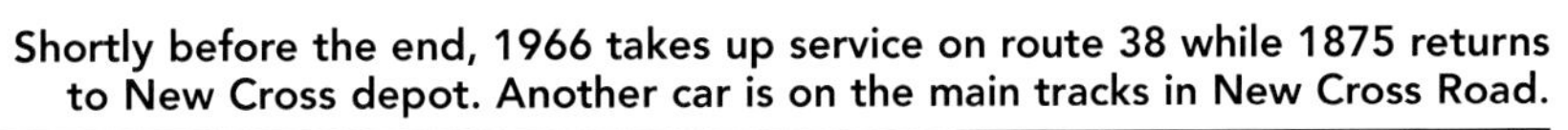

Shortly before the end, 1966 takes up service on route 38 while 1875 returns to New Cross depot. Another car is on the main tracks in New Cross Road.

The trams that had formerly belonged to West Ham Corporation had advertisement panels that precluded the use of Last Tram Week posters. This fact is clearly seen on 299 at the 44 terminus of Middle Park Avenue on 17th May 1952. (Clarence Carter)

187 sits peacefully at the Southwark Bridge terminus of route 46 on Monday 30th June 1952. This tram was to feature in far from peaceful scenes during the last tram rites at New Cross six days later. The ladies looking out over the River Thames show no interest in a car that is part of London's tramway history. (Clarence Carter)

Thursday, June 26, 1952

From All Quarters

SOUVENIR LAST TRAM TICKETS

Souvenir tickets will be issued on London trams from next Monday to mark the last week before London's tram routes are finally scrapped at midnight on July 5. The tickets will have pictures of the first horse tram and the present day car.

About 180 trams on services 36, 38, 40, 72, 44 and 46 will take part in the finale. Their replacement by buses completes a £9 million post-war transport scheme.

The last tram, a route 40 car, will leave Woolwich on Saturday week, arriving at New Cross at 12.29 a.m. It will be driven part of the way by Mr. J. Cliff, deputy chairman of London Transport Executive.

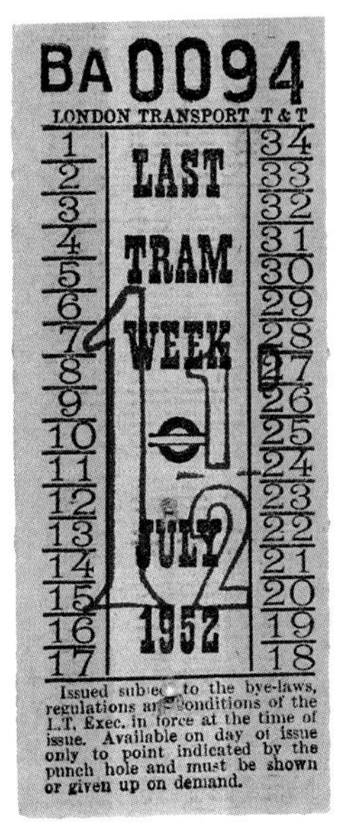

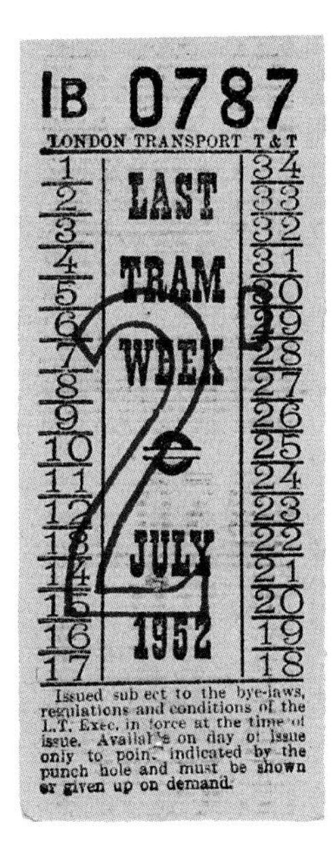

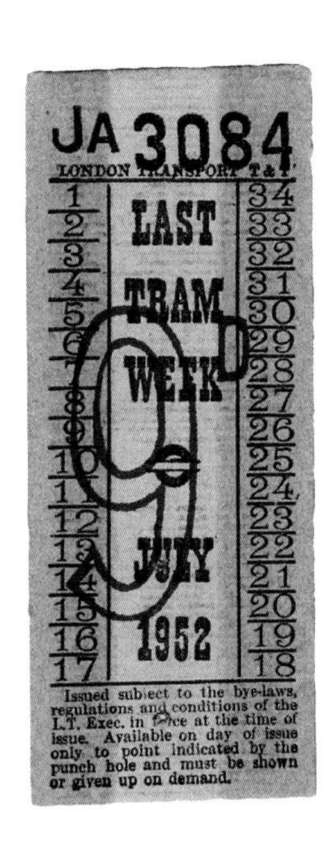

BUSES FOR TRAMS

Tram Route 74 will
Station and Farringd
Old Kent Road, Eleph
On Sundays, Grov

ASK CONDUCTO

1251—2674E—415/6 chgs. (80) TRAMS

This car was number 70 in the East Ham Corporation Tramways Fleet; it was renumbered 100 by London Transport and is seen in Eltham on its way to Beresford Square. Both the East Ham and West Ham tramcars did not use route number plates - linen route blinds were used.' (Jack Wyse)

RTING ON JANUARY 6

replaced by BUS ROUTE 179 Grove Park
Street via Catford, Brockley Rise, New Cross,
& Castle and Blackfriars Bridge (weekdays)
ark Station and Elephant & Castle only

A LEAFLET GIVING TIMES OF FIRST AND LAST BUSES

The Baynard Press

Starting on January 6, 1952

BUSES
FOR
TRAMS
(Stage 6)

TIMES OF FIRST
AND LAST BUSES

LONDON TRANSPORT
55 Broadway S.W. 1 ABBey 1234

Starting on April 6, 1952

BUSES
FOR
TRAMS
Stage 7

TIMES OF FIRST
AND LAST BUSES

LONDON TRANSPORT
55 Broadway S.W. 1 ABBey 1234

Starting on July 6, 1952

BUSES
FOR
TRAMS
Final Stage

TIMES OF FIRST
AND LAST BUSES

LONDON TRANSPORT
55 Broadway, Westminster, S.W.1
ABBey 1234

1981 is seen opposite the Yorkshire Grey public house and just west of Westhorne Avenue. Route 72 operated between Savoy Street, Strand and Woolwich. 1981 is turning short at Middle Park Avenue so must be running late. (Jack Wyse)

295 is also seen at the Yorkshire Grey. Route 44 was the shortest route operating on Last Tram Day. Due to the complex track and overhead arrangements at this location, movements had to be completed slowly. (Jack Wyse)

1908 and 1931 were used by the LRTL on 5th July 1952; the tour commenced at Southwark Bridge where both cars are seen. 1931 has arrived first; for obvious reasons 1908 will lead the pair away. Note the temporary bridge in the background, and the two crew members with their white caps. (Jack Wyse)

The LRTL tour on 5th July saw the break for the crew and participants being taken on the stub track outside Abbey Wood depot. In the background, overhead wires lead into the depot. All told, six trams were used for private hire purposes on this day. Their total mileage was 223, the number of passengers carried was 810, with the total cost of hiring them being £47 1/6d. (Jack Wyse)

578 is in Blackfriars Road at 9.30 am on 5th July 1952. A route 36 plate is not in position. This is probably due to a shortage at New Cross depot rather than it having been taken as a souvenir – the collectors were not out until later in the day. The background is typical of early post-war London. (Clarence Carter)

E3 179 was on route 38 on Last Tram Day; it is seen alongside RT 3853 which is on route 109, a tram replacement service. The permanent tram stop makes the dolly bus stop look second class. 179 achieved notoriety by being the last tram to be broken up at Penhall Road scrapyard in January 1953. This view was taken opposite Temple Station on the Victoria Embankment. (Clarence Carter)

1858 was working on route 72 on 5th July 1952; seen on the Victoria Embankment at 10am, it will shortly arrive at Savoy Street terminus. Only those 'in the know' that day were aware that it had been bought privately. As is well known, 1858 spent some years at Chessington Zoo before moving to the East Anglia Transport Museum at Lowestoft where people can ride on this tram. Thank you very much Peter Davis for spending your hard-earned wages on purchasing this precious vehicle. (Clarence Carter)

Former Leyton car 180 halts at Lee Green change pit on the last day of tramway operation in London. The car will soon be driven slowly forward to pick up a plough, thus allowing it to continue on its journey on route 72 to Savoy Street, Strand. Once the plough has been inserted beneath 180, the trolley pole will be placed under its retaining hook. Unusually for 5th July 1952, the car does not have many passengers on board. (Peter Mitchell)

There was a lot of late running on Last Tram Day and 1990, on route 46, has been turned short at Academy Road near Shooters Hill. The tram has had its trolley arm placed on the London-bound overhead and the driver is about to take 1990 over the crossover. London trams are not normally associated with the greener area of the capital; Woolwich Common, however, was one of these places. (Peter Mitchell)

1863 approaches the Yorkshire Grey roundabout on Last Tram Day; it is working on route 46 to Beresford Square. This location was one of the few in London where track points and overhead frogs were operated by drivers who gave two notches of power on the controller to operate them. (Peter Mitchell)

Southwark Bridge terminus was a quiet backwater compared with the busier parts of the tram system of Inner London. Waiting for passengers on the last day is the penultimate highest numbered car in the fleet – 2002. Soon it will set off for its Beresford Square terminus at Woolwich on route 46. (Peter Mitchell)

Tram 83 in the London Transport fleet had formerly been East Ham Corporation 53; it is seen on Saturday 5th July 1952 at the Middle Park Avenue terminus of route 44. The trolley pole has been placed on the eastbound wire; it looks as if the conductor is releasing the handbrake for 83 to commence its next trip – to Beresford Square. A car on route 72 waits for 83 to cross over; in the background, two other trams can just be seen. During traffic hours, there was always a lot of tramway activity at this location. (Peter Mitchell)

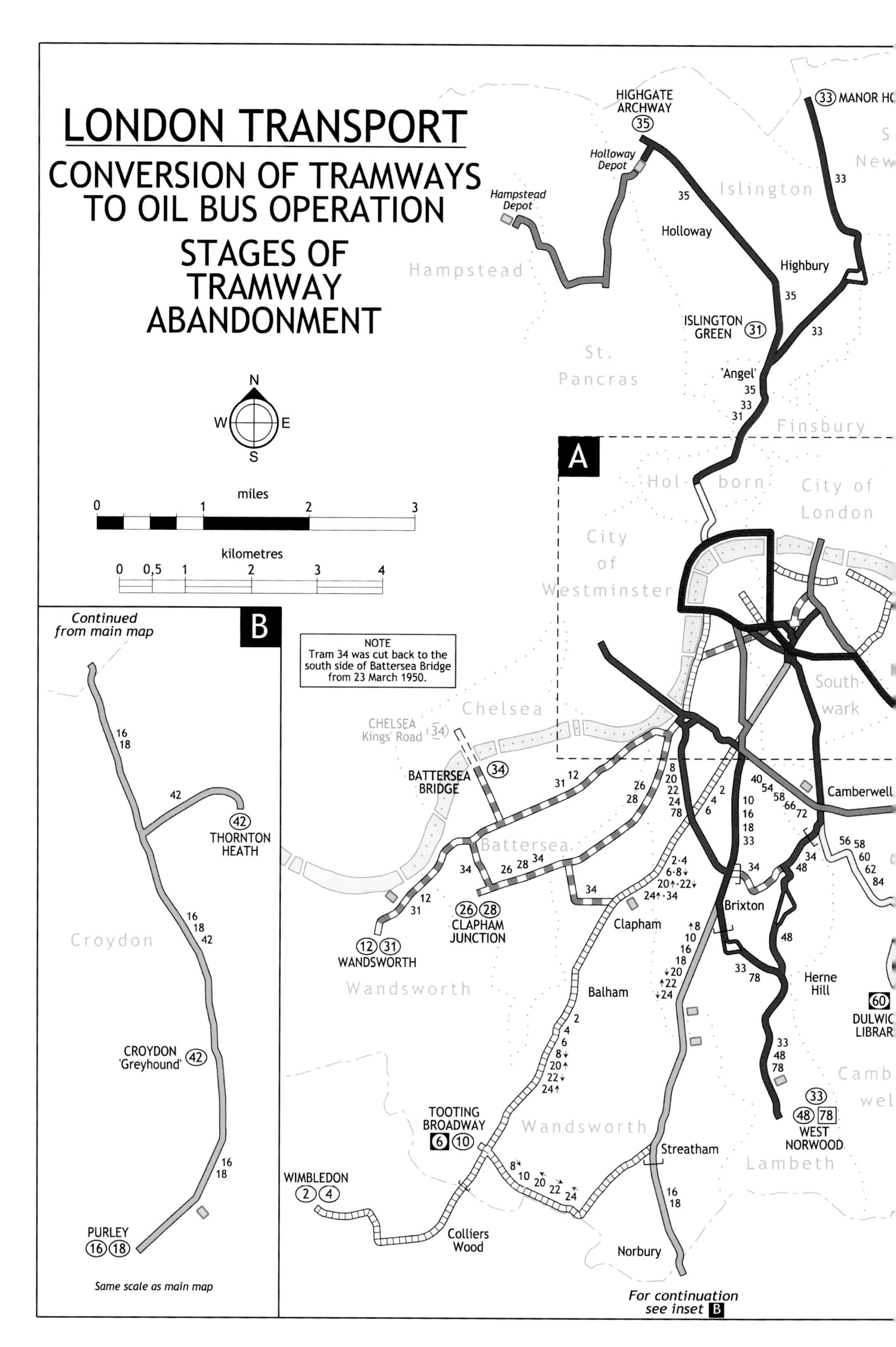

LONDON TRANSPORT
CONVERSION OF TRAMWAYS TO OIL BUS OPERATION
STAGES OF TRAMWAY ABANDONMENT
N
W
E
S
miles
kilometres
Continued from main map
B
A
NOTE
Tram 34 was cut back to the south side of Battersea Bridge from 23 March 1950.
HIGHGATE ARCHWAY
Holloway Depot
Hampstead Depot
Hampstead
Islington
Holloway
Highbury
ISLINGTON GREEN
St. Pancras
'Angel'
Finsbury
Holborn
City of London
City of Westminster
Chelsea
CHELSEA Kings' Road
BATTERSEA BRIDGE
Battersea
South-wark
Camberwell
CLAPHAM JUNCTION
WANDSWORTH
Wandsworth
Clapham
Brixton
Herne Hill
DULWICH LIBRARY
Balham
WEST NORWOOD
Lambeth
TOOTING BROADWAY
WIMBLEDON
Streatham
Colliers Wood
Norbury
THORNTON HEATH
Croydon
CROYDON 'Greyhound'
PURLEY
Same scale as main map
For continuation see inset B

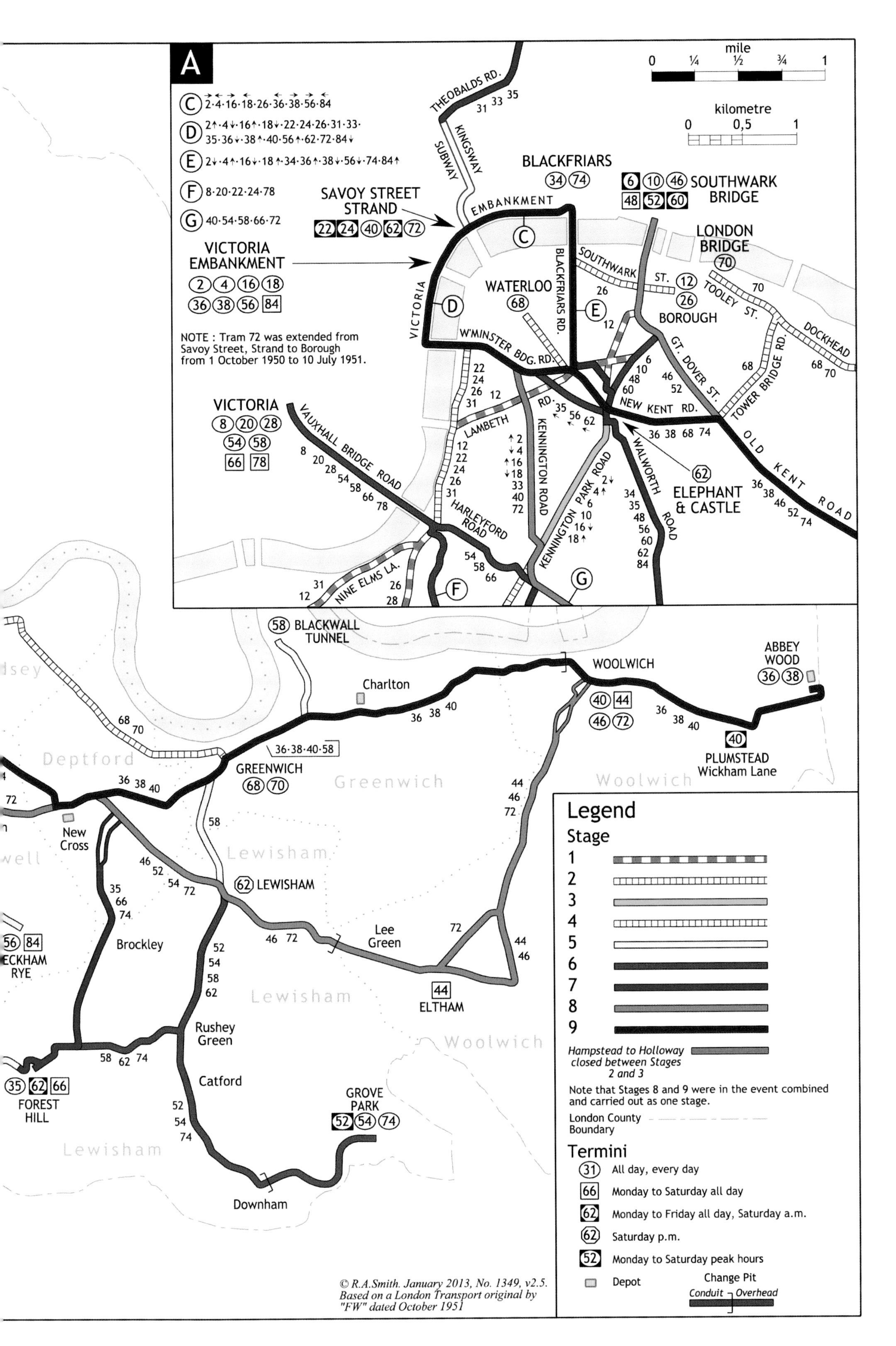
A
C 2·4·16·18·26·36·38·56·84
D 2↑·4↓·16↑·18↓·22·24·26·31·33·35·36↓·38↑·40·56↑·62·72·84↓
E 2↓·4↑·16↓·18↑·34·36↑·38↓·56↓·74·84↑
F 8·20·22·24·78
G 40·54·58·66·72
VICTORIA EMBANKMENT
NOTE : Tram 72 was extended from Savoy Street, Strand to Borough from 1 October 1950 to 10 July 1951.
VICTORIA
SAVOY STREET STRAND
BLACKFRIARS
SOUTHWARK BRIDGE
LONDON BRIDGE
WATERLOO
BOROUGH
ELEPHANT & CASTLE
THEOBALDS RD.
KINGSWAY
SUBWAY
EMBANKMENT
BLACKFRIARS RD.
SOUTHWARK ST.
TOOLEY ST.
DOCKHEAD
TOWER BRIDGE RD.
GT. DOVER ST.
NEW KENT RD.
OLD KENT ROAD
W'MINSTER BDG. RD.
LAMBETH RD.
KENNINGTON ROAD
KENNINGTON PARK ROAD
WALWORTH ROAD
VAUXHALL BRIDGE ROAD
HARLEYFORD ROAD
NINE ELMS LA.
mile
0 ¼ ½ ¾ 1
kilometre
0 0,5 1
BLACKWALL TUNNEL
Charlton
WOOLWICH
ABBEY WOOD
PLUMSTEAD Wickham Lane
Deptford
GREENWICH
Greenwich
Woolwich
New Cross
LEWISHAM
Lewisham
Brockley
Lee Green
ELTHAM
PECKHAM RYE
Rushey Green
Catford
FOREST HILL
GROVE PARK
Downham
Legend
Stage
1
2
3
4
5
6
7
8
9
Hampstead to Holloway closed between Stages 2 and 3
Note that Stages 8 and 9 were in the event combined and carried out as one stage.
London County Boundary
Termini
31 All day, every day
66 Monday to Saturday all day
62 Monday to Friday all day, Saturday a.m.
62 Saturday p.m.
52 Monday to Saturday peak hours
Depot
Change Pit
Conduit Overhead
© R.A.Smith. January 2013, No. 1349, v2.5.
Based on a London Transport original by "FW" dated October 1951

LRTL 1082

TRAM No. 1.

15th MAY, 1938.

AND RETURN.

To be cancelled on Tram and shown when required.

Extra tickets as souvenirs may be obtained on the tram for 6d. each. Send them to your friends.

L.R.T.L. 3325

TRANSFER.

5/-.

CAR A.

Pemberton Gardens. | Manor House. | Kingsway Subway. | West Norwood.

When Working. | Penhall Road. | New Cross. | Forest Hill.

LIGHT RAILWAY TRANSPORT LEAGUE in conjunction with London Transport Executive.

Valid only for SPECIAL TOUR on the last day of tramway operation via KINGSWAY SUBWAY, Saturday, 5th April, 1952. To be cancelled on tram at stage boarded and to be shown on demand.

L.R.T.L. 4419

CAR. A.

City & Southwark | Elephant & Castle | Lee & Beresford Sq. | Abbey Wood

Addington Street | Embankment via Blackfrs. | Penhall Road | Eltham Church

LIGHT RAILWAY TRANSPORT LEAGUE in conjunction with the London Transport Executive.

Valid only for SPECIAL TOUR on the last day of tramway operation in London-Saturday, 5th July, 1952, departing from City Terminus (Southwark Bridge) at 2.30 p.m.

To be cancelled on tram at stage boarded and to be shown on demand.

BUSES FOR TRAMS

Stage 4

On and after July 11

Tram Route 68

will be replaced by

BUS ROUTE 188

Greenwich Church & Chalk Farm (L.T. STN.)

via Waterloo, Aldwych, Kingsway, Russell Square and Camden Town

Bus Route 68A Chalk Farm (L.T. STN.) and Norwood Jct. WILL BE WITHDRAWN

and

Route 196 Tufnell Park & Waterloo Stn. WILL BE EXTENDED to Norwood Jct.

Tram Route 70

will be replaced by

BUS ROUTES 70 & 70A

70 Greenwich Church and Waterloo Station

via Tooley Street, London Bridge Station, Southwark Street and Stamford Street

70A Greenwich Church and Embankment (HORSE GUARDS AVENUE) (Monday to Friday peak hours only)

via Tooley Street, London Bridge Station, Southwark Street, Blackfriars Bridge and Victoria Embankment

Tram Route 72

will be withdrawn between

SAVOY ST. & LONDON BRIDGE (Borough)

Full details of the new services from the TRAFFIC ENQUIRY OFFICE London Transport, 55 Broadway, S.W.1 ABBey 1234

LIGHT RAILWAY TRANSPORT LEAGUE.

For those interested in Tramways and other Light Railways. Catering for all tramway grades and the general public. Full details from J. A. Pullen, Hon. Secretary, 67, Denman Drive, N.W.11.

Read "The Modern Tramway," post free 2½d. per month.

Printed by W. J. FOWLER & SON Ltd. Publicity Experts.

245-7, CRICKLEWOOD BROADWAY, N.W.2. GLAdstone 1234.

London Scraps whilst others build Modern Cars, Systems and Subways.

This ticket is issued on the distinct understanding that the holder or any other person taking part in the excursion has no claim on the Light Railway Transport League, its officials or members, or the Transport Undertaking for any injuries received, however caused, during the excursion or upon any vehicle or in any premises of the Transport Undertaking.

LIGHT RAILWAY TRANSPORT LEAGUE.

Advocating Tramway Development.

245, CRICKLEWOOD BROADWAY, LONDON, N.W.2.

The car on which you are riding finishes its life of service to the travelling public to-day. It has given many years of useful work, and, were it not for overriding interests, would continue to do so. The Light Railway Transport League deplores the abandonment of tramways in London. With imagination and public spirit uppermost, the tramway systems of many cities in our country could have been modernised and turned into a passenger-carrying service second to none. **You believe in tramways—let people know it—advertise trams.**

LIGHT RAILWAY TRANSPORT LEAGUE.

Advocating Tramway Development.

245, CRICKLEWOOD BROADWAY, LONDON, N.W.2.

CHARLTON WORKS EMPLOYEE

Ken Thorpe

My earliest memory of London's trams was in the early years of the last war when, with my mother and father, I was at the Woolwich Common tram stop one evening waiting for a tram to Eltham. A convoy of trams came from the Woolwich direction at a very slow pace, in pitch darkness, with no lights on in varying states of damage, i.e. broken windows, burnt paintwork. I can only assume that Abbey Wood depot had been bombed, and that these trams were being transferred to New Cross depot for repair and were going via Eltham and Lewisham to avoid Greenwich and Deptford.

I had been interested in transport from a very early age, so it was natural that I joined London Transport (in 1948) to take up a five-year apprenticeship at the Central Repair Depot, Charlton where trams and trolleybuses were overhauled. This meant I could observe the many aspects of work first-hand - one was the straightening of twisted and bent tramcar underframes, in-situ. Standard cars had an exposed side frame and by placing a tram on a single track section between two buildings, a correction was made by placing screw jacks between the side frame and wall and screwing in and out as necessary - adjustment was by sight-line until straight again. As an enthusiast there was the clandestine excitement of waiting for daylight in winter; I hid my box-camera within a boiler suit and ventured into the yard, on my breaks, to take pictures. Because the end was in sight for the trams, it was deemed not to be useful for my apprenticeship to work on them, but to concentrate on trolleybuses instead. However, there was one enjoyable exception when I was asked to produce some general arrangement drawings of Radial-Arm HR/2 trucks, as these were required for the workshop staff in Alexandria, Egypt, to whom the 101-159 series of bogies had been sold and shipped to. I went down to Penhall Road where I measured up and provided the necessary plan.

A remarkable upsurge in repainting took place in 1952 - this kept the paint shop staff fully occupied in the run-down period. With fewer passenger-carrying trams to overhaul, some of the works fleet came in for attention. Unusual was stores van 05 which came in to have a broken lifeguard repaired; it had a board on each end in painted lettering in 'copperplate' style stating that "This tram must not be operated over the Kingsland Road side-slot conduit section." Snowbrooms 035 and 037 were also dealt with. Not so fortunate was snowbroom 016 from Abbey Wood depot; it was not painted but was sent to 'Penhall' where it caused chaos at the scrapyard entrance. It had a fixed plough carrier; the lad driving it was unaware of this and everything was jammed-up when the plough was wrenched out of the car at the plough-pit. Such was the high standard of workmanship at CRD, that in their final years the trams still looked good; in fact, those with a provenance as far back as 1907 were kept going (even until January 1952) while motorbuses built in the early 1930s were being scrapped.

Although the withdrawal of the trams was well in sight as 1952 dawned, overhauling still took place. Generally speaking, large organisations would not countenance unnecessary expenditure and many of the municipal tramways that were closing performed minimal maintenance on their cars. However, London Transport employed a large workforce at CRD and although staffing levels were being run down through retirement and redeployment, work had to be found for others. This was partly met by an intensive trolleybus overhaul programme and work being carried out for the Road Haulage Executive's lorries. Overhauling of trams was to continue - as it was, parts were in stock and labour accounted for. The last one overhauled and returned to everyday service was 1909 which was out-shopped on 25th March 1952 (it might even have had a stint or two through the Kingsway subway). A remark made at the time was 'trams

The upsurge in overhauls even saw old E1s being dealt with. 1369 is travelling from Charlton Works to Norwood depot and is at New Cross. Despite its venerable age, 1369 does not need external body bracing. (Fred Ivey)

With the scaling down of tram maintenance came an increase in failures; in some instances there were 'trams on fire'. 1312 suffered this fate in early 1951; it awaits a second conflagration, this time formally in Penhall Road scrapyard – a sad end to a tram that survived two world wars. (Fred Ivey)

are being overhauled and sent straight to the scrapyard.' This was not quite right, but was an understandable statement as some spent less than four months on the tracks.

With so many cars having been recently overhauled, when it came to 'Last Tram Day,' there were a good number of smart looking trams on the road. For those who had lovingly overhauled them in 1952, it was soul-destroying to see their good work literally go up in smoke a few months later. To give an idea of waste, 570 had a partial overhaul in March 1952 and was in the scrapyard the following month.

I recall two very fast runs on HR/2 non-trolley trams. Travelling from Victoria terminus on a route 58 very late at night, with no other car 'in section,' it never left top notch until it got to Vauxhall Cross at an estimated speed of 45mph. Another time during the day a tram departed from Oval tube station and ran top notch to Camberwell Green, passing over the crossover and points outside Camberwell depot so fast that a cloud of dust came up through the floor hatches in the lower saloon. I was severely shaken by this, fearing a high speed derailment (crossings and points were restricted to a 5mph speed limit). There was an instance when an HR2 which had come from Peckham Rye and which was turning into Walworth Road at Camberwell Green conduit junction, became 'stuck on the dead.' The driver leaned out and asked the driver of the following 'ST' type bus to push them off it. It was achieved slowly and seemed not to have harmed the radiator of the bus on the tram's buffer.

Advertising – I remember riding a couple of times on the only ex-East Ham tram to have various colour-tinted advertisements in the opening ventilator top-lights in the lower saloon. There was one advert in particular that caught my attention – i.e. "The Tramcar and Omnibus Scripture Mission" (with a London address) proclaiming "Mark 8:36 – For what shall it profit a man to own the whole world if he loses his own soul?"

A friend of mine, John Wills, loved trams and spent many hours observing the intricacies of driving them; this put him in good stead on 5th July 1952 when a motorman asked if he'd like a 'spin on the handles.' John did not need to be asked a second time and drove 331 the last half mile on top notch into Southwark Bridge terminus. With the end of the trams, John was presented with more opportunities of driving them; he got to know the watchman at Penhall Road and on Sunday mornings would take a couple of bottles of stout to give to this individual who had no hesitation in allowing him to drive up and down the tracks. John had acquired some controller keys and was driving trams until November; while there were lots of cars in the yard, he was inconspicuous but when there were just a few left, eyebrows would be raised if 'car driving' was seen four months after abandonment. 'Penhall' also produced bounty for John; the older cars had been around for well over forty years and by looking under seats and between panels, he found many tickets from the LCC as well as those from Croydon, East Ham, Walthamstow, and West Ham Corporations; a number of coins were also there. John purchased a destination box from London Transport; it had been fitted to one end of former East Ham 89 whose original box had been damaged – the 'new' box came from an old LCC car. The contraption had three coloured lights to denote its route – many people could not read at the time the car was constructed, and routes were designated by colour. It had been converted by taking off the lenses and replacing them with three circular wooden discs. John and I carried the box from Penhall Road to Blackfen via Maze Hill and Avery Hill; it took four hours and we got some strange looks from bus crews on the way. He restored the woodwork and rewired it to house voltage; I then repainted it.

Thanks to regular routine maintenance, breakdowns on the extensively used conduit system were rare until about

West Ham Corporation tramcar 102 was renumbered 290 by London Transport; it was withdrawn in March 1938. It was selected for preservation; having had its plough carrying equipment removed by then, it was towed via Bloomsbury and the Kingsway Subway to eventually end up in New Cross depot. Seen in the south-east corner of New Cross depot at 3.40pm on 6th May 1950, a suave Mr Peter Davis poses at the controls of 290.

Seen shortly after leaving Charlton Works, and seeing tram tracks for the last time, 290 is on its way to Reigate Bus Garage on 6th May 1952. In the left view, one of Cohens 600 group lorries coincidentally scurries ominously about. Once 290 arrived at Reigate it will not see the light of day for many years. (Roy Hubble/London County Council Tramways Trust collection)

When this photograph (below) of 1025 was taken at Catford Bridge Station on 8th September 1951, the photographer would have had no idea that this tram would be preserved by London Transport. 1025 works on route 74 to Blackfriars. (Peter Mitchell)

Fortune smiled on 1025 which was selected by London Transport to represent a typical London tram; it was overhauled before despatch to Reigate country bus garage – there was plenty of space there with the location being deemed safe for their collection of historic vehicles. 1025 is in Charlton Works with final touches being made to the paintwork – this will be the sign-writer's last job on trams. The car is on lifting jacks – the trucks have already been removed. Both trolley retaining hooks were inverted so that they would not foul any obstructions on its journey into Surrey. (Ken Thorpe)

1950 when overhauling and maintenance was scaled down – the occasional broken plough was the only item of note before this time. From then on more serious disruptions occurred and queues of trams would be held up if a disabled one could not be pushed or towed away; culprits tended to be the 552-601 series of E/1s, mistakenly referred to as 'reconstructed subway cars'. These cars had new bodies but were mounted on the old subway car trucks; considering that they were manufactured in 1905/6 those that lasted until 5th July 1952, did well. There were two occasions when I saw these cars with broken truck-sides (made of cast steel) at 'Yorkshire Grey' roundabout; they were parked on one side of a triangle so other cars could be shunted around the remaining two sides. It was probably the fact that although designed to take only the weight of single-deck cars, the extra weight of double-deck trams caused the problems.

Records show that on 21st June 1950 the Chief Mechanical Engineer advised that a LUT UCC type trolleybus (56-seater)

Seen in Reigate on a Pickford's low-loader, 1025 is not far from the garage where it will be stored for many years. The trucks were separated from the body and are on the back of the lorry; the date is 21st April 1952. (London Transport Museum U3346)

The last staff car in use was 2055 which is seen in its usual position on the stub track outside CRD. There is bracing on the lower exterior panels; this was necessary on many cars in later years so as to keep the bodies in serviceable condition. Both trolley booms are at the same end – this was not unusual. (Don Thompson)

With the contraction of the tram system, the number of staff cars was reduced from three to one. 330 is on its regular run and is seen one afternoon in Plumstead heading towards Abbey Wood where it will stable overnight. (Fred Ivey)

The last two non-passenger cars in use were wheel-carrier 011 and ex-Walthamstow staff car 2055. Both are seen above at the exit of Charlton Works, with the crew of 011 posing for the camera. (Don Thompson)

in London United livery, a LCC class E1 tramcar in LCC livery and a "Metropolitan" UCC Tramcar (Feltham) in "Metropolitan" livery should be retained for museum purposes. London Transport saved the first two, albeit in London Transport livery; it was left to the tramway preservation movement to restore a Feltham in Metropolitan livery. Prior to this, London Transport had put aside for preservation former West Ham 290; withdrawn in 1938 it was stored in West Ham depot for a time. There is a line of thinking that it may have been towed to Hampstead depot where it spent the war; what is known though, is that it went to New Cross depot at some stage where it languished for many years. It was towed to Charlton works in 1951; on arrival, a shunter had been told where to put 290 and placed its trolley pole on the wire – it sprang to life immediately despite no power being taken for thirteen years. A full paint job was then completed; even the truck was removed and repainted. 290 entered the works for overhaul on 5th March 1952 and left on 6th May, the day it went to Reigate bus garage for safe keeping. Acting on the CME's advice, two E1s were selected as possible representatives of the London tram fleet. Sent to CRD from New Cross depot on 8th January 1952 (categorised 'for final selection and storage') were 1025 and 1038; the latter had been the first car to be rehabilitated back in 1935. Richard Elliott, who was in a senior position at Charlton Works, and who had a great interest in trams was asked to adjudicate; he decided that 1038 was not representative and 1025 would stay the course. Put into the overhaul system on 6th February, 1025 received a very good repaint to the extent of taking off the black half-round beading below the windows and burning off many years of paint in the forge. The trucks were completely dismantled and as many new parts that could be found were fitted – even the wheels had new tyres fitted and then turned on the wheel lathe. If the tyre treads could be touched by hand now, the slight grooves would be felt. 1025 was out-shopped on 21st April 1952 and transported to Reigate the same day. New advertisements were fitted to both cars. The less fortunate 1038 was driven 'down the road' to Penhall on 14th May 1952. The cost of overhauling 290 and 1025 was £330.

For Charlton works staff who lived some distance away, transport was provided in the form of three ex-West Ham

NEW CROSS
Two Cars to be transferred (for final selection and storage)
for Museum to.................CHARLTON WORKS

1025, 1038.

Well before the trams finished, one of the tramway societies had a tour which embraced a visit to New Cross depot; a short ride on 011 in the confines of the depot and on the traverser took place. Maybe it was this concept of carrying passengers on 011 in New Cross depot that gave rise to its use by Charlton Works staff on 5th July 1952. An East Ham car has been 'in the wars' (Online Transport Archive)

CRD staff arranged for a Last Tram Week poster to be positioned on both sides of 2055. They have adapted it by deleting the words 'Week' and 'On July 5' so that it reads: 'LAST TRAM WE SAY GOODBYE TO LONDON'.

bogie cars (326, 327 and 330). They arrived from Hampstead depot, unscreened and with longitudinal seats the length of the lower saloons; all received a repaint and screens, but the seating was not altered. Paper farecharts for either ex-West Ham route 10 (withdrawn in 1934) or 65 and 67 were fixed to a sheet of aluminium in the fare cabinets. These cars worked regular routes: 326 to Clapham (cut back to Camberwell on closure of Clapham), 327 to Southend Village where it reversed and went to New Cross, and 330 to Abbey Wood direct. I decided one evening to ride on a staff car to Grove Park whose path took in the abandoned 58 route via South Street, Greenwich. Coming down to the Obelisk at Lewisham to join the 46 route, we encountered a freshly laid tarmac zebra crossing right across the track and roadway. After discussion it was decided to plough through the obstruction; with the help of the policeman on point duty, who held up trams and traffic coming from New Cross, we charged full speed into the crossing, hoping that the plough would cut a new slot. Happy to say, this was achieved, though Lewisham Borough Council would not have been too pleased, having been notified that the 58 route had ceased to operate. From the following day, an STL bus was used. From January 1952, two former Walthamstow trams took over the staff car duties.

Being an established employee I (and my mother), along with other members of staff and their friends, were invited to a farewell 'get together' at Charlton works in the evening of Saturday 5th July. After light refreshments in the staff canteen, we were offered a ride on wheel-carrier 011 to

Many works staff and their families wait to board 011 and 2055 at the entrance to CRD on the evening of 5th July. There will not be room for everyone and only those with permission will be allowed on board. For passengers to ride on a wheel carrier was highly illegal; someone must have approved it though. (London Transport Museum U14645)

87 is at Eltham Church at 1.30pm on the last day; many attempt to board the car which is heading east to Beresford Square on route 46. This is a very interesting picture as 87 would pass this way at about 2.30am on Sunday 6th July, having got the better of two other trams whose crews were hoping to be 'Last car in". (Clarence Carter)

Penhall Road scrapyard. Climbing aboard via a pair of portable steps especially provided for the occasion, we waited while the side boards were put back in place; moveable seats had been fitted in its open area for the one mile run to Penhall. Although there were about thirty five people, including myself, standing with nothing to hold on to (apart from the sides and ends) it was the smoothest ride I've ever had on a tram. This was due, I imagine, to the fact that the non-standard Mountain and Gibson truck was only ever oiled and greased; combine this with its relatively low mileage and the only sound was the wind rushing past our ears! The one remaining staff tram (ex-Walthamstow 2055) followed – it was garlanded with white lights. We left at about 8pm, arriving twenty minutes later and alighted at the entrance to the yard; 'shooting' its plough, 011 was followed by 2055 into 'the place of no return'. STL buses took us back to the works where we arrived at about 10pm. As a matter of interest, 011 and 2055 are recorded by London Transport as being transferred from Central Repair Depot (Charlton Works) to Penhall Road on 7th July 1952.

Later in the evening I cycled to New Cross depot where I arrived at about 11.30pm. Showing my staff pass to an official, I parked my cycle in a rack at the back of the depot. Along with thousands of others, I watched the last rites; 1951 came in with 187 turning up outside the depot a little later. Time to cycle home. Shortly after passing the Marquis of Granby pub at New Cross I observed another tram which I thought was heading for the depot (it turned out to be 87, an ex-East Ham car). I thought "How many other trams are there roaming the streets?" Having had such a long day, I continued my ride home, passing through Lewisham and Lee. Cycling via the erstwhile 46 and 72 tram routes, I looked at the shiny rails and felt very sad that there would never be any more trams and that within a day or so the rails would become rusty. At the 'Yorkshire Grey' roundabout at Westhorne Avenue, I was ready to turn off to Middle Park Avenue when I became aware of the presence of a tram – I could hear it coming. Seconds later, 87 on route 46 came into sight and, to my great surprise was carrying passengers. I said to myself: "What on earth is this doing at this time of the morning?" It was now 2.20am. I turned my bike round and followed the lonesome tramcar. I just had to see the outcome.

87's crew may have been aware that on Friday July 4th, a local or national newspaper had published an article titled 'The forgotten tram' and the crew appended this statement to this journey. A clued-up journalist had obtained information that the last tram of the night was due into Abbey Wood depot at 12.34 am on the Sunday – three minutes after the last service car was due at New Cross depot. The accompanying article stated that while much pomp and ceremony would occur as London's official last tram entered New Cross depot, another, unhonoured and unsung, would be lumbering and creaking its way through the darkness somewhere on the road between New Cross and Abbey Wood (what the journalist didn't know was that the Abbey Wood depot runs that night were cancelled). London Transport commented 'We consider the number 40 tram to be making the last journey because it leaves Woolwich at 11.57 pm. It actually starts later than the 72* which leaves New Cross at 11.32pm. Driving the 'forgotten tram' was Mr William Crosk of 140 Dursley Road, Blackheath; conductor was Mr John Whitefield of 131 Alabama Street, Plumstead – they had 28

* London Transport wrongly quoted route 72 – it was a 46.

FRIDAY, JULY 4, 1952.

THE FORGOTTEN TRAM

Last on Road–But No Fuss

There will be much pomp and ceremony at New Cross tomorrow (Saturday) night as London's official last tram (a number 40) enters the depot. The V.I.P.s will be there for speech-making and a ceremonial farewell.

But even as this taking place, another, and forgotten tram, a 72, will be lumbering and creaking its way through the darkness—somewhere on the road between New Cross and Abbey Wood.

This will be the last tram carrying passengers on the London roads. It is due to enter the Abbey Wood depot at 12.34 a.m.—five minutes after the "official" tram enters New Cross depot.

Explained London Transport this week: "We consider the number 40 tram to be making the last journey because it leaves Woolwich at 11,57 p.m. It actually starts later than the 72 which leaves New Cross at 11.32 p.m."

Driving this "Forgotten Tram" will be Mr. William Crosk (28 years' service) of 140, Dursley-road, Blackheath. His conductor is Mr. John Whitefield (33 years' service) of 131, Alabama-street, Plumstead.

TRAM-DRIVER EX-MAYOR AT THE CONTROLS

Another "ceremonial" tram will be taking Lord Latham, chairman of London Transport, and other V.I.P.s, from Charlton to New Cross depot earlier in the evening.

This will be driven by an ex-Mayor of Woolwich, Councillor A. E. Jago, who was a tram driver for over 40 years. At Wednesday's Council meeting he recalled the beginnings of the "Ol' Faithful" tram and told the council how the first 44 route service started between Woolwich and Eltham in 1910 and of the many distinguished personalities he himself had transported. "The trams have done a good service to Woolwich and the London public," he declared.

Other Councillors also paid tribute to Mr. Jago and the tram. One humorously remarked, "One thing we can say about Councillor Jago is that he has never gone off the rails."

The special tram arranged by the Infantile Paralysis Fellowship — with Pearly Kings, students in old-time costume and "old crock" car—will leave Westminster at 7.57 p.m. for Woolwich and return at 9 p.m.

Other last tram details:—

Last from Embankment (route 40) leaves at 11.38 p.m.; arrives New Cross, 12.11 a.m.

Last down Old Kent-road (38) leaves Embankment at 11.30 p.m.; arrives New Cross, 11.56 p.m.

and 33 years service to their credit respectively.

Why was 87 running so incredibly late? Its previous trip had been extensively delayed by well-wishers on what should have been a forty-five minute run and it arrived at Woolwich after midnight – many staff would have called it a day. The crew, not through any determination to be the last tram, were intent that they should cover their mileage and decided that, "the last 46 must run", however late that might be. On its penultimate eastbound journey they would have told the man at Lee ploughshift to stay until they returned as they would require his services when heading back to New Cross; he could go home after that as there would be no need for him to be there on their return as westbound cars 'shot the plough'. 87 would not have been seen by those travelling on 187 which was on route 72 – even if anyone had given 87 a second glance, its blind display of BERESFORD SQ would not have aroused interest. On arrival at Woolwich, 87 turned back to take up its last journey. The tram that London Transport had gone to great lengths to avoid being 'last one home' was going to be 'last in service'. Inadvertently, Crosk and Whitefield had set a trap – the big-wigs were to be upstaged by a usurper which ironically was to be a car not from the mighty LCC empire, but from one of the municipalities.

"This must be the very last tram – I must see what's happening". At a tram stop I went over to the driver to ask why it was still running: the reply was "We're the forgotten tram". It wasn't a special – it was the normal service car which was running extremely late. The driver then said "We're the last scheduled tram – we must run." I asked if I could put my bike on the platform but my request was denied; however, I decided to pursue it. On the way up Eltham Hill things got out of hand as people were throwing light bulbs out of 87; it was stopped by a police car whose officers were concerned about this. Having quelled the 'revellers', the tram continued on its way uphill and down dale at a fair lick of speed, and I had great difficulty keeping up with it; one policeman rode the tram "shotgun" style while his colleague drove behind. Although still a young man I found it quite an effort to keep up with 87 as it had full line voltage

As stated in my account, I followed 87 for miles on my bicycle. None of the on-lookers outside Penhall Road scrapyard would have been aware that the car beside them had been London's last passenger carrying tram; in the process she was also the last to use a conduit change pit on the public highway. It is approximately 3am on 6th July and 87 is about to take her final bow. In the background an RT bus is ready to take London Transport staff home. (D.W.K. Jones)

and there was the very hilly nature of the route to contend with; passengers were being set down all the way between Westhorne Avenue and Woolwich. A few stayed on as it proceeded around the little used 'Ordnance Curve' and then on to Woolwich Ferry where it arrived at approximately 2.45am (scheduled time was 12.17am at Beresford Square).

Without a doubt those still on board were the last fare-paying passengers on a London tram. At Market Hill, trams change from the overhead to the conduit, and the crew looked in vain for the plough shifter; he had gone home a while back making a reasonable assumption that all trams requiring his services had gone through (that night, London Transport officials and servants alike did not really know what trams were where). I parked my bike; for about fifteen minutes, 87's conductor and driver deliberated as to what should be done. Tram crews were never ordinarily involved in plough changing; presumably 87's driver and conductor had never done it before although they would have seen the procedure first-hand on many occasions. I was in two minds as to whether I should approach them as I knew what to do, but thought "they're uniform" and considered it best that they should deal with the situation. There were no facilities to get any advice, and wanting to get home at a reasonable hour, they eventually decided that they would try and 'plough-up' the tram themselves. The conductor had a vague idea of what to do and having spoken about the procedure one to the other, the crew were hopeful that they could get it right first time; after all they didn't want to get 'jammed up' The implements required for plough changing were kept in a large green wooden box adjacent to the change pit. As per normal procedure, the plough shifter had left the box unlocked and they were able to obtain a fork, and a lever with a hook that would lift a plough. Cautiously the conductor put the hook on to the lug on top of a plough that was still in the stub and lifted it on to the fork. Meanwhile the driver moved 87 up until he reached the place where his conductor was standing and between them they gingerly got the plough beneath the tram; the trolley arm was removed from the overhead and placed under the retaining hook.

There were a few other enthusiasts waiting in the shadows; at their request they were allowed to travel on 87 which arrived at Penhall Road at about 3.10am. 87 travelled to Church Lane crossover where it reversed and headed east; another reversal at the entrance to the yard and 87 shot the plough that its crew had successfully inserted at Woolwich Ferry. 87 was then placed at the end of a long line of other cars, which I saw next morning. Having witnessed all this first hand, I found myself at Church Lane crossover where I saw two empty cars from New Cross approaching; I was desperately tired by now, jaded in fact and enough was enough. Again I thought to myself "How many more trams are there to come?" I didn't get home until about 4am.

At some stage, 87's crew were ferried back to Abbey Wood; daylight had broken by the time London's last tram crew got home.

TRAM 1858

Peter Davis

Peter Davis lived in Dulwich for many years and had an affinity with the local trams and the routes on which they ran. They were part of the highway and byway of everyday life for him; he had used them as a child to visit relatives and later to and from work. Occasionally he hitched a lift on his bike up Dog Kennel Hill holding the ledge on the nearside front of the main body of the tram until it got to the top. Normally he did this when the car was on the outside track, but now and again did it when it was climbing the inner track – he was bumping over cobbles at these times. On occasions, he acted as unofficial pointsman at Goose Green so if a 56 or 84 came along bound for Peckham Rye, he would yank the point lever over. He became known well enough by the drivers to be trusted not to let the lever go before a tram had cleared the points – it also saved the conductor having to get off and hold them over if there was no regulator there. In October 1951, the Dulwich routes, on which HR2 class trams ran, were abandoned though most of the 'hilly route' cars survived the conversion. They were transferred from Camberwell to New Cross depot where, at the time, it was anticipated that they would survive for another twelve months.

Mr. Davis Hires a Tram For a Sentimental Journey

" Evening News " Reporter

A SPECIAL tram will draw up at Camberwell threequarters of an hour after midnight on Sunday to mark the end of seven more tram routes operating over 56 miles of track.

The tram has been hired by Mr. P. J. Davis, of East Dulwich-grove, Camberwell. He will take friends as passengers on the sentimental journey.

Mr. Davis, a tram enthusiast, intends to take them for a 32-mile tour of the routes which are being abandoned through Westminster, Victoria, Camberwell Green, Dulwich, Lewisham, Forest Hill and back to Camberwell.

The last service tram will be a No. 58, which will arrive at Camberwell a few minutes before the " special."

The No. 58 will be driven by Mr. J. Gregory, of Camberwell. He will have Mr. James Lale, of East Dulwich, as conductor.

At 3.4 a.m. the first bus on the new route, 185, will run from Denmark-hill to Catford and afterwards operate between Blackwall Tunnel and Victoria via Forest Hill.

The change-over to buses marks the half-way stage in the big London Transport scheme to be completed in the next 12 months.

Of particular interest is the passing of the trams from Dog Kennel-hill, which is unique in having four sets of tracks, set up following a runaway tram accident in 1912 when the Board of Trade ordered that no more than one tram should be on the same set of rails on the one-in-eleven gradient at any time.

A total of 109 buses will replace the 99 trams. And, says London Transport, "there is no fear of the buses not being able to take the hill, because they climb stiffer gradients elsewhere."

Peter takes up the story.

"I knew a few other people (mainly in tramway societies) who were also interested in trams and all we could do was watch the remainder of the system being dismantled – route by route, car by car. In 1952, the first murmurings were being made about tramcar preservation, and although I was aware that London Transport was keeping two cars, neither was a 'Dulwich tram'. I had organised two London tram tours; HR2, 120 on the last day of the Dulwich routes, the other on the last day of the subway services, 5th April 1952. Six trams were hired that day. 195 and 199 by the Light Railway Transport League – I hired 1931, the borough of Holborn had 173, the borough of Lambeth hired 197, and 210 was used by the West Norwood Chamber of Commerce. The thought now came to me about buying a tram; I really wanted an HR2 re-habilitated car but they had all gone by April. In that month, I wrote to London Transport asking if it was

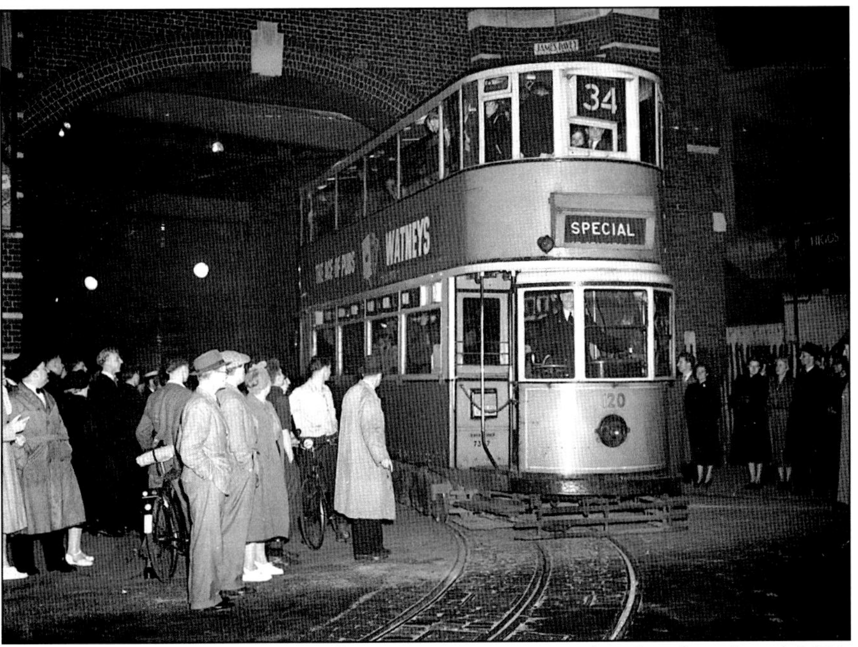

"I hired trolley-less HR2 car 120 for a tour over routes to be abandoned on 6th/7th October 1951; this was late at night and 120 arrived back at Camberwell depot after normal services had finished. I was charged £20 for the job." Route 34 was withdrawn at stage one, but a stencil has been procured for that service; 120 leaves Camberwell depot for its last stint on Dog Kennel Hill. (London Transport Museum U52251)

Peter Davis is quoted as saying "I would have preferred to preserve one of the rehabilitated HR2 cars." An ideal candidate would have been 1887 which is seen at Denmark Hill Station working on route 56 to Peckham Rye on 22nd September 1951. (Peter Mitchell)

possible to buy a tram – whoever opened my letter must have looked at it in incredulity. They replied that they were happy to sell me one. I did not consider buying a trolley-less car as even then I was hoping that any tram I bought would eventually run again at some time – therefore buying a car fitted with trolley poles was a necessity. I was quoted £60 for an HR2, £70 for an E3 and £80 for an E1. I replied, accepting their quotation for an HR2, but I wanted to choose which car it would be. I went along to New Cross depot one evening and introduced myself to some of the maintenance staff; they were not bothered about people going around the depot and had got used to me looking around. Surprised that I wanted to buy a tram, one of their questions was "Where are you going to put it?" Although they could not pick out a specific car which they knew was very good, I decided to choose 1858 as it seemed to be the one in the best condition in the depot at the time; despite its last overhaul being recorded as long ago as 31st May 1949 it still looked very smart. London Transport could sell a tram to anyone other than Cohen's if they wanted to; I told them I wanted to purchase 1858. The £60 quote was the amount London Transport considered they would have recovered if it had

1866 is only going to Elephant & Castle on route 62. This powerful car climbs Dog Kennel Hill, using the nearside of the two 'up' tracks. 'Up' was also tramway terminology for 'towards London'. (Peter Mitchell)

I got in touch with the *Daily Mirror* and asked if they would be interested in photographing the tram I was purchasing. They were, and came along to New Cross depot where 1858 was especially parked for me. The New Cross maintenance staff accommodated me fully as I prepared to take possession of 1858.

For its last nine months of service, 1858 saw a number of places that it had not seen before. 1858 is in Well Hall Road, approaching Shooters Hill on 5th July 1952; at the moment, only 'TA TA' has been chalked on the dash – later on more slogans will appear. When this view was taken this car belonged to a Mr P.J. Davis; bit of a liberty London Transport using his tram for fare paying passengers! 1858 ran well into the night and did not reach 'Penhall' until 6th July.

SALES ORDER NUMBER 1182

LONDON TRANSPORT EXECUTIVE AWRA C16/61.

Telephone
AMBassador 3444

Telegrams
PASSENGERS
NORWEST LONDON

GRIFFITH HOUSE
280 MARYLEBONE ROAD
LONDON N.W.1

4th July, 1952.

P.J.Davis Esq.,
23, East Dulwich Grove,
Dulwich,
London, S.E.22.

SALES ORDER

The undermentioned material will be handed over to you upon presentation of this authority to ~~the Storekeeper~~

Mr. Hodges,
Penhall Road Site,
Woolwich Road,
S.E.7.

A signature for receipt of the goods will be required at the time of your taking delivery.

QUANTITY					Particulars
Number	Tons	cwt.	qr.	lb.	
1					Tramcar No. 1858. This vehicle is sold subject to the conditions set out in letter dated 4th July, and/without guarantee and in the condition in which it is handed over.

NOTE—LOADING IS ALLOWED ONLY BETWEEN 8 A.M. AND 4 P.M. MONDAY TO FRIDAY.

139.
102/8
(M/500 6.51-S11- Stock)

W.HILTON.
PURCHASING OFFICER

LONDON TRANSPORT EXECUTIVE

C 37907

RECEIPT

55 BR...
WESTMINSTER
LONDON, S.W.1

Date	Receipt number	Received from	Amount
5 JUL 52	C 37,907.	P.J. DAVIS	80. 0. 0

For the LONDON TRANSPORT EXECUTIVE

704/95 (1)
(1m 8/50 B3)

2d

TREASURER

been broken up for scrap. However, between the time of the initial agreement and the time that payment was requested, I was told that the scrap value had risen. I considered that a firm contract had been made when I accepted their original quote – I did not want to lose 1858 to scrap so paid the £80 under protest. Correspondence between myself and LTE took place and I was refunded the extra £20 with assistance of my local Member of Parliament.

On 5th July 1952, I was talking to some of the maintenance staff in New Cross depot when I was told that 1858 had just gone by on route 72 towards Lewisham (running number 16). I pursued it on my bicycle and overtook it just before Lee; I parked and locked my bike at Lee change-pit and boarded 1858. I showed my sales receipt to the conductor who agreed that I didn't need to pay a fare seeing it was my tram. 1858 was running late and turned short at Dickson Road (in Well Hall Road); I helped turn the seats. The conductor meanwhile told the driver that, in effect, they were driving a tram that was on hire to London Transport as my sales receipt was for 4th July (London Transport's records state 'Tram 1858 sold 2nd October 1952 to Mr P.J. Davis of 23 East Dulwich Grove, London, SE22'). The driver then said "Well if it's yours, you'd better drive it". After traversing Well Hall roundabout, he let me take the controls and I drove it almost to the 'Yorkshire Grey' roundabout where there was a regulator. The driver took over for a while and, once past the roundabout, I carried on again up to the junction with the A20; I was very pleased at having had two whirls 'on the handles'. I reckon I

1858 crosses Westminster Bridge on its final day in service. Apart from Peter Davis, most of its passengers that day will not have known that it had been purchased for preservation.

1926 on route 40 and 1858 on route 72 pass at Camberwell Green on 5th July 1952. A number of people board 1926; one crew member has placed their white cap in the traditional way – in the 'rear driving cab'. As stated in the text 'SOLD' has been chalked on to 1858's dash by its purchaser. (Geoffrey Ashwell)

1858 was segregated from the 'scrappers' at the Penhall Road site and is next to snowbroom 022 which is restored to its original condition of LCC 106; both operate at museums in England. 1858 last ran on route 72; somebody has put a 40 plate up. 297 was less fortunate and, despite an attempt to preserve it, was scrapped in December 1952.

LONDON TRANSPORT EXECUTIVE

Telephone
Works
GREENWICH 0862

CHARLTON WORKS,
WOOLWICH ROAD,
LONDON, S.E. 7

P.J. Davis, Esq.,
23, East Dulwich Grove,
Dulwich,
S.W.22.

1st September, 1952.

Our Ref.C27/JS/2589.

Dear Sir,

I wish to refer to the movement of Tramcar No.1858 from our Penhall Road site to Charlton Works.

This will take place between 11 p.m. and midnight tomorrow, Tuesday 2nd September, and whilst I have no objection to any of your group members being present, I should like to make it quite clear there must be no demonstrations of any character.

You will no doubt be getting in touch with me shortly regarding completion of the site at Chessington, together with delivery of your trailer, so that I may load the vehicle and despatch same as quickly as possible.

Yours faithfully,

Works Manager
(Trams & Trolleybuses)

With a trolley arm placed on live overhead, 1858 was driven out of Penhall Road on Tuesday 2nd September 1952. Having reached Woolwich Road, it stands there all lights blazing. A breakdown tender has been backed up to 1858. The men in charge are in the process of positioning a tow-bar between the two vehicles; once 1858 is secured the trolley will be lowered and 1858 will be towed 'wrong road' to Charlton Works. It is approximately 11pm – the movement had to be that late in the day as this was the time when vehicular traffic was light.

drove it for about a mile, albeit without a tram driver's licence! I alighted at Lee Green where I chalked SOLD on to the dash; I then made my way to Addington Street where I joined the LRTL tour which was using 1908 and 1931. This took two trams off service, but with premium prices being charged for car-hiring, London Transport probably made more from the tour than if it had been taking passengers. Even though 1858 was running late into the night on 5th July, I do not recall seeing her again that day; on the following morning I visited Penhall Road site to check on her; she was fine. Word had got through to LT staff there that it had been bought privately so, in due course, she was placed away from cars due to be scrapped; it was positioned next to 022, another preservation prospect. I was happy with it being stored at Penhall; she was safe and sound and I kept an eye on her from time to time.

Prior to buying 1858, I had given thought as to where to store it. My uncle knew the manager at Chessington Zoo who agreed that it could be put out to pasture there. There were no facilities for a tram to be loaded at Penhall Road and arrangements were made with London Transport for them to return 1858 to Charlton works for loading there – I agreed to their £30 quote for the move to CRD and for the loading of the tram to Chessington. I was informed that the move would occur on 2nd September between 11pm and midnight. I turned up at about 10pm to find 1858, with all of its lights on in the Woolwich Road; it had been positioned there by one of the LT employees at the yard who had been asked to stay on and assist with the operation. 1858 had been driven out on the overhead – the accompanying photograph shows her in a blaze of glory; it was amazing to see this sight, almost two months after the abandonment of London's tramways. While I knew that the trams that worked on 5th/6th July 1952 were the last in service, to me 1858 was London's last tram as it did operate on the street tracks, albeit for a few yards that evening. The trolley boom was stowed and having been hitched up to a LT towing wagon, the duo left at about 11pm when there was little traffic on the road. Spring-back points were fitted to the entrance to the scrapyard (so that condemned cars could go straight in) so the towing crew had to wedge them to the 'straight' position to make sure 1858 didn't enter the yard again!

With the departure of the final trams from CRD on 5th July 1952, the works staff thought that they had seen the last of them. There must have been a number of surprised faces when they turned up for work on 3rd September to find that one had returned. (Ken Thorpe)

It was towed 'wrong road' to Charlton; at the approach to CRD, the service vehicle had to 'run round' and tow her in from its other end. I followed on my bike; a few enthusiasts were aware of what was occurring and were able to ride on 1858. It did not take long to get to CRD and once there, one of 1858's trolley arms was placed on the overhead. The lights came on straightaway, a controller key was produced and a London Transport man drove her on to a siding. I bought a considerable number of spares from London Transport – mainly redundant, reconditioned stock from Charlton Works. These included a traction motor, a set of tyres, brake parts, brake blocks, controller parts, windscreen woodwork, linkages etc. I also purchased three ploughs (one of which was a long-lead type). Many of these items have been extremely useful in returning the car to working order. I also considered purchasing E3 179, but bearing in mind the problems I had in finding somewhere to keep 1858 I had to let the idea drop; therefore 179 was the last to be burnt at Penhall Road scrapyard.

I engaged Evan Cooks, transport specialists and consultants, to move 1858 to Chessington; it all happened on 2nd October 1952. Owing to its height, 1858's trucks were separated from the body at CRD; the body went on a low-loader, with the trucks going on a wagon. The charge for the job was £80; that meant a total outlay of £170 not counting sundry expenses. Re-assembly was by Evan Cooks with the aid of a pair of tower jacks borrowed from LT. A group of us laid a pair of 45ft rails (from Croydon) for the car to stand on at Chessington. However, after nearly twelve years, the zoo required the land for bison and I was given notice to quit; I had a few offers from people who wanted to use the tram as a dwelling – these were not taken up. It was a strange situation – I had a tram but not a car! At the time, the East Anglia Transport Museum at Carlton Colville near Lowestoft was an embryo organisation and the founder, 'Dick' Bird, who was preserving a Lowestoft tram, offered 1858 a home there. Transport to Lowestoft by low-loader took three days (8th-10th April 1964); the journey was not without problems as some under-height telephone wires caught in the trolley bases and some panes of glass in the top deck were broken by overhanging trees. The tram went as one unit, hence the problems; the first wires brought down were at Hampton. The GPO was alerted to the situation and we saw a number of their vans heading in the opposite direction! One of the 'low loader men' was on the roof for some time; with gauntlets on, he lifted telegraph wires when necessary. However, safe and sound and after much renovation, 1858 now operates regularly at the museum where she is a popular performer; I am very pleased that my initial £60 investment gives pleasure and brings back memories to many people. Most years I manage to spend a week at the museum driving it, re-enacting my experience in Westhorne Avenue on 5th July 1952."

I engaged Evan Cooks to move my 1858 from CRD to Chessington Zoo. This was a one-off job for them, transporting a London tram. In the top view, 1858 leaves CRD; in the lower view, the towing wagon takes her out of Fairthorn Villas and on to Woolwich Road.
(Jack Law/Online Transport Archive)

I saw 179 in Penhall Road scrapyard many times; although I made enquiries to save the car I had to abandon my attempt as there was nowhere to keep it. Even if it had been saved, a vestibule would have been required for one end of it. This view was taken on 17th January 1953; twelve days later 179 will be the last of hundreds that went up in smoke and perished in the 'flames of Penhall'. (Clarence Carter)

1858 is in Walthamstow en route to its new home in Lowestoft. The body was not separated from the trucks; this made the height of the load very tall and caused a number of telegraph wires to be pulled down. After that a man was positioned on the roof, armed with a piece of wood to lift any more GPO property. During the journey some windows fell out. Safety glass was not used on trams and shards of glass fell into the road; Peter says: "we just left them". (London and Essex Guardian Newspapers)

"Camberwell was 1858's home depot and it was from here that I first saw her operating. It is appropriate therefore for my chapter to conclude by illustrating her working from there." The HR2s were built for use on hilly routes (Highgate Hill and Dog Kennel Hill), hence their class designation; however, they worked on other Camberwell routes. In Battersea Park Road 1858 is heading for Battersea Bridge, not Blackfriars. The conductor has probably changed the blind prematurely, and follows 1730 with a blank destination display. (Fred Ivey)

SUNDAY 6th JULY 1952 AND BEYOND

By daybreak on Sunday 6th July, all of the trams that were due for withdrawal the previous day were under lock and key in Penhall Road scrapyard. Abbey Wood and New Cross depots had to retain all manner of spare parts until the end; now they would return all tramway orientated items to Charlton Works who would arrange for the disposal of what was now redundant material. Ploughs removed from cars arriving at Penhall Road on Last Tram Day would be returned to CRD. With no more tracks to maintain, the remaining permanent way yards were de-commissioned.

The *Daily Mail* of Monday 7th July had a piece titled 'PEACE BREAKS OUT IN OLD KENT ROAD' AND THE LAST TRAM MEN 'GO RURAL'. The Old Kent Road was almost peaceful when Mr Fred Cutler went to work last evening. Overnight the tramcars had gone forever, taking with them the screeching and clanging and banging which had been work-day music to Mr Cutler for 38 years. And overnight 63 year-old Mr Cutler, spry and smiling, had changed from Tram Conductor T6875, with 38 years experience to Bus Conductor N34243 with no experience at all. But Mr Cutler was not worrying. He had to admit of course that there had been something of a lump in his throat the night before when he conducted one of the last trams to the "graveyard" at Charlton. Now that was finished. "Today I'm happy," said Mr Cutler rattling his money bag and studying his new tickets. "For all those years I've been bumping up and down London riding down the Old Kent Road and never getting any farther than Eltham Church. Today is different. With my old driver, Bill Appleton – we were the oldest tram team – I shall go past Eltham Church stop out into the country all the way to Farningham. Quite a thrill it will be too." Mr Cutler studied the notice boards at New Cross garage, once the home of the trams. Chalked instructions told the new boys what to do, and a large sign said "Good Luck." "My driver and I have had 32 years together" said Mr Cutler "and we have discussed this change. It's a good thing. It will be more comfortable for us and the passengers – and safer. Now we can pull into the kerb to pick them up. It always worried me the way they had to dash into the road to get aboard the trams."

To give an idea of the money spent on accessories at each stage of the conversion programme, the following estimated expenditure was made for stages 8/9. This consisted of:

Removal of 375 tramway stop posts and signs	£1050
Removal of 27 redundant trolleybus stop posts and signs	£33
Removal of 154 redundant bus stop posts and signs, and 47 'Weekdays only' and 'Queue' signs	£419
Removal of two redundant tramway shelters from Victoria Embankment, delivery to new sites and reinstatement of footway	£235
Provision of 206 stop posts and 376 stop signs including 46 queue plates, 1440 route plates and 60 hoods (metal covers over bus stop flags)	£4277
Provision of 40 posts to replace tramway poles	£344
	£6358

No trams were scrapped in the days following Last Tram Week – it was as if Cohen's gave their men a holiday as they had cleared the yard for the mass influx that would arrive on 5th July. The only remnants of London's great tramway fleet to be seen at Penhall Road on 28th November 1952 were: 95, 180, 335, 336, 341, 342 and 1859 awaiting immediate scrapping; 179 and 593 used as stores: four E3s used as spark shields and four used for ancilliary purposes. Interestingly, four of the remaining complete trams were ex-West Ham cars. Recently dismantled were 2 and 297 which were one-time preservation prospects. Power to the overhead would have been switched off sometime in late December 1952/early January 1953. The last batch of cars was sold to Cohen's on 27th January 1953; this comprised 179, 1231, 1727, 1730 and 1768. E3 179 was the last to be burnt; this occurred on 29th January 1953. London Transport vacated this part of the site on the appointed date: September 1953. Taking down the overhead, removing traction standards, power cables and removing tram tracks was a lengthy process. Although at one time discussions were made with the permanent way department, arrangements were made with Cohen's who on behalf of London Transport levelled the site. It was suggested that Cohen's remove the traverser; it is not known whether they or London Transport dismantled it. The traverser pit (on the long lease part of the yard) was to be retained as there might be a use for it in the future. London Transport removed the rails, sleepers and overhead equipment at a proposed cost of £1870; it was estimated that the value of the recoverable scrap would be £4190. The long lease carried through into the 1960s and in 1959 a total of eighty-six London trolleybuses were scrapped on the site. In the summer of 1953, London Transport looked into the possibility of buying the land and using it as a bus garage; the main site was retained as insurance in case it became necessary to abandon Plumstead owing to subsidence. It was stated that this would only be temporary but that it would cost about £16,000 to acquire the site – nothing occurred though. The channels in which the tram tracks had been laid remained for many years and were a vestige of the grim task that had taken place at the 'Tramatorium'.

A priority for the overhead department was to remove all tram-orientated equipment on the section between Woolwich and Abbey Wood; this would embrace not only the running wires but also a number of frogs and crossings. Once this equipment was removed, trolleybuses would have a free overhead line path in this area. London Transport staff also removed tramway overhead equipment in the other areas where the trams had run. The task should have been completed by the end of 1952 but was considerably delayed. On 26th May 1955 the final expenditure was quoted as £17,342; it was stated that the work in some instances had proved more difficult and taken longer than expected, requiring much overtime to be worked. Tram track would gradually be removed from the streets but even in the second half of the 1950's, London Transport and the LCC were still haggling about who was paying what. Some negotiations were quickly resolved with one being the removal of tracks over Battersea, Vauxhall and Westminster bridges.

At the commencement of the 'South London Tramway Conversion' the LTE was responsible for the maintenance of 205 single track miles of tramway (157 on the conduit system and 48 on the overhead system). However this excluded the Kingsway Subway tracks but included the disused single line between Holloway and Hampstead car sheds, the latter having been retained during the last war for the storage of spare trams. In October 1950 the first length of track was abandoned; tracks ceased to be owned by the LTE in September 1952. Of the twenty-four highway authorities having tram tracks in their area, only three (Holborn, Lambeth and Westminster) assumed responsibility for their removal. In some cases special track-work at road intersections was carried out in these three boroughs by the LTE who were requested (under the Conduit Undertaking of 1936)

These photos show the stripping and cutting of 1951 which was the official last tram on the night of 5th July 1952. The third view shows the car about to be torched. London Transport and George Cohen & Son had no room for sentiment and she was burnt on 14th July – a mere nine days after her time in the spotlight. Many of the last arrivals of stage eight were parked nearer the scrapping area than those that had arrived earlier in the day; consequently they perished first.

by the boroughs of Camberwell, Islington, Southwark and Wandsworth to remove conduit special work and sub-surface construction at main intersections – the major items were the complicated junctions at St George's Circus, Elephant and Castle, and Tooting Broadway. As a result of negotiations with the local authorities nearly all sub-surface equipment was left in position and the LTE relieved of the cost of this work. It was formally stated that the removal of tracks by the Executive commenced in late summer 1951 and was completed by August 1953. The LTE removed fourteen percent with the bulk of the work being in Lambeth. The authorities responsible for removing the track were required to reinstate the road areas concerned.

Alternative work had to be found for those whose grade was lost with the end of the trams. On the engineering side it was: brakesmen, tinsmiths, truckmen, traversermen, shunters, tyre setters, hammermen, spindle hands, armature winders, coil winders, blacksmiths, armature banders, foundry foreman, controller repairers and chainmen. On the permanent way there were tarpotmen, conduit cleaner gangers, paviors, leading paviors, checkburners, plate layers, point adjusters, welders, mobile gangers and points foreman. Still on the permanent way, one watchman did not retire until December 1952 - maybe he kept an eye on abandoned tracks. One Deptford Wharf employee retired in September 1952, implying a tidying-up exercise until then.

A number of staff at Charlton Works retained their tram status for a number of years. Truckman, F. Wheatley retired in May 1956; the last man to retain a tramway grade was Mr C. Baggett, a plough repairer who retired in August 1959 after completing fifty-seven years service - what were these men doing for their last few years? Maybe the question can be answered thus: in 1961, a few enthusiasts working at 55 Broadway decided to visit the now-closed CRD. Obtaining appropriately headed paper and using a 'departmental signature' a letter was sent to Charlton stating that a visit would take place one Saturday afternoon - this was confirmed by telephone. On arrival, the watchman waved the party through. A number of tramway items were still on the premises, the most noticeable being a number of refurbished ploughs stacked against a wall; bearing in mind that some can be seen at museums today, indicates that maybe, just maybe this was what Mr Baggett was doing for some of this period. In reality he had retained that grade for pay purposes, so for his last seven years of service was working on trolleybuses. Although by 1961 the works had been closed for two years, other remnants were wooden route boards that had been cut in three; they had been used as benches and showed route 65 which had been withdrawn in 1940. An early form of recycling!

The South London tram scrapping programme saw the removal of various practices; most affected staff. Interestingly, one featured trolleybus drivers' licences. Tram drivers who had been upgraded to this position in the 1935-1940 era had their licences endorsed with a codicil saying that they could also drive trolleybuses. When they renewed their licences (every three years) the same conditions applied and it was not until 1952, that these 'grandfather' rights ceased. Two premises that had not been used by trams for about fifteen years also fell by the wayside; taken out of commission at stage seven was the permanent way yard of the northern division of the tram and trolleybus department - it was situated at the rear of Walthamstow depot. The tram to trolleybus changeover in the 1935-1940 period contributed to a lack of space to store tramway items; used thereafter was the former Metropolitan Electric Tramways Works at Hendon; this facility now came to an end, just as the final curtain on the London tramway system came down when car 87 dropped off its last passengers outside Penhall Road scrapyard at about 3am on Sunday 6th July 1952.

MESSAGE FROM CONTROLLER
(CENTRAL ROAD SERVICES)

To A.H. GRAINGER ESQ.
Date 24.6.52. Place OUTSIDE NEW CROSS DEPOT.
Route No. Tram) Garage –
Time received
Time occurred 8.45 a.m.

PERSONAL INJURY TO TRAM DRIVER ON DUTY.
Driver Lovett, Badge No.9726 of New Cross Depot was boarding his car (1917 - Route 38) on the offside front platform, when he found the platform chain was around the centre handrail. He leaned back to release the chain, but was struck by Tram No.1926 on Route 72 travelling in the opposite direction, and was knocked to the ground. He was taken to the Miller Hospital suffering from head wound and is detained for X-ray.

Six minute delay was caused on both tracks.

OFFICE OF THE OPERATING MANAGER (CENTRAL ROAD SERVICES)
402/120 (3)
(20/150 10/51-D20)

MONDAY, JUNE 30, 1952

TRAM DRAGS WOMAN

Eileen Crowley, aged 43, with an address in West London, was knocked down and dragged by a tram on the Embankment at Horse Guards-avenue, Westminster, to-day. She was taken to hospital.

Tram injures woman

Mrs. Eileen Crowley, 43, was knocked down by a tramcar on Victoria Embankment this afternoon. Firemen released her, and she was taken to hospital.

POSITION OF CARS, PENHAL

ROAD NUMBER 7A

104
101
102
103

ROAD NUMBERS

8	9	10	11	12	13	14	15	16	17	18	19
					1966	2055	181	175	91	1948	83
1730	169	176			1923	011	1875	183	1964	335	312
1768	1977	344			298	334	1855	1908	184	1984	1903
10727	1965	598		022	297	560	100	1935	1927	92	185

TRA

ROAD NUMBERS

1	1A	2	3
			168
		87	1904
		1950	1936
	187	1987	342
1952	1998	340	1993
1909	592	1913	1916
1995	1946	1922	1932
1988	1912	309	94
1951	1931	1863	1859

CASUALTIES

MESSAGE FROM CONTROLLER
(CENTRAL ROAD SERVICES)

To A.H. GRAINGER ESQ. 70 — Time received

Date 30.6.52. Place VICTORIA EMBANKMENT, HORSE GUARDS AVENUE.

Route No. Tram Route 38. Garage New Cross Depot. Time occurred 1.25 p.m.

PERSONAL INJURY.
A tram on Route 38 was proceeding on the "up" track towards Blackfriars when a woman, who was wearing a deaf aid, stepped out from behind a central bus proceeding in the opposite direction into the path of the tram. She was knocked down by the front of the tram, and picked up on the lifeguard. She was taken to Charing Cross Hospital where she is detained for X-ray.

OFFICE OF THE OPERATING MANAGER (CENTRAL ROAD SERVICES)
402/120 (3)

LAST TRAM ACCIDENTS

And the trams did not go without taking their last toll in accidents on the road.

On their last day, Saturday, eight - year - old Christopher Heath, of 83, Mayday-gardens, Eltham, was knocked down by a motor-cycle while getting off a tram. He was taken to hospital with leg injuries.

And the day before, Pte. Mary Jones (20), of the W.R.A.C., was knocked down by a pedal cycle in Academy-road, Woolwich, while dismounting from a tram. She was taken to Herbert Hospital with cuts to face, injuries to the ribs and shock.

Eight-year-old Derek Purser, of 105, Glengall-road, Camberwell, was a victim of the crush outside the New Cross Depot. He was pushed by the crowd on to a stationary bicycle and injured his thigh.

OAD, SUNDAY 6th JULY 1952

1	22	23	24	25	26	27	28	29	30	31	32	33
30	1915	1953	180	1999	1857	1854	2002	1940	1969	86	84	173
05	1996	1928	1981	1961	1920	1906	165	1877	1911	578	85	332
6	2000	1979	1974	1873	1989	1871	1991	1910	2003	1917	311	82
9	1856	186	1934	1907	196	1980	1869	1945	1942	295	565	577

RSER

4	5	6	7
	179	304	90
1926	1939	1971	1937
305	88	1941	343
337	99	1970	559
341	339	200	307
1955	1954	1864	89
1962	1858	1994	302
1933	1938	1947	1862
1979	2	1867	1872
1956	1861	2001	97
1921	96	95	1231

APPENDIX 1

Snow Clearance

This appendix has been prompted by two memos, one of which is shown below. It would appear that the Divisional Superintendent of the South-West Division was not 'up to speed' with the events of 5th July 1952 as he sent an instruction dated 24th September 1952 to bus and tram controllers in his district detailing traffic arrangements for the winter of 1952/3 in respect of fog, ice and snow. Details are given with regard to the use of snow ploughs when necessary and that arrangements should be made for staff to man snow brooms should a request be made from a highway authority.

In response to the above instructions, the Permanent Way Engineer (Trams) at Bowles Road sent J.B. Burnell Esq, Operating Manager of Central Road Services, instructions for dealing with tram services during the winter of 1952/53.

E.104/HAW.

J.B. BURNELL, ESQ.,
OPERATING MANAGER,
(CENTRAL ROAD SERVICES)
55, BROADWAY.

PERMANENT WAY ENGINEER (TRAMS)
BOWLES ROAD DEPOT.

7th October 1952.

TRAFFIC ARRANGEMENTS - WINTER 1952/53.
FOG, ICE AND SNOW.

In connection with the instructions now being issued by your Divisional Superintendent, I would advise you that the following anti-frost materials are available at Bowles Road Permanent Way (Trams) Depot and must be cleared before March 31st 1953:-

Approx: 5 Tons Freezing Salt
" 200 Galls. "Froidene" anti-frost liquid for road surface dressing.

I would be pleased if arrangements could be made to transfer these materials to your depots.

9/3

HAW

Snow clearance was a highly organised operation and necessary to keep tram services running in severe weather conditions. The main items to deal with were important junctions and crossovers and the lifting and cleaning of plough hatches. Mobile gangs were available and lorries would stand-by for the emergency conveyance of men and materials. Details were available to supervisors of the necessary equipment and vehicles required. Lists were compiled of men who could be called upon to assist; with few having access to a private telephone line many had their doors knocked on, sometimes at an unearthly hour. Grades used on this work were: gangers, platelayers, leading platelayers, paviors, rammermen, labourers, tarpotmen, check burners, point adjusters, point and conduit cleaners.

Tools required were: brooms, shovels, point brushes and point irons; all were reserved purely for snow clearing and not general work. Gangers were responsible for the safe custody of the tools. Anti-frost liquid was available with cans of this at points and hatchways.

MEMORANDUM
OFFICE OF THE
PERMANENT WAY ENGINEER (TRAMS)

TO

DEPOT FOREMAN CHILCOTT

Ref: E.104/

Date 1 NOV 1951

SNOW CLEARING 1951/52
INSTRUCTIONS TO DEPOT FOREMEN - HEAVY LORRIES

In the event of a heavy fall of snow occurring any time between the finish of normal shift and resumption the following morning, the Traffic Branch may require the use of heavy lorries for hauling defective cars. It is intended that these lorries shall stand by in your depot awaiting instructions from the Traffic Department or Central Distribution Service.

Welding lorries will also stand by for distributing Permanent Way men to defects as directed by the District Foreman on duty at Bowles Road Depot.

It is necessary for you to make yourself familiar with the general snow clearing instructions.

Memo issued for the trams' last winter!

Snowbroom 037 is seen amid snow and slush in the last days of March 1952. It is allocated to Highgate depot and is at Archway terminus; a 35 tram can be seen in the background. (Peter Mitchell)

APPENDIX 2

Notes on the Last Hours of London's Tramways

by Alan Jackson

Beresford Square, Woolwich, 11.45pm: large crowds of local people, many a little alcoholic, singing and dancing, paper hats etc. Large numbers of police and police cars. A man takes a ticket rack from a tram conductor and distributes tickets free to all. Pennies placed on the rails for the last trams to flatten. Car 340 left for Abbey Wood in service 11.58 pm, 5 July 1952. Tram 1987 came in from London and turned at Perrott St 12.05, returning to New Cross in service. Motor cycle club out in full force, probably glad to see end of trams. Veteran motor cars still running around after Infantile Paralysis Fellowship procession earlier in the evening. Last official car leaves Woolwich at 12.10am 6 July – car 1951. Lurid yellow flare burning from top deck; man taking cine films from open window at back of top deck. Motors and motor cyclists follow. However this was by no means the last car to run through Woolwich as will be seen. Cars were running in service after 12 midnight as noted below, so last day of London trams was 6 July 1952. Breakdown wagon followed car 1951 westwards 12.12.

Left Woolwich on bicycle for Abbey Wood 12.15am. Passed 305 going westwards (towards Woolwich) in service in Plumstead High Street 12.21. Huge crowds at Bostall Hill/Basildon Rd Corner 12.30. At Abbey Wood (12.35) car 340 on road outside depot waiting to leave for Penhall Rd (it had come in service). In the depot was car 592 alone. I was told it would be moved down to Penhall Road at 2.30am. Meanwhile people were endeavouring to move souvenirs from 340. One man climbed up and carefully prised out the destination blind, only to have it torn from him by the crowd below! 340 left Abbey Wood for Penhall Rd with a policeman on the platform at 12.50am. Meanwhile car 309 had come into Abbey Wood terminus from Woolwich in service at 12.53am. It left for Penhall Rd out of service at 1.5am. This still left 592 in Abbey Wood depot. Buses using tram traverser!

Left Abbey Wood for Penhall Rd on bicycle 1.15am. All the crowds had dispersed although 592 had still to come through from Abbey Wood. The change pit in Woolwich Market Hill was still manned and the operator told me he was waiting for 592. Arrived at Penhall Rd 1.55am. Huge crowd awaiting it, including a drummer and various inebriates who were entertaining the crowd with songs and mock speeches about the trams ("a cheer for some good old friends who saw us through in wartime"). I was told that there were still five cars to come from New Cross; the staff did not seem to realise that there was still one car at Abbey Wood also. 187 and 1998 arrived from New Cross in that order and about 300 yards apart at 2.15am. Crowd at Penhall Rd dwindling. At 2.27am. 592 came in from Abbey Wood, thus being the last car in London to run east of Penhall Rd and the last car in London to pass through a normal change pit. It ran up to Church Lane to reverse and reluctantly entered the scrapyard at 2.35am. Penhall Rd crowd growing smaller, entertainers and lady with cross and wreath had left. Various rumours as to the number of cars still at New Cross. I left at 3am and still nothing had come through from New Cross since 187 and 1998. *A number of tram enthusiasts slept at my house overnight and when Mrs Jackson opened the living room floor on Sunday she was met by a number of people sleeping on the floor.*

The following, which completes the account, was had from a spectator outside Penhall Rd at 10.30am. on Sunday morning 6 July. I cannot therefore claim that the facts are correct but he appeared to have been an eyewitness and I think reliable enough. The last cars to run in London came from New Cross to Penhall Rd in convoy. There were nine of them and they arrived at Penhall Rd about 3.20 am 6 July. Their numbers were: 1946, 1912, 1951, 1995, 1863, 1952, 1909, 1988 and 1931. The last car to run in London and the last to enter Penhall Rd was 1931 (the car League members had ridden on earlier). It entered Penhall Rd at 3.35am after speeches and my informant told me that it was driven by Lord Latham. Car 1931 was parked first on the second siding from the left looking in when I visited the yard at 10.30 am 6 July and car 1951 first on the first siding from the left looking in. The other seven cars listed above were behind these two in these two sidings.

3am at 'Marquis of Granby' New Cross – Sunday 6th July 1952. Two hours earlier this place had been swarming with people seeing London's last trams off the streets; shortly before this photograph was taken, the last out-of-service trams passed this point on their way to Penhall Road. (John Gillham)

Nothing would deter John Gillham from photographing important landmarks in London Transport's history. Even on his birthday of 5th July he took many photographs, continuing into the small hours of the following morning. This view was taken at Lambeth North looking north-west at 4am on 6th July 1952. (John Gillham)

By the time that the last batch of New Cross cars arrived, the crowd at Penhall Road had dwindled. 1909 is fourth last. With its interior lights out, 1952 enters the yard. Even at this late hour, some of the onlookers are children. (D.W.K. Jones.)

3.30 am on Sunday 6th July 1952 and the last straggler arrives at Penhall Road from New Cross – 1931 which was reputedly driven into the scrapyard by Lord Latham. The A sticker on the windscreen indicates 1931's use by the Light Railway Transport League the previous day. Both of 1931's trolley arms at the same end of the car; one will be raised to allow it to enter the yard. (D.W.K. Jones)

Twenty-four hours previously they had been the centre of attention in the capital; now the last of London's vast tram fleet await the scrapman. This is the position in which the last cars ran into the yard on 6th July were parked; this view was taken that morning. Notable are 1951, seen on the left and 1931 on road 1A. Next to 1859 are a number of the cars' toolboxes which will be returned to CRD despite there being no further use for them. London Transport just about got it right when estimating how many cars could fit into the yard in one go; as can be seen, there was only room for a few more. Inside are 158 passenger trams and ten miscellaneous specimens. (D.W.K. Jones)

This photograph was taken at 2.30pm on Sunday 6th July; it is a view that will raise much conjecture. By comparing it with the one above, it will be noted that three cars have been moved to another part of the yard, enabling 1931 to move up three cars' length. It has acquired a 46 route plate, and a trolley arm is on the overhead. There was no need for any car to move as all trams meant to be in the yard on conversion night were there. What then is the reason for these movements, and who drove them? As a guess, London Transport staff who turned up for work in the daylight, became aware that there was room for a few cars to be positioned in spaces on nearby tracks and moved the trams accordingly.(Clarence Carter)

APPENDIX 3

Notes Made by Fred Ivey of the Last Night of the London Tram System

TIME	PLACE	CAR	DESTINATION & ROUTE
9.31	Glenton Road	200	Southwark 72
9.35	Lee Green	1954	New Cross Gate 46
9.38	Courtlands Road	304	To Penhall Road 44
9.40	Yorkshire Grey	307	To Penhall Road 44
9.41	Ditto	2	City 46
9.42	Eltham Church	298	Eltham Green 44
9.47	Well Hall Stn	343	Eltham Green 44
9.47	Ditto	1993	City 46
9.47	Ditto	90	Eltham Green 44
9.51	Odeon	598	Eltham Green 44
9.52	Ditto	337	City 46
10.03	Ditto	1929	City 46
10.08	Well Hall Road	298	Eltham Green 44
10.09	Ditto	1941	Beresford Square 46
10.09	Ditto	343	Beresford Square 44
10.10	Well Hall Stn	341	Last City 46
10.10	Ditto	598	Beresford Square 44
10.13	Eltham Church	339	Beresford Square 46
10.13	Ditto	342	Beresford Square 46
10.18	Yorkshire Grey	341	Last City 46
10.19	Ditto	1950	New Cross Gate 72
10.20	Ditto	89	Beresford Square 46
10.24	Ditto	1861	Beresford Square 72
10.33	Odeon	1858	Beresford Square 72
10.34	Ditto	89	Beresford Square 46
10.37	Ditto	1954	Beresford Square 46
10.38	Ditto	87	Beresford Square 46
10.40	Ditto	90	Eltham Church 44
10.42	Ditto	307	Eltham Church 44
10.43	Ditto	559	Beresford Square 44
10.44	Ditto	1941	New Cross Gate 46
10.48	Well Hall Road	342	New Cross Gate 46
10.55	Woolwich Barratt St	1858	New Cross Gate 72
10.57	Woolwich Post Office	1954	New Cross gate 46
11pm	Beresford Square via lefthand spur	559	To Penhall Road
11pm	Beresford Square	1932	Abbey Wood 38
11.02	Beresford Square	343	To Penhall Road
11.04	Ditto	2001	Turning on route 40
11.07	Plumstead High Street	99	New Cross Gate 36
11.18	Abbey Wood	1926	36/38

TIME	PLACE	CAR	DESTINATION & ROUTE
11.21	Abbey Wood depot	592	Out of service
11.35	Abbey Wood	1922	Last 38 to New Cross Gate
11.35	McLeod Road	1951	40 southbound special
11.52	Beresford Square	339	Awaiting to proceed to Penhall Rd
	via spur.		
11.55	Change pit	340	Abbey Wood 36
11.58	Woolwich Road	1987	Eastbound
12.01	Warspite	1913	Turning on route 40
12.04	Penhall Road	2	Entering yard
12.04	Woolwich Road	309	Abbey Wood 36/38
12.05	Woolwich Road	1858/1938/1954	To Penhall Road
12.09	Woolwich Road Park	1939	To Penhall Road
12.09	Tunnel Avenue	179	To Penhall Road
12.12	Christchurch, East Greenwich	1956	To Penhall Road
12.13	Maze Hill	1929	To Penhall Road
12.20	Deptford Bridge	1933	To Penhall Road
12.20	Brookhill Road	1962	To Penhall Road
12.21	Deptford Broadway	1955	To Penhall Road
12.24	New Cross Gate Station	1926 & 1932	To Penhall Road
12.29	New Cross Gate outside depot	1916 & 1993	To Penhall Road
12.30	Ditto	1922	New Cross Gate38
12.31	New Cross Gate	1936	New Cross Gate72
12.32	New Cross	1913	New Cross Gate 40
12.36	New Cross	1987	New Cross Gate 40
12.37	New Cross	1950	New Cross Gate 72
12.43	New Cross Gate Station	1904	To Penhall Road
12.47	Ditto	168	To Penhall Road
12.49	Ditto	1992	To Penhall Road
12.50	Ditto	1913	To Penhall Road
12.52	Ditto	1987	To Penhall Road
12.54	Ditto	1950	To Penhall Road
1.03	Ditto	1951	New Cross Gate 40
1.10	Ditto	1863	To Penhall Road
1.20	Ditto	1951	To depot (1931 assisted)
1.25	Ditto	1951	At depot entrance
1.33	Ditto	187	Last 72 New Cross Gate; passed depot westbound – reversed to eastbound.
1.35	New Cross depot	1951	To traverser
1.45	New Cross	187	Reversed back to westbound to Queens Road
1.48	New Cross	187	Reversed and used lefthand curve to Old Kent Road; reversed to eastbound thence to Penhall Road.
1.52	New Cross Gate	1998	To Penhall Road
2.48	Ditto	1946	To Penhall Road
2.49	Ditto	1912 & 1951	To Penhall Road
2.50	Ditto	1952 & 1909	To Penhall Road
2.51	Ditto	1995	To Penhall Road
2.52	Ditto	1988	To Penhall Road
2.56	Ditto	1931	To Penhall Road

A typical view of a tram driver as seen by passengers; his job required him to stand up all day long. This picture was taken in the Old Kent Road.

WITH THE PASSING OF THE TRAMCAR MANY FAMILIAR SIGHTS AND SOUNDS DISAPPEARED FROM THE LONDON SCENE. THESE TWO PHOTOGRAPHS ILLUSTRATE THIS.

A tram driver's workplace: E3 class car 1918. Electrical equipment was provided by a number of different manufacturers – one was English Electric. To drive a car forward, the controller key was inserted into the control switch on the left; to supply electricity to the motors, the controller handle was rotated clockwise, passing over series notches. To gain more speed, the handle was rotated a further four notches – this was known as running in parallel. To stop, the driver turned the controller handle back to the off position, and then further anti-clockwise to the brake notches seen on the right. On the right is the handbrake handle which was wound on to hold trams at stopping places. The driver could warn other road users of his presence by using the gong pedal on the floor. (Don Thompson)

GOODBYE LONDON TOWN

Many newspapers focussed on the fact that Tom Monk would drive 'Last tram from town'; he is with conductor A.E. Harris and two London Transport officials. Harris has a whistle attached to his uniform jacket – he will have used it many times during his tram career. As soon as the photographer has moved out of the way, Monk will take 1863 over Savoy Street crossover and back to New Cross. Somebody has chalked 'Cohen's Special' on the dash; once 1863 reaches New Cross it may well be Monk and Harris who take it to Penhall. The destination blind and route plate have already gone. This is not only 'Last 40 from Savoy Street' but also 'Last tram from Central London'. (London Transport Museum U53463)

1863 was not going without as many people as possible getting a ride; some cling to platform handrails, others perch precariously on the back fender – hopefully these dare-devils will jump off once it has crossed Westminster Bridge. 1863s rear blind has gone as well as its front one; presumably the route plate has been stashed away by a member of the public. The trolley boom is not under the retaining hook; maybe a reveller has pulled it out of the hook, played around with it and then tied it to the cleat. (London Transport Museum U53457)

Hoping to get a ride on 5th July, a number of people have assembled in the middle of the road at the junction of Peckham High Street and Rye Lane – hardly a safe procedure but something that will not be happening tomorrow. A bus conductor hitches a lift to Peckham bus garage; this may be the last time he travels on a London tram. 1926 is only running as far as New Cross Gate. Most of the ladies look towards the photographer – can't miss an opportunity to have their picture taken can they! (Jack Wyse)

Heading along the Embankment for Abbey Wood on route 36 is a former Leyton Corporation tram – it is now London Transport 181. A poet described the Embankment as where trams clang and tramps sleep. None of the LAST TRAM WEEK posters seem to have survived.

List of routes in operation on 30th September 1950

ALL ROUTES DAILY UNLESS STATED OTHERWISE

Route		
2	Wimbledon – Tooting – Clapham – Embankment (Circle)	*Clockwise around Embankment*
4	Wimbledon – Tooting – Clapham – Embankment (Circle)	*Anti-clockwise around Embankment*
6	Tooting Amen Corner – Balham – Clapham – City Southwark	Monday to Saturday peak hours
8/20	Victoria – Clapham – Tooting – Streatham – Victoria	*Route 8 anticlockwise; Route 20 clockwise*
10	Tooting – Streatham – Brixton – City Southwark	
12	Wandsworth – Battersea – Vauxhall – London Bridge	
16	Purley – Croydon – Embankment (Circle)	*Clockwise around Embankment*
18	Purley – Croydon – Embankment (Circle)	*Anti-clockwise around Embankment*
22	Savoy Street – Vauxhall – Clapham – Tooting Broadway	Monday to Saturday peak hours
24	Savoy Street – Vauxhall – Brixton – Streatham – Tooting Bdwy	Monday to Saturday peak hours
26	Clapham Junction – Vauxhall – Westminster – London Bridge	
28	Clapham Junction – Vauxhall – Victoria	
31	Wandsworth – Westminster – Bloomsbury – Islington	
33	West Norwood – Westminster – Islington – Manor House	
34	Battersea Bridge – Clapham – Camberwell – Blackfriars	
35	Highgate – Islington – Westminster – Camberwell – New Cross – Forest Hill	
36	Abbey Wood – Woolwich – New Cross – Elephant& Castle – Embankment	*Anti-clockwise around Embankment*
38	Abbey Wood – Woolwich – New Cross – Elephant& Castle – Embankment	Clockwise around Embankment
40	Plumstead – Greenwich – Camberwell – Savoy Street	
42	Croydon – Thornton Heath	
44	Woolwich – Eltham	Monday to Saturday
46	Woolwich – Eltham – Lewisham – New Cross – City Southwark	
48	West Norwood – Camberwell – Elephant & Castle – City Southwark	
52	Grove Park – Lewisham – New Cross – City Southwark	Monday to Saturday peak hours
54	Grove Park – Lewisham – Camberwell – Kennington – Victoria	
56	Peckham Rye – Camberwell – Westminster - Embankment	*Clockwise around Embankment*
84	Peckham Rye – Camberwell – Blackfriars – Embankment	*Anti-clockwise around Embankment*
		Monday to Saturday
58	Blackwall Tunnel – Forest Hill – Camberwell – Victoria	
60	Dulwich – Camberwell – Elephant & Castle – City Southwark	Monday to Saturday peak hours
62	Lewisham (Saturday) – Forest Hill – Westminster – Savoy Street	Monday to Saturday
66	Forest Hill – New Cross – Kennington – Victoria	Monday to Saturday
68	Greenwich – Surrey Docks – Bermondsey – Waterloo Station	
70	Greenwich – Surrey Docks – Bermondsey – London Bridge	
72	Woolwich – Lewisham – Camberwell – Savoy Street	
74	Grove Park – New Cross – Elephant & Castle – Blackfriars	
78	West Norwood – Brixton – Vauxhall – Victoria	

NIGHT SERVICES

Saturday night Sunday morning excepted

Route	
1	Blackfriars – Brixton – Tooting – Blackfriars
	Westminster – Clapham – Tooting – Westminster
3	Battersea – Westminster – Blackfriars
5	Downham – Lewisham – New Cross Gate – Savoy Street
7	New Cross Gate – Camberwell Green – Elephant – Savoy Street
26	Clapham Junction – Vauxhall – Westminster Stn – London Bridge
35	Highgate – Highbury – Islington – Bloomsbury – Westminster